JUDGMENT DAY

This book demonstrates how, after many years of inactivity after the World War II tribunals, judges at the Yugoslav, Rwanda and Sierra Leone tribunals, and to a lesser extent the ICC, have seized the opportunity to develop international law on war crimes, crimes against humanity, and genocide. Aloisi and Meernik argue that judges are motivated by a concern for human rights protection and the legacy of international criminal justice. They have progressively expanded the reach of international law to protect human rights. They have used the power of their own words to condemn human rights atrocities. Judges have sentenced the guilty to lengthy and predictable terms in prison to provide justice, deterrence of future violations and even to advance peace and reconciliation. Aloisi and Meernik show that, on judgment day, judges have sought to enhance the power of international justice.

Rosa Aloisi specializes in research on international justice, international courts, international human rights, and gender issues in international politics. She currently co-leads a Trinity University International Criminal Justice Study Abroad Program to The Hague and to Poland.

James Meernik specializes in research on international justice and international courts, post-conflict peace building, and United States foreign policy. He co-leads a UNT Study Abroad Program to the International Criminal Tribunal for the Former Yugoslavia that won the 2007 American Political Science Association award for the most innovative course in the United States. He won a Fulbright Specialist grant to the Autonomous University of the State of Mexico (UAEM) in 2009 and another Fulbright Specialist award with Soochow University in Taiwan.

Judgment Day

JUDICIAL DECISION MAKING AT THE INTERNATIONAL CRIMINAL TRIBUNALS

ROSA ALOISI

Trinity University, San Antonio

JAMES MEERNIK

University of North Texas

CAMBRIDGE
UNIVERSITY PRESS

CAMBRIDGE
UNIVERSITY PRESS

University Printing House, Cambridge CB2 8BS, United Kingdom

One Liberty Plaza, 20th Floor, New York, NY 10006, USA

477 Williamstown Road, Port Melbourne, VIC 3207, Australia

4843/24, 2nd Floor, Ansari Road, Daryaganj, Delhi – 110002, India

79 Anson Road, #06-04/06, Singapore 079906

Cambridge University Press is part of the University of Cambridge.

It furthers the University's mission by disseminating knowledge in the pursuit of
education, learning, and research at the highest international levels of excellence.

www.cambridge.org
Information on this title: www.cambridge.org/9781107173156
DOI: 10.1017/9781316779835

First published 2017

Printed in the United States of America by Sheridan Books, Inc.

A catalogue record for this publication is available from the British Library.

Library of Congress Cataloging-in-Publication data
Names: Aloisi, Rosa, author. | Meernik, James David, author.
Title: Judgment day : judicial decision making at the international criminal tribunals / Rosa
Aloisi, Trinity University, San Antonio, James Meernik, University of North Texas.
Description: New York : Cambridge University Press, 2017. | Includes bibliographical
references and index.
Identifiers: LCCN 2017002749 | ISBN 9781107173156 (alk. paper)
Subjects: LCSH: International criminal courts. | Judgments. | Judicial power. | Criminal
procedure (International law). | Human rights. | Criminal justice, Administration of.
Classification: LCC KZ7230 .A44 2017 | DDC 345/.0238 – dc23
LC record available at https://lccn.loc.gov/2017002749

ISBN 978-1-107-17315-6 Hardback
ISBN 978-1-316-62573-6 Paperback

Contents

Tables

Acknowledgments

The authors would like to acknowledge the invaluable research assistance of Lee Rathbun, Melissa McKay and Ayal Feinberg. We are especially grateful to the many individuals who have worked at the ICTR and the ICTY who have always been so helpful and welcoming whenever we visited.

1

Judgment Day at the Tribunal

INTRODUCTION

"May justice be done lest the world perish"

Presiding Judge Almiro Rodrigues of Trial Chamber I of the International Criminal Tribunal for the Former Yugoslavia begins the delivery of the Trial Chamber's judgment in the case of General Radislav Krstic with this stirring quote from Hegel.[1] The general stands accused of numerous crimes, not the least of which is the crime of all crimes – genocide – for the massacre of Bosnian Muslim men in Srebrenica in 1995. The world did perish for those eking out a horrible existence in this UN-declared safe area in the hot summer months of that year as the Bosnian Serb forces made their final push to end the Bosnian war. The world perished for the thousands of boys and men who were systematically massacred by the Bosnian Serb forces. The world perished for the women, children and elderly who were bussed out of Srebrenica to an uncertain future without their husbands, fathers, sons, and brothers. They did not know then, and would not know for months, even years in many cases what happened to these men. Some months earlier, when one Bosnian Muslim woman, known only as Witness DD, testified at the ICTY (International Criminal Tribunal for the Former Yugoslavia), the general's usual stoic demeanor seemed to momentarily escape him as he was confronted with this mother's appeal. Judge Rodrigues had asked the woman at the conclusion of her testimony if she wanted to say anything else:

> I would like to appeal to you to ask Mr. Krstic, if you can, whether there is any hope for at least that little child that they snatched away from me, alive, because I keep dreaming about him. I dream of him bringing flowers and saying, "Mother,

[1] The quote has also been attributed to others.

1

I've come." I hug him and say, "Where have you been, my son?" and he says, "I've been in Vlasenica all this time." So I beg you, if Mr. Krstic knows anything about it, about him surviving some place . . . [2]

As the summary judgment was read out in open court that day in early August 2001, however, General Krstic mostly maintained his composure as the judge described the crimes the Bosnian Serb forces had committed and whether he himself bore responsibility for their actions.

That day, the opening of Trial Chamber I's session to read the summary judgment, proceeds like all other openings of public sessions of the trial chambers at the ICTY. The various lawyers for the prosecution and defense, the staff of the Registrar's Office, which handles the administrative functioning of the Court, the UN security guards and eventually the defendant assemble in their assigned places. The defendant and his lawyers sit on the left hand side (when viewed from the public gallery) and look across the courtroom to the prosecution on the other side while the Registry staff are positioned in the middle and the judges sit, elevated at the head of the room. The public is allowed to view from a gallery walled off from the courtroom by thick glass. But even that barrier can seem very thin and ephemeral when one sits in the front row on that left side and catches the eye of a defendant. Everyone in the courtroom and the public gallery are instructed to rise as the three judges enter the courtroom. UN security guards will admonish those in the public gallery who do not stand up. The presiding judge pronounces, "Please be seated" and the summary judgment is read.

The public sessions of the international criminal tribunals are often quite dry and dull. Much time is occupied by lawyers debating the finer points of international law, the routine business of court administration and the excruciatingly exacting dissection of witness testimony. It is not uncommon to see people nodding off in the public gallery, who are then gently nudged by UN security in order to maintain proper decorum. Repeat offenders may be asked to leave the gallery. But on that day the audience in the public gallery is fully engaged with the events taking place beyond the glass in front of them as Judge Rodrigues reads the summary judgment against General Krstic, which provides the kind of history of the horrible events of Srebrenica that will speak to a wider audience beyond the courtroom. He explains just what the judges can say with certainty about the events at Srebrenica. He outlines the responsibility of the Bosnian Serb leadership and their forces that organized and committed the massacres and ethnic cleansing at Srebrenica. He calls and rules it as genocide – the first time that the ICTY has made such a determination. For once the official words of the Tribunal express a more profound and human understanding of these events:

---

[2] Witness's DD testimony is found in the documentary produced by the SENSE News Agency, Triumph of Evil. A transcript of the documentary, including her testimony, can be found at http://www.sense-agency.com/documentaries.43.html.

One needs to remember the shelling, including the shelling of the United Nations base in Srebrenica. One needs to imagine thousands of people crowded into a few buildings without water or food other than a few pieces of candy thrown in by General Mladic in front of the cameras and, we were told, taken back once the cameras had left. One must imagine the heat. One must picture the dozens of soldiers and Serbian armed men coming and going shouting out discriminatory insults. One must see the houses set on fire, the night falling and the rising screams. The witnesses described to the Trial Chamber the prevailing atmosphere of terror, the rapes and murders and the mistreatment so pervasive that some of the refugees committed suicide or attempted to do so.[3]

Throughout the reading of the judgment summary most of those in the courtroom seem to be focused intently on Judge Rodrigues's words. As most are listening to the simultaneous translation from French (Judge Rodrigues is Portuguese) they look at their computers or something else as they concentrate on his words. The courtroom is very quiet and very still.

Judge Rodrigues describes the events leading up to the massacre at Srebrenica.[4] Srebrenica was a United Nations declared "safe area" in which civilians were to be protected and fighting was not to occur. After the safe area was declared on April 16, 1993, by the United Nations Security Council, thousands of individuals from around Srebrenica and the towns and villages of eastern Bosnia, which Serbs were systematically cleansing of their Muslim populations, moved into this small zone of "peace". They fled to escape the violence and destruction that their government and the international community seemed powerless to stop. They endured horrible and cramped living conditions for months because the alternatives were far worse. For approximately twenty months until January 1995, a tenuous stalemate existed between the Bosnian Serb forces, which sought to link up their conquests in eastern Bosnia to create their greater Bosnian Serb Republic and the forces of the Bosnian government (ABiH or Army of the Republic of Bosnia and Herzegovina and also known as the Bosnian Muslim army). But as the Bosnia Serb leadership determined to finish the war on their terms that year, their political leader, Radovan Karadzic, in Directive 7, ordered that "By well thought out combat operations, create an unbearable situation of total insecurity with no hope of further survival or life for the inhabitants of Srebrenica and Zepa."[5]

On July 6, 1995, the attack by Bosnian Serb forces on Srebrenica was launched. Their armies quickly overran the meager defenses offered by the Bosnian government forces and conquered the Srebrenica safe zone. General Ratko Mladic

---

[3] International Criminal Tribunal for the Former Yugoslavia Press Release, The Hague, August 2, 2001, OF/P.I.S./609e, p. 4. as found at http://www.icty.org/x/cases/krstic/tjug/en/010802_Krstic_summary_en .pdf.

[4] The account that follows is drawn principally from the Krstic summary and full judgments, which can be found on-line at http://www.icty.org/case/krstic/4.

[5] Ibid, p. 3.

triumphantly entered the town of Srebrenica and can be seen on video speaking directly into the camera to declare, "We give this town to the Serb nation as a gift. The time has come to take revenge on the Turks."[6] But the town was deserted as many of the men had already fled into the hills to hide, suspecting what fate likely awaited them from the Serb forces. The rest of the population moved to the nearby UN outpost at Potocari in the hope that the Dutch battalion there would protect them. They were sadly mistaken as the UN Protection Force (UNPROFOR) offered nothing of the kind. Videos showing General Mladic talking to representatives of the UN Dutch Battalion demonstrate the failure of the international community to protect the Muslim population. In one of the videos shot inside the Fontana Hotel in Bratunac, close to the town of Srebrenica, the day after the fall of what was supposed to be a UN-protected safe haven, Mladic declared "You can survive or you can disappear."[7] The UN peacekeepers were at the mercy of the Serb forces as well – forces that had seized UN peacekeepers as hostages before. Meetings were organized among the Bosnian Serb military leadership, including General Krstic, the leaders of the Dutch battalion and hastily appointed representatives of the Bosnian Muslim refugees. Mladic demanded that the Bosnian Muslim representative, a school teacher, arrange for the Bosnian government forces to lay down their arms. He demanded that the UN forces organize a transport of the women and children out of Potocari.

Meanwhile somewhere between ten and fifteen thousand Bosnian Muslim men sought to escape the advancing Serb forces by heading into the hills around the safe zone and making their way to Bosnian Muslim territory. Most were from the Twenty-Eighth Division of the Bosnian government army, although many were also civilians fleeing the chaos and violence. Somewhere between eight thousand and nine thousand Bosnian Muslim males ranging in age from those just barely entering their teens to men in their sixties were captured by the Serb forces. Many were lured to come out of hiding by trickery and promises of safety. On July 13, 1995, the mass executions began.

They occurred in many places across several days. In fact, there is a first-hand account of the massacres by a member of the Bosnian Serb forces, Drazen Erdemovic. Erdemovic was a twenty-three-year-old member of the Serb army who surrendered himself to the ICTY after having taken part in the killings. On the morning of July 16, 1995, Erdemovic and seven members of the Tenth Sabotage Unit of the Bosnian Serb army were ordered to Pilica farm near Zvornik. Bosnian Muslim men, who had surrendered, were to be brought there. Then, beginning at 10:00 that morning, the captured men were led off buses in groups of ten, ordered to stand with their backs against the firing squad and systematically executed. The executions continued until 3:00 that afternoon, and although Erdemovic protested that he did

---

[6]   As found at http://www.bbc.co.uk/news/world-europe-18099008.
[7]   As found at http://www.pbs.org/wnet/cryfromthegrave/about/intro.html.

not wish to take any more part in such actions, he was threatened with his life if he did not participate. Erdemovic estimated there were about twenty buses that came that day each carrying fifty to sixty men and boys. He believed that he was responsible for the deaths of dozens of Bosnian Muslim men with his automatic weapon. After taking part in this execution, Erdemovic was ordered to begin executing other civilians, but he, along with two of his fellow soldiers, refused the order.[8]

Erdemovic was later shot by one of his Bosnian Serb compatriots and wound up in a hospital in Belgrade. He later confessed his actions to a journalist, to a local Serbian court (in Yugoslavia), and ultimately to the ICTY. Erdemovic's testimony not only provided the ICTY and the world with a first-hand account of the massacres at Srebrenica, his cooperation with the Tribunal shed new light on the execution sites and helped the Office of the Prosecutor (OTP) develop evidence in other cases pertaining to Srebrenica, like the *Krstic* case.

Returning to the summary reading, Judge Rodrigues carefully describes all the events that led up to the Srebrenica massacres and what took place those fateful days in July. His voice is even and steady and throughout the lengthy reading of the summary of the judgment, General Krstic remains largely impassive. Judge Rodrigues describes how the Bosnian Serb army is responsible for these events. He tells of the implementation of one massacre after another from a few killed early on in one incident to the mass execution sites scattered across the region. After the bodies were hastily disposed, there was a subsequent attempt to better conceal evidence of these crimes and so in the fall of 1995, bodies were dug up and reburied. Ironically, all the digging, hauling and moving at the original sites was visible in satellite photography and helped the Office of The Prosecutor determine more precisely where the original burial sites were located.

The statutes of the ICTY, ICTR (International Criminal Tribunal for Rwanda) and ICC (International Criminal Court) all restate significant and substantial passages from the 1948 Genocide Convention that outlaw various acts, such as murder, causing serious bodily or mental harm, forcefully transferring children and seeking to prevent births when, "committed with intent to destroy, in whole or in part, a national, ethnical, racial or religious group, as such".[9] While the Rwandan Tribunal had issued several verdicts in which leaders of the genocide against the Tutsi population were found guilty, no one had been found guilty of genocide in regard to the events in the former Yugoslavia. Indeed, until the ICTR issued its first verdict in September 1998, no one had ever been found guilty of genocide by an international tribunal. There was debate over whether genocide had occurred at Srebrenica since only Bosnian Muslim men were targeted; such individuals were only a part of a larger

---

[8] Details of Erdemovic's story can be found at http://www.icty.org/x/cases/erdemovic/tjug/en/erd-tsj961129e.pdf.

[9] ICTY Statute, Article 4 as found at http://www.icty.org/x/file/Legal%20Library/Statute/statute_sept09_en.pdf.

Bosnian Muslim population, and it wasn't clear if there was a conscious genocidal intent on the part of the perpetrators. While certainly international crimes had been committed – whether or not they were to be ruled as acts of genocide by the ICTY was not clear until Judge Rodrigues read his opinion.

Interestingly, the decision to commit these acts of genocide was not part of a long-standing and organized plan, as we saw with the Holocaust or the Rwandan genocide. Rather, Judge Rodrigues accepts that the plan to annihilate Bosnian Muslim men of fighting age around Srebrenica was devised only after the Serb forces transferred out the women, children and the elderly. Why the determination was made that the males should all be killed is not clear. The judge concludes, "By deciding to kill all the men of Srebrenica of fighting age, a decision was taken to make it impossible for the Bosnian Muslim people of Srebrenica to survive." This is what constitutes an act of genocide. It was not necessary for the plan to have been well-thought-out, or that some passage of time elapsed between the decision and the action, only that the decision was made to kill the men with the knowledge that this would lead to the destruction of the Bosnian Muslim community in Srebrenica. The men would be dead and all others would be ethnically cleansed.

Judge Rodrigues comes third and finally to the crux of the matter – does General Krstic bear some responsibility for the genocide at Srebrenica. General Krstic was second in command of the Drina Corps of the Bosnian Serb army at the beginning of the attack on Srebrenica and was later promoted in the course of the offensive to the top commanding position of that army. Judge Rodrigues acknowledges that several, different Serb forces were involved in the offensive and that while the Drina Corps was not responsible for all the killings, it took part in these efforts. It appears at this point in the reading of the judgment summary that the Trial Chamber is about to find Krstic guilty. General Krstic and his lawyers had argued during the trial that the General had already been dispatched to begin another offensive when the massacres began and that he was not present at the scenes of the crimes. Furthermore, they alleged that he was unable to communicate effectively with his superiors to understand what was happening. His lawyers had also argued that there was a parallel chain of command that led up to General Ratko Mladic and excluded General Krstic. The defense contended that it was this chain of command that was responsible for the genocide at Srebrenica. The Trial Chamber is not persuaded of this argument and finds that the General must have known what was happening as his own forces were involved in the transportation and execution of the Bosnian Muslim men. The Trial Chamber's finding at this point in the reading of the judgment summary regarding General Krstic's guilt is obvious.

Judge Rodrigues asks General Krstic to please rise, but quickly lets the General know that if, because of his injuries from the war, he cannot stand, he can remain seated. The General rises, balances himself on his desk and then sits back down. And while these proceedings are often lacking in drama and emotion, the language of the judgment summary is surprisingly forceful and dramatic:

The Trial Chamber does not dispute that you are a professional soldier who loves his work. The Trial Chamber can accept that you would not of your own accord have taken the decision to execute thousands of civilians and disarmed persons. Someone else probably decided to order the execution of all the men of fighting age. Nonetheless, you are still guilty, General Krstic. You are guilty of having knowingly participated in the organised forced transfer of the women, children and old people in Srebrenica at the time of the attack on 6 July 1995 against the United Nations safe area.

You are guilty of the murder of thousands of Bosnian Muslims between 10 and 19 July 1995, whether these be murders committed sporadically in Potocari or murders planned in the form of mass executions. You are guilty of the incredible suffering of the Bosnian Muslims whether these be the ones in Potocari or survivors of the executions. You are guilty of the persecution suffered by the Bosnian Muslims of Srebrenica. Knowing that the women, children and old people of Srebrenica had been transferred, you are guilty of having agreed to the plan to conduct mass executions of all the men of fighting age. You are therefore guilty of genocide, General Krstic.[10]

Judge Rodrigues recalls the words of Kant and declares that if justice is ignored, life on earth has no value. Before pronouncing the sentence, however, Judge Rodrigues strives to make clear that the Tribunal is not holding the Serbian people accountable but rather those who were directly responsible. He asserts that in July 1995 General Krstic agreed to evil and he is therefore being sentenced to forty-six years in prison. This was the longest sentence imposed to that date at the ICTY.[11]

With the reading of the judgment summary concluded, the audience is again instructed to rise as the judges leave the courtroom and the proceedings conclude. The ICTY has since heard several more cases pertaining to the genocide at Srebrenica and is now finally, at the time of writing, adjudicating the responsibility for military mastermind of the crime, the Bosnian Serb General, Ratko Mladic.

In the public gallery many Bosnian women watched and listened on their headsets for nearly an hour and a half. Women in Bosnia, watching the proceedings at the Association of Mothers of Srebrenica and Zepa Enclaves, expressed their feelings as someone was finally held accountable for the crimes committed at Srebrenica. One woman declared, "Today, among the mothers with wounded souls, I do not see even a bit of satisfaction at the length of his sentence."[12] Munira Subasic, who

---

[10] Supra note 3, pp. 9–10.

[11] The sentence was later reduced to thirty-five years in prison after the Appeals Chamber found that the Trial Chamber had made several findings in error, most notably in declaring that General Krstic shared the genocidal intent of other top Bosnian Serb leaders in Srebrenica, such as General Mladic. Rather, the Appeals Chamber concluded that General Krstic must be found guilty not as a principal perpetrator of genocide but rather as an aider and abettor of genocide by permitting the use of his troops in the commission of genocide.

[12] "Reward, Not Punishment." CNN.com as found on September 6, 2012, at http://edition.cnn.com/2001/WORLD/europe/08/02/widows.reaction/index.html.

headed the association argued, "Even if he had a thousand lives and each one were taken away from him there would be no justice. I am not satisfied with 46 years. I don't think he will live that long but I still expected to hear the words 'life imprisonment'."[13] Many Serbs expressed anger at the verdict. The Serb chairman of Bosnia-Herzegovina's multi-ethnic presidency, Zivko Radisic, stated, "I express disagreement with the qualification of the verdict in which Krstic was found guilty of genocide." He accused the ICTY, as many Serbs do, of bias against his people.[14]

The judgment pronounced that day on August 2, 2001, is but one of many handed down by international criminal tribunals since their re-emergence in world affairs in the early 1990s. The ICTY, established by the United Nations Security Council in 1993 and the International Criminal Tribunal for Rwanda, created just one year later after the Rwandan genocide in 1994, were the first international tribunals since the World War II Nuremberg and Tokyo tribunals. Those tribunals, organized to try the authors of the Nazi and Japanese atrocities, were seen in that era as the beginning of a renewed and more committed effort to hold accountable those who violated international humanitarian law. Along with the ratification of the Geneva Conventions on war crimes (1949) and the Genocide Convention (1948), the quest to hold individuals accountable for these crimes seemed to herald a new era in international law. As the US Prosecutor at Nuremberg, Judge Robert Jackson, proclaimed:

> The wrongs which we seek to condemn and punish have been so calculated, so malignant, and so devastating, that civilization cannot tolerate their being ignored, because it cannot survive their being repeated. That four great nations, flushed with victory and stung with injury stay the hand of vengeance and voluntarily submit their captive enemies to the judgment of the law is one of the most significant tributes that Power has ever paid to Reason.[15]

Sadly, despite such auspicious beginnings and lofty words, the promise of a new era in international law that would attack the long-standing impunity enjoyed by those who ordered and carried out horrific crimes floundered and died on the shoals of Cold War politics. Indeed, governments continued to commit massive crimes and massacres of their own people with little to fear from the international community. The Chinese Great Leap Forward and Cultural Revolution, the massacres in Algeria

[13] Ibid.
[14] "Krstic conviction puts spotlight on fugitive war crimes suspects," Agence France Presse, August 3, 2001, as found at http://groups.yahoo.com/group/decani/message/56922 on September 6, 2012. Such divisions of opinion on ICTY judgments regarding the genocide at Srebrenica persist. Bosnian Muslim opinion generally leans toward supporting the tribunal and its punishments, although a vocal minority often criticizes many sentences as too lenient (Clark 2009, 476). Serbs, by contrast, have been mostly critical of these and other verdicts and argue the ICTY is biased against them and has not taken their claims of self-defense seriously.
[15] Opening Address by US Chief Prosecutor at Nuremberg, Robert Jackson as found at http://fcit.usf.edu/holocaust/resource/document/DocJac01.htm.

by the French, the repression in Eastern Europe by the communists during the Cold War, and the myriad large and small crimes that occur across the globe by dictators and tyrants demonstrated that human rights atrocities were gathering strength, not winding down.

It was not until the end of the Cold War that political conditions were ripe for renewed attention to the development of a system of international criminal justice. The United States and the Soviet Union with their zero-sum view of global politics were unlikely to both agree on the need to condemn, let alone prosecute the large scale human rights violations that were endemic throughout this period. But with the collapse of the Soviet Union and the emergence of horrific violence in Europe in the former Yugoslavia, criminal prosecution not only became possible, it became desirable given the lack of will to take more aggressive measures to stop civil war violence. The International Criminal Tribunal for the Former Yugoslavia was established by the United Nations Security Council on May 25, 1993, acting under its Chapter 7 powers to maintain peace and security. The Security Council may have established the ICTY in part because it was incapable and generally unwilling to take stronger measures to address the violence in the former Yugoslavia, but any such lack of normative commitment to international justice could be overlooked at that time. The International Criminal Tribunal for Rwanda, created on November 8, 1994, by the Security Council, further embedded international tribunals and international humanitarian law into the fabric of international society.

That two such institutions were up and running in such a short amount of time presaged that once the international "justice cascade" (Sikkink 2011) had begun, either more ad hoc tribunals would need to be established, or a permanent court created, especially given the scale of atrocities occurring in the world. Thus, subsequently and strongly influenced by the lessons and legacy of the ICTY and ICTR, the nations of the world met in Rome in 1998 and drafted the treaty that eventually led to the creation of the International Criminal Court. In 2002 an agreement between the United Nations and the Government of Sierra Leone created the Special Tribunal for Sierra Leone to prosecute some of the most serious violations of international humanitarian law committed during the decade long war that had ravaged the country. In 2013 the Sierra Leone Tribunal delivered its last and most prominent judgment, confirming the fifty-year jail sentence against former Liberian president Charles Taylor. Now these judgments that determine the responsibility and punishment to be apportioned to those who violate international law are here to stay. But what is so important about these judgments? What do they tell us of the impact of international justice and the goals of their authors?

THE LEGACY OF JUDGMENTS

The judgments of the tribunals are the ultimate and most important product of the international criminal tribunals. Rarely do such opportunities present themselves for the judges to give voice to their mission and to their collective wisdom about international law. These judgments are the most far-reaching actions the judges can take (Freeman 2006; Harmon and Gaynor 2007). The reading of the *Krstic* verdict described earlier was a watershed moment in the history of the ICTY, as was the first guilty verdict for war crimes handed down by the ICC in the case of Thomas Lubanga Dyilo. To imagine the central importance of judgments in the life of an international tribunal one need only remember the tragic end of the trial of former Yugoslav leader, Slobodan Milosevic, who stood trial at the ICTY as mastermind of the wars of the former Yugoslavia. Not a few commentators described how he cheated justice by dying during the middle of his trial. After all the hours and hours of witness testimony, expense and years of labor that went into his prosecution, when all was said and done, there was nothing really to show for the efforts. Justice and the world had both been deprived of the proper and rightful conclusion to the trial – a judgment.

Judgments are the climax of the quest for justice, retribution and deterrence. The victims and those who live in the affected nations look to these judgments to right wrongs and to balance the scales of justice. Many victims certainly want more than just justice – they also may desire reparations, apologies and remorse – but justice originates in a verdict that corroborates their history and suffering and vindicates their struggles. Judgments are handed down for the victim that lost her whole family. They are for the community whose destruction was sought. And justice is for the world. These are crimes against "humanity." The entire world is the community which justice seeks to protect through these judgments in small and large ways. They are intended to quiet the voices calling for vengeance. As the renowned Italian jurist and former ICTY President, Antonio Cassese, wrote, "they act on behalf of the whole international community and are therefore entitled to pronounce upon crimes that offend universal values" (2007–2008, 9). They are intended to counter the opinions of those who claim that entire peoples and nations are "the problem." They are the hope that a message is being sent that the world will no longer tolerate what brutal rulers do to their own people and to others. They are supposed to be another nail in the coffin of impunity. They are these things and more in the eyes of those who demand international justice and those who support it. Not all peoples and not all observers of international tribunals might make such claims or pin such hopes on their judgments. But whether rightly or wrongly, many people from all continents and all walks of life seek the verdicts of international justice.

To be sure, there are many critics of these tribunals and the type of justice they deliver as we describe in subsequent chapters (Mendeloff 2004; Snyder and Vinjamuri 2003; Zacklin 2004). Thus, because the judgments are so important; because there are many and disparate voices that offer differing opinions of the work of the tribunals; and because there is a lack of theory building and systematic evidence regarding the rationale behind these judgments and their consequences, it is time to explore them in much greater depth and understand their role in realizing the goals of the judges who write them. We begin by outlining the reasons why these judgments are so important in the context of the development of international law. Subsequently, we address the purposes of this book.

The Importance of Judgments

Developing and Filling In International Law

The creation of the three international tribunals for the former Yugoslavia, Rwanda and Sierra Leone symbolized the newfound goal of the international community to prosecute those responsible for the most egregious violations of international humanitarian law. But as the tribunals dusted off the precedents of Nuremberg and Tokyo and looked carefully at their statutes, it became clear that international law was full of holes and ambiguities. International judges have sought to address these gaps and ambiguities in a rapidly changing international environment. As former ICTY President Theodor Meron has written, "Their judgments have filled the gaps in international procedural and evidentiary law left by the Nuremberg decisions, and their success serves as an example for national prosecutions of those who commit atrocities" (2006, 578). Today, judgments represent the result of complex legal reasoning and highlight the struggle of judges to balance their judicial role of delivering verdicts and their role as developers of international law.

The importance of an in-depth analysis of their judgments is substantial. First, international tribunals have created an incredible corpus of jurisprudence that has significantly filled in the lacunae present in international criminal law. Analyzing the judgments of international criminal tribunals provides international criminal law scholars and practitioners with a comprehensive understanding of the innovations of international law and the active role played by judges in the development and consolidation of international crimes and types of intent and liability. Second and most importantly international judgments have become the product against which the tribunals' legacy will be assessed after the completion of their mandate. They represent the living and constantly evolving jurisprudence of international criminal and humanitarian law. They embody the spirit of international criminal justice, and are intended to establish the truth, historical record and precedents from which the future work of the International Criminal Court can draw.

Given the lack of prior jurisprudence and the vagueness of the statutes of the ad hoc international tribunals judges have often resorted to expansive legal interpretations trying to fill the gap left open by a Swiss cheese corpus of international law. Since the beginning, the tribunal judges have been pronouncing decisions for extraordinary crimes while lacking a detailed statutory framework akin to what we now see with the ICC. Judges have adopted discretionary powers in the determination of sentences, while walking the fine line between the interpretation of legal principles and the creation of novel criminal elements. It is not rare while reading the judgments of the ad hoc international tribunals to find instances of creative judicial interpretation, such as their efforts at enlarging the scope of the definition of crimes (Darcy and Powderly 2010). The reading of the summary on "judgment day" very often becomes the moment through which judges have articulated advances in international law in front of a large audience and have emphasized to the international community the importance of their opinions on crimes and responsibilities.

The international community has witnessed several occasions in which judges have through their decisions revitalized the structure of an international criminal law that had been left dormant for a long period of time. For example, on July 22, 2002, as the Appeals Chamber began the delivery of the summary of the Judgment in the case of the *Prosecutor v. Kunarac et al.* (widely known for its landmark ruling on sexual enslavement), Judge Claude Jorda made the following statement:

> The Appeals Chamber of the ICTY [. . .] judgment elucidates the definition of several crimes under the jurisdiction of the tribunal and in particular clarifies the status of rape as a crime under Customary International Law.[16]

The ICTY Appeal Chambers decision in the case of the *Prosecutor v. Kunarac et al.*[17] dedicated several pages of the Appeals Judgment to the crime of rape and how the crimes and violations in the Statute of the Tribunal included some element of the crime of rape. Rape was reshaped, redefined and reconceived as a crime against humanity, as a violation of the law of wars, and as a "recognized war crime under international criminal law."[18] Perhaps one of the judgments that best highlights the importance of the legal and historical values of international judicial decisions is the trial judgment handed down by the ICTR in the case of the *Prosecutor v. Jean-Paul Akayesu.*[19] Akayesu was found not only guilty of genocide, but also rape. For the first time since the adoption of the Convention for the Prevention and Punishment of the Crime of Genocide in 1948, an international criminal tribunal found someone guilty of genocide, but also rape as a type of genocidal crime. The judgment was also a landmark ruling on the crime of rape and its legal definition.

Although rape represents one of the international crimes whose circumstantial and legal elements have been mostly developed by the ICTY and ICTR, trial and appeals judgments provide numerous other examples of judicial innovations that have brought energy and new life back to the international criminal law system. Many cases have dealt with the meaning of command responsibility; others have focused on the definition of joint criminal enterprise; yet others have specified and characterized the mental element (*mens rea*) and material elements of many crimes. Verdicts and punishments have become the expression of a law that has progressed

---

[16] http://www.youtube.com/watch?v=EqPn4AoGmRQ   http://www.icty.org/x/cases/kunarac/acjug/en/kun-aj020612e.pdf.

[17] The Prosecutor v. Dragoljub Kunarac, Radomir Kovac, and Zoran Vukovic, Case No. IT-96–23/1-A, June 12, 2002.

[18] Ibid, para 195.

[19] The Prosecutor v. Jean-Paul Akayesu, Case No. ICTR-94–4-T, September 2, 1998.

considerably and that represents the legal basis for the work of the International Criminal Court.

One recent example of the importance of the development of law articulated by the judges at the ad hoc tribunals is the verdict handed down by the ICC bench in the case against Congolese warlord and former Vice President of the Democratic Republic of Congo Jean-Pierre Bemba. Building considerably upon the jurisprudence established by the ICTY and the ICTR, the ICC found the indictee criminally responsible as a commander for failing to take the necessary measures to prevent the troops under his effective command from committing the crimes of murder, rape and pillaging against the civilian population.[20] In a decision which has been welcomed by multiple organizations – including the UN[21] – as groundbreaking, the ICC for the very first time since the beginning of its operations has furthered the mission of the judges of the ICTY and ICTR, by sending a clear message to all parties involved in a conflict that impunity for the crime of rape has definitely come to an end.

The acceptance of international judicial decisions as an instrument of innovation, which was indispensable and desirable given the circumstances faced by international judges, has been and still is incomplete. Reactions to the decisions handed down by international judges have been diverse. Many academics and international law practitioners have welcomed such decisions as long awaited and necessary steps forward in the establishment of precise international law rules (Askin 2002 and 2004; Cassese 2004; Mose 2005; Wald 2010). Critics, by contrast, have noted the perils of judges acting with unfettered and quasi legislative power (Karnevas 2011; Olusanya 2005; Swart 2010; Zacklin 2004). When the Security Council created the ad hoc international tribunals for Rwanda and the ex-Yugoslavia there was a clear understanding among its members that judges could not engage in law making (Danner 2006). However, although judges were called to apply treaties, conventions, general principles of law, or customary international law they were quickly challenged by hearing cases and assessing events that had not been prosecuted by international or national courts since the end of World War II and within a political context radically different from the post-war period. International judges had to adjust quickly and respond to the void left by an incomplete international legislative process to avoid running the risk of pronouncing *non liquet*[22] decisions and letting international criminals run free. Following the events that led to the establishment of the ICTY and ICTR, it was particularly evident that some form of judicial "activism" was especially important at the international level to address the poor specificity of international law. The Appeals Chamber in the *Celebici* case made sure that the

---

[20] Prosecutor v. Jean-Pierre Bemba Gombo, Case No.: ICC-01/05–01/08, March 21, 2016, para 752.

[21] See UN Secretary General Ban Ki-moon statement at http://www.un.org/apps/news/story.asp?NewsID=53523#.VyU3bzArLIU.

[22] Non liquet, which literally translated from Latin means "not clear", refers to the situation in which judges do not have legal standards applicable to the case under their examination.

superior interests of international law that judges and judicial decisions must serve did not go unnoticed. By quoting the separate opinion of Judge Shahabuddeen in the case the *Prosecutor v. Laurent Semanza* at the ICTR,[23] the judges of the Appeals Chamber at the ICTY stated:

> [...] so far as international law is concerned, the operation of the desiderata of consistency, stability, and predictability does not stop at the frontiers of the Tribunal. [...] The Appeals Chamber cannot behave as if the general state of the law in the international community whose interests it serves is none of its concern.[24]

In examining the role of the judges at the international tribunals it becomes evident that they had to overcome several obstacles while trying to address the shortcomings of international humanitarian and criminal law. They faced two different tasks: creating the rules of procedure and evidence that would administer their work within novel institutions and revisit rules of international humanitarian law that had remained unused for decades. Judges had to pay close attention to procedures of international criminal law to regulate trials and inflict punishments on individuals found guilty of crimes, while at the same time re-establishing a system of humanitarian law often relying on unwritten rules (*jus cogens*), praxis and general principles. Within these two initial tasks it became immediately evident to many in the international community that international tribunals were equipped with a pool of judges who were approaching the law with an innovative mind-set and expansive judicial activism to fill the legal deficit left open by vague or absent legislation and inadequate jurisprudence (Van Schaack 2008).

The Legitimacy of the Tribunals

There are multiple reasons why judgments have become such a vital contribution to the development of international criminal law and the legacy of international tribunals. International judgments are the instruments through which the legitimacy and legal importance of international institutions are reaffirmed and defended by judges. From the very beginning of the tribunals when the ICTY, in the interlocutory opinion in the *Tadic* case, ruled on the legality of the Tribunal's very existence and legitimacy[25] to the numerous challenges that have arisen regarding the criminality of certain actions, tribunal judges have vigorously defended the legitimacy of their institutions and judgments. This is especially important as the judges have expanded the reach of international law by choice or because of the inadequacy of the prevailing jurisprudence. Such activity has opened up the judges to charges

---

[23] Separate Opinion of Judge Shahabuddeen, appended to Decision, The Prosecutor v. Laurent Semanza, Case No. ICTR-97-20-A, App Ch, May 31, 2000, para 25, as cited in Celebici appellate judgment of February 20, 2001, para 24.

[24] Prosecutor v. Zejnil Delalic, Zdravko Mucic, Hazim Delic and Esad Landzo, Case No. IT-96-21-A, Appeals Chamber Judgment, February 20, 2001, para 24.

[25] Prosecutor v. Dusko Tadic Decision on the Defence Motion for Interlocutory Appeal on Jurisdiction, October 2, 1995.

of judicial legislating, which might undermine their legitimacy. Although scholars have recognized that judges engage in some forms of lawmaking behavior (Shapiro 1986), tribunal decisions have been criticized for overstepping boundaries vital to principles of legality.

The adjudication of crimes for the very first time in front of international judges has been questioned as a violation of the principle of *nullum crimen sine lege certa* (Ginsburg 2005) by both critics and defendants. The latter in particular have raised claims of violations of their rights based on the principle that only an activity criminalized at the time of its commission can be punished. Thus, international judicial decisions have been the instruments through which judges have answered the many challenges of legitimacy and authority raised by defendants and critics of these international institutions. Questions about the nature of the crime, the very existence of a criminal element, and grounds of responsibility have been continuously raised by defendants. Notably, in the *Celebici* case the defendants had asked the court to dismiss the counts that alleged the commission of "willfully causing great suffering" and "cruel treatment" because they violated the principle of specificity required to consider a *lege certa*.[26] Similarly, in the "Lasva Valley" case of the *Prosecutor v. Kupreskic et al.*[27] the defendants asked for the dismissal of the count alleging the commission of "crimes against humanity" under the definition of "other inhumane acts" for the violation of the international criminal law principle of *nullum crimen sine lege*. In both cases[28] the judges answered by claiming a purposive logic behind the open interpretation and elusive categorization of crimes against humanity in order for the judges applying the law to reach a variety of conditions and modes of conduct.[29] Lastly, in the case of the *Prosecutor v. Norman* in front of the Special Court for Sierra Leone, the defendant moved for the dismissal of the crime alleging the conscription of children under the age of fifteen into the armed forces to participate in the hostilities "since the crime of child recruitment was not part of Customary International Law at the time of the indictment," adding that the Geneva Conventions Additional Protocol II[30] may have created an obligation on

---

[26] Prosecutor v. Zejnil Delalic, Zdravko Mucic, Hazim Delic and Esad Landzo, Case No. IT-96–21-T, Trial Chamber Decision, November 16, 1998, paras 503–515.

[27] The Prosecutor v. Kupreskic et al., IT-95–16-T, Trial Chamber Decision, January 14, 2000.

[28] Prosecutor v. Zejnil Delalic, Zdravko Mucic, Hazim Delic and Esad Landzo, Case No. IT-96–21-T, Trial Chamber Decision, November 16, 1998, para 515. The Prosecutor v. Kupreskic et al., IT-95–16-T, Trial Chamber Decision, January 14, 2000, para 563.

[29] See also, The Prosecutor v. Milomir Stakic, Case No. IT-97–24-A, Appeals Chamber Judgment, March 22, 2006, paras 314–315, "the notion of "other inhumane acts" contained in Article 5(i) of the Statute cannot be regarded as a violation of the principle of *nullum crimen sine lege*." Also, in the Prosecutor v. Galic, Case No. IT-98–29-T, December 5, 2003, para 133, the judges had to specify the crime of terror against the civilian population as a crime prohibited by the Geneva Conventions, but not specified in its elements.

[30] Article 4(3)(c) of the 1977 Additional Protocol II to the Geneva Conventions provides that: "Children who have not attained the age of fifteen years shall neither be recruited in the armed forces or groups nor allowed to take part in hostilities."

the part of states without criminalizing the activity.[31] The SCSL judges stated that the continuous attention and condemnation of the international community over a certain period of time to enlisting and conscripting children within armed forces, was an indication that the behavior had become criminalized and part of customary international law.[32]

Judgments have become the means by which judges have reaffirmed, re-interpreted and to some extent brought back to life, the sources of international law and judicial interpretation. Judgments have become the vehicle through which traditional principles of interpretation provided by the Vienna Convention on the Law of Treaties, customary international law principles, the Convention on the Punishment and Prevention of the Crime of Genocide, and the general principles of international law have been applied for the first time in decades. Thus, judgments are an important archive of general principles of law. Rulings often include references to the important principles of *jus cogens* which apply to the international community as a whole. More importantly, judgments have changed and reinforced the principle of legality at the international level. Specifically, the reference to customary international law and the judicial issuance of landmark decisions using rules that are not necessarily engraved in written documents have strengthened the principles of international humanitarian and criminal law.

Internationalizing National Laws

International judgments also represent the passage of principles from national to international jurisdictions and an instrument of reinforcement of domestic legal principles. In making their decisions, international judges frequently resort to the domestic jurisprudence, legal sources and constitutions of many countries. In doing so, international judges achieve two different goals. On the one hand, they provide legal reasoning and foundations for some of the crimes that are prosecuted at the international level and for which the international law sources might be silent or equivocal. Resorting to general principles of law has become a way for judges to avoid the obstacles of *nullum crimes sine lege*. In the ICTY case *Prosecutor v. Furundzija* judges have claimed that:

> no elements other than those emphasised may be drawn from international treaty or customary law, nor is resort to general principles of international criminal law or to general principles of international law of any avail. The Trial Chamber therefore considers that, to arrive at an accurate definition of rape based on the criminal law principle of specificity (*Bestimmtheitgrundsatz*, also referred to by the maxim "*nullum crimen sine lege stricta*"), it is necessary to look for principles of criminal

---

[31] The Prosecutor v. Sam Hinga Norman, Case No. SCSL, 2004–14-AR-72(E), May 31, 2004, para 1 (a) and (c).

[32] Ibid, para 20.

law common to the major legal systems of the world. These principles may be derived, with all due caution, from national laws.[33]

As well, by introducing principles of domestic jurisdictions into the framework of international law, judges provide a validation of those domestic principles that have been violated. We believe that by referring to general principles of laws, judges generate a "boomerang effect" (for a discussion on the boomerang effect as understood in the human rights context, see Keck and Sikkink 1998). By bringing domestic law into international courtrooms, decisions, and judgments, judges interpret its principles, reinforce its validity, and confirm its importance both as domestic law and foundation of international crimes. International judges signal to the domestic jurisdictions and in particular to those nations in which crimes have occurred that they have a criminal and constitutional law structure that can be applied to these violations, and they show a path to rebuild justice systems in the aftermath of conflict. International judges take laws that have often remained dormant for a long period of time and reinforce their legal value, while sending a message to perpetrators that certain behaviors are not only morally deplorable, but are unlawful.

In this regard, the analysis of judgments provides an insight into the difficulties faced by judges in interpreting and applying international law principles, while at the same time offering the basis for the future application of international humanitarian law. Indeed, international judges of the ad hoc tribunals have laid the foundations of the use of interpretative instruments and have provided the systematic categorizations of the sources of international criminal and humanitarian law. By embedding these international law principles, especially as they pertain to human rights in national law, the tribunals buttress national law just as their references to such laws provides further justification for the use of such principles at the international level.

An Expression of Universal Values

Lastly, judgments carry an incredible expressive power and very often address the broader social and political context in which international crimes occur on the local and international level. In so doing, these judgments can transcend the facts and opinions that are their principal focus to highlight important moral principles and values. For example, judges have often reinterpreted crimes and elevated them to the ranks of customary international law by referring to such concepts such as "human and personal dignity." While redefining the crime of rape and expanding its interpretation based on the initial criminalization of the conduct by the ICTR in the *Akayesu* case,[34] the ICTY judges in *Furundzija* stated that:

---

[33] The Prosecutor v. Furundzija, Case No. IT-95-17/1-T, December 10, 1998, para 177.
[34] The Prosecutor v. Jean Paul Akayesu, Case No. ICTR-94-6-T, Trial Chamber Judgment, September 2, 1998.

The essence of the whole corpus of international humanitarian law as well as human rights law lies in the protection of the human dignity of every person, whatever his or her gender.... This principle is intended to shield human beings from outrages upon their personal dignity, whether such outrages are carried out by unlawfully attacking the body or by humiliating and debasing the honour, the self-respect or the mental well being of a person.[35]

Through the analysis of judgments we discover the nature of the "international judge" and the rationales behind rulings and opinions. We uncover the human dimension of international criminal law, in which crimes are not only seen through the lenses of criminal reasoning, but also through moral and social values. While adjudicating serious violations of international humanitarian laws, judges apply these larger moral values to speak on behalf of the international community whose laws have been violated. In explaining the great task with which international judges are charged and in justifying their expansive interpretation of principles and criminal responsibility, Judges McDonald and Vohrah stated that:

we are not, in the International Tribunal, concerned with ordinary domestic crimes. The purview of the International Tribunal relates to war crimes and crimes against humanity committed in armed conflicts of extreme violence with egregious dimensions. [...] We are concerned that, in relation to the most heinous crimes known to humankind, the principles of law to which we give credence have the appropriate normative effect upon soldiers bearing weapons of destruction and upon the commanders who control them in armed conflict situations.[36]

Judgments have sent moral and legal messages at the same time. International judges have often reasoned according to principles that would overcome the absence of written and specific law and would instead give priority to condemning crimes that shock the conscience of the international community, invalidate human dignity, and threaten international peace and security. As powerfully noted by Justice Jackson in his opening statement at the Nuremberg Trials, the impact of international justice is not only to be considered by an isolated judgment or case, but within the greater effort to make the world more peaceful and secure. To this end, Justice Jackson, in addressing the judges, stated:

The real complaining party at your bar is Civilization.... The refuge of the defendants can only be their hope that International Law will lag so far behind the moral

[35] The Prosecutor v. Furundzija, Case No. IT-95-17/1-T, December 10, 1998, para 183.
[36] The Prosecutor v. Erdemovic, Case No. IT-96-22-A, Joint Separate Opinion of Judge McDonald and Judge Vohrah, October 7, 1997, para 75. See also the Prosecutor v. Tadic, "the *moral gravity* of such participation is often no less – or indeed no different – from that of those actually carrying out the acts in question." Case No. IT-94-1-A, July 15, 1999, para 191 in which judges have specified and applied for the first time individual criminal responsibility as the consequence of Joint Criminal Enterprise.

sense of mankind that conduct which is crime in the moral sense must be regarded as innocent in law.[37]

International tribunals today represent the focal point of humanity's efforts to prosecute crimes with the aim of promoting justice and peace, as well as demonstrating liability. International judges do so knowing that what is at stake is something more than the punishment of criminals. There is the need to rediscover values and morals that should inform legal principles, making sure that, what is immoral becomes illegal and what violates human dignity and human rights becomes criminal. Drawing on moral values and concepts such as human rights and human dignity, judges have often been able to fill the gaps of international criminal law and, with their decisions, reach beyond the main goal of punishment.

Judgments represent the newfound importance of creating an international criminal law in the absence of written rules and are, as we argue, the embodiment of the image of an entrepreneur international judge. Through analysis of the judgments we discover the tension among judges about the interpretation of their role and the extension of their judicial creativity (Darcy and Powderly 2010). International judges are aware their roles have changed over time from rigorous followers of international rules to lawmakers, and of the presence of a blurred line between judicial interpretation of pre-existing legal principles and judicial creation. The delivery of judgments has become a critical moment through which judges have fulfilled the unwritten mandate to fill the void of international criminal and humanitarian law left open by the deficit of international "legislation." In judgments we find the creation of exhaustive and precise criteria through which crimes should be identified, individual criminal responsibility ascertained, and international jurisdiction established, which in turn provides the basis for the future implementation of consistent international law. By analyzing the judgments of the ad hoc tribunals, we can better understand the future decisions of the International Criminal Court, which now can rely on authoritative precedents and overcome the burden of probing the existence of crimes for the prosecution of violations of international humanitarian law.

THE PLAN OF THE BOOK

Our most fundamental purposes are to explain how international criminal tribunals punish individuals for committing the worst crimes known to civilization, and how judges use their decisions to progressively develop international law and utilize its expressive capacity. *It is our central contention and theoretical contribution that judges have seized the opportunities presented in delivering their judgments to progressively*

---

[37] Opening statement of Justice Robert H. Jackson, Chief of Counsel for the United States, November 21, 1945, in the Palace of Justice at Nuremberg, International Military Tribunal in Case No. 1, The United States of America, the French Republic, The United Kingdom of Great Britain and Northern Ireland, and the Union of Soviet Socialist Republics v Hermann Wilhelm Gorina, et al.

develop the scope and depth of international law and utilize the expressive power of the law to raise moral arguments and speak to the collective values of those who suffered as well as all humankind. We conceive of the progressive development of the law as that which, in general, expands the range of crimes, modes of liability and punishment for violations of human rights. As Wessel (2006, 387) argues, progressive development of the law occurs when courts recognize " . . . new legal obligations that govern previously unregulated behavior." This definition also comports with the conception of international judicial decision making as expanding the types of conduct that fall under the purview of international humanitarian law (Scobbie 1997; Wessel 2006). The expressive value of these judgments refers to their purpose as statements of moral principles and observations that transcend their adjudicative function.

We argue that what makes these judgments so remarkable is that judges achieve these goals within the legal and political limits that have been established by international bodies, such as the United Nations Security Council, that authorized their creation. Judgment day thus brings with it not just the pronouncing of verdicts and the meting out of punishment, but often, the expansion of international law and the expressive power of the law. While scholars have commented on these developments (e.g., Darcy and Powderly 2010; Sloane 2007a; Swart 2010), we develop a theoretical framework within which to understand and explain such behavior and utilize empirical methods to test our expectations.

We contend that judges are judicial entrepreneurs who must work within an international criminal justice system whose political and legal boundaries necessarily limit the extent to which they can expand and fill in the gaps in law. However, because international humanitarian law, international human rights law and international criminal law are such nascent areas in international legal development, and judges are being called upon to interpret and implement such laws for the first time since the World War II tribunals, substantial opportunities exist for judges to use their discretion to advance the law and speak to its higher moral purposes when possible and appropriate. The central portion of our book develops this theory in depth and identifies the circumstances under which judges develop the law and utilize its expressive power.

We develop our theory of entrepreneurial judicial decision making in Chapter Two. We contend that judges seek to use their opinions not only to determine guilt and punishment, but also for expressive purposes and to advance the development of international law. Judges, however, must work within the statutory and political parameters determined by their superiors and the international legal community. In our theory of entrepreneurial judicial decision making we identify two compelling forces that encourage judges to go beyond merely pronouncing verdicts and punishments to use the law to realize these aims. First, we argue that because of their interest in human rights, judges will seek to condemn such behavior both to acknowledge the suffering of the victims and to further erode the norm of impunity. Judges will use the expressive capacity of their opinions to demonstrate moral outrage at such conduct (e.g., when defendants commit especially heinous acts and show no remorse), and will further develop international law to ensure that such actions will henceforth fall within the ambit of their jurisdiction and be considered a violation of international law (e.g., finding that rape is a prosecutable offense under the Genocide Convention). Second, because the tribunals have been such novel experiments in international relations and are part of the "justice cascade" (Sikkink 2011) judges will also generally be conscious of the need to create a legacy. We believe that the motivation to establish a legacy for future generations will also encourage judges to utilize their judgments for expressive purposes and further develop international law.

Furthermore, we also assess when such entrepreneurial decision making is most likely to occur. We argue that where international humanitarian, criminal and human rights laws are emerging, ambiguous or where gaps exist in the coverage of crimes, modes of liability and so on judges will likely perceive the opportunity and need for further jurisprudential development. International humanitarian, international human rights and international criminal law are embryonic fields that must be clarified, expanded upon and interpreted by judges to reach verdicts and determine punishment. Indeed, until the creation of the ICTY in 1993 and the ICTR in 1994 there had been little jurisprudential development in this area of international law since the Nuremberg and Tokyo Tribunals of the post–World War II era.

Judges are not, however, free agents with unfettered discretion to weigh into all aspects of international law and the conflict situations over which the tribunals exercise jurisdiction. Rather, the international tribunals are intended to serve a diverse array of constituents including the international community, broadly defined, the peoples whose conflicts they adjudicate, an international legal community whose work is informed and guided by the tribunals, and those who authorized their creation. We stress that the tribunals are like other political institutions – their methods and goals reflect primarily the interests of their designers – principally the major, Western powers and the United Nations Security Council – and their professional community – the international legal community (King and Meernik 2011). The tribunals depend upon the former group of powerful actors for resources and political support, while their aims, jurisdiction and fundamental operating principles have been outlined in the founding statutes authored by these powers. Their judgments must be interpreted and ultimately given force by the lawyers, judges and experts who comprise the international legal community. Therefore, we contend that the legal and political reach of the judges' opinions are circumscribed by the interests of these actors. For example, the ad hoc tribunal judges are confined to matters of customary international law by their founding powers (Ratner, Abrams and Bischoff 2009) and thus may not stray into certain, developing areas of the law, such as the crime of aggression. Trial chamber judges must anticipate the possible objections of their appeals chambers and so strive to maintain some measure of consistency with precedent; avoid unusual interpretations of international law that may be overturned; and avoid giving the defense grounds on which to make successful appeals that may undermine their more fundamental purposes. But while all judges must operate within the boundaries of what is politically permissible, judges will use the expressive power of the law, and further develop its meaning and reach to the extent possible given these constraints. We discuss both the legal and political conditions that create opportunities for international tribunals to progressively develop international law and to employ its expressive power, and those conditions that circumscribe such efforts. We describe how the judges exploit such opportunities when they arise, but have managed to stay within the lines of authority outlined by their founding statutes. We contend that our theory of judicial decision making enhances and expands upon traditional accounts of international legal development that tend to focus on textual analyses and do not conceptualize the judges as making strategic choices regarding their judgments in a political environment (Federova 2012).

In Chapter Three we test our theory of judicial decision making and the progressive development of international law. Among many of the difficulties that international judges face in administering justice, one of the greatest is the "novelty" of many of the crimes committed, and the relative absence in international law of practices, guidance and norms that could be applied to specific cases. We contend that this "legal vacuum" has given international judges an extraordinary opportunity to not only deliver justice but also to break new ground in the development of international criminal law by filling in those areas of international law that are vital to their administration of justice. Thus, while the mandate behind the creation of international criminal tribunals may have focused on the apprehension, prosecution, and accountability of individuals responsible for war crimes, crimes against humanity and genocide, the actual work of international judges has called upon them to generate an extensive jurisprudence, which has further developed the extant corpus of international criminal law.

We suggest that international judges seize the opportunity of developing international criminal norms by (re)defining and developing elements of crimes, modes of responsibility, as well as expanding the application of these concepts and norms to other forms of international crimes. We also contend that most of the landmark decisions have been made by the appellate chambers where judges, utilizing the grounds of appeals, develop general statements that create groundbreaking precedents. We assess the development of key innovations in international law, including: development of international jurisprudence on bias crimes such as genocide[38] and persecution, the origins of the Joint Criminal Enterprise forms of liability[39] and command liability,[40] and sentencing issues.

---

[38] The Prosecutor v. Akayesu, Case No. ICTR 96–4-T, Judgment, September 2, 1998.

[39] The Prosecutor v. Duško Tadić, Case No. IT-94–1-A, Appeal Judgment, July 15, 1999.

[40] Prosecutor v. Zejnil Delalic, Zdravko Mucic, Hazim Delic and Esad Landzo, Case No. IT-96–21-Abis Appeal Judgement, April 8, 2003.

We then take a novel approach to understanding when and how judges seize the opportunity to further develop international law through an empirical analysis of appellate chamber decisions. We suggest that appellate chamber judges will engage in the progressive development of international law when issues arise that pertain to: (1) lack of clarity in the definitions of elements of crimes; (2) the need to consider new and novel forms of liability; (3) the need to recognize new and novel types of crimes that fall within the spirit, but not the current status of treaty and customary international law. Thus, not only do we provide a legal and textual analysis of the evolution and impact of these key areas of international law, we also show through statistical analysis of appeals chamber decisions just when such developments are most likely to occur, and which opinions have been cited most frequently.

Chapter Four focuses on how the judges utilize the expressive capacity of the law to move beyond facts and legal developments to pronounce value judgments. To sit in judgment where the guilty have committed unspeakable atrocities; where the victims expect justice and recognition for their pain and suffering; and where the international community seeks condemnation of the violation of its laws gives judges tremendous power to speak to the morals, values and conscience of the world. Do international tribunal judges seize this opportunity to use the expressive power of their judgments to acknowledge the violence done to society and affirm there will be no impunity for the guilty? Scholars have argued that judges can and should use the "expressive" potential of their opinions to make such grandiloquent proclamations (e.g., Sloane 2007a, see also DeGuzman 2012). We take a novel approach to answer this question by analyzing all the language used in the tribunals' judgments to determine the frequency with which judges make statements that express values and morals; that condemn behavior; that speak to ending impunity; and other similar pronouncement that go beyond the recitation of evidence and legal analysis. This research will, for the first time, shed empirical light on judicial decision making that has heretofore been confined to speculation and normative arguments.

Our analysis of the determinants of tribunal sentences is the focus of Chapter Five. In the previous chapters we explain and demonstrate how judges act as entrepreneurs and utilize opportunities in cases and the spare language in their statutes and founding documents to progressively develop the law and employ its expressive capacity. In this chapter, we explain the other major purpose of judgments as pronouncements of guilt and punishment, which are grounded in a reliance to their founding documents that provides them with substantial power to make such determinations. Hence, judges advance important international principles, such as retribution and recognition of the horrific impact of these international crimes through utilization of the broad discretion given them in their statutes and rules of procedure and evidence.

Perhaps the most fundamental purpose of international criminal tribunals is the administration of international justice through the application of international law. However, due to the special nature of the crimes international criminal tribunals prosecute, their mandate reaches beyond that of domestic criminal courts, and international judges encounter greater challenges than domestic judges. International justice is intended to facilitate the realization of retribution, deterrence, rehabilitation, as well as the "restoration and maintenance of peace"[41] by bringing to justice and holding responsible individuals who have committed international crimes. The implication of the scope of international judgments suggests that the standards by which the international community will ultimately evaluate the effectiveness of the work of international tribunals in administering justice will be measured in part against their ability to apprehend war criminals, deliver fair verdicts, and hand down the appropriate sentences.

How do international tribunal judges fare in providing justice and meting out punishment that respect the rights of the accused while at the same time addressing the desire for retribution and "justice" by the victims and the international community? Many scholars and observers have called into question the fairness and consistency of the sentences meted out by these tribunals (Drumbl 2007a; Harmon and Gaynor 2007; Olusanya 2005; Weinberg de Roca and Rassi 2008). We contend, however, that judges seek to fulfill their mandate by issuing verdicts and sentences that (1) reflect the guidance of their statutes and rules of procedure and evidence; (2) are consistent across defendants; and (3) will withstand the scrutiny of their appellate chambers. We approach the study of the administration of international justice by looking at judgments handed down by international tribunals over time, and assess the fairness and consistency of sentences based on the type of crime, individual level of responsibility, and the mitigating and aggravating factors considered by the judges. We empirically analyze and evaluate sentences by the ICTY, ICTR and SCSL to estimate the impact of these criteria and assess whether, through consistency and fairness, judges are able to provide justice for all. We find through empirical analysis of all the sentences handed down to date by the tribunals, as well as the results of appeals of sentences by the tribunals' appellate bodies, that it is possible to identify a small set of sentencing determinants to accurately explain judicial decision making. Thus, contrary to the arguments made by many scholars, we find that judges act within their powers and consistently, and arguably, properly sentence those found guilty. We also argue that because the judges were given so little guidance regarding sentencing, their judicial entrepreneurship could safely remain within the wide parameters permitted by their statutes.

We conclude in Chapter Six. Our analysis comes at a fascinating time in the history of the international criminal justice system. The creation and functioning of the International Criminal Court, new investigations into violations of international humanitarian law, and the challenges posed by new crimes require new research. In addition to providing a summary of our major findings and the ways in which

---

[41] United Nations Security Council Resolution, 808, 1993, p. 2, establishing the International Tribunal for the former Yugoslavia.

our research informs the study of international law and transitional justice, we also discuss the importance of the results in our understanding of international judicial decision making as well as the legacy of the tribunals' jurisprudence.

We contend that it is of pivotal importance to understand how international judges seize, when necessary, the opportunity to develop and innovate international criminal law; utilize its expressive capacity to speak to victims and other international audiences; and punish the guilty. We suggest that judges engage in entrepreneurial decision making to achieve these goals and have sought to go beyond the letter of the law when necessary in order to increase the strength, understanding and legitimacy of international criminal law. Some studies have already begun to explore the possibility of promoting a more active role of the international judge (Danner 2006; Zarbyiev 2012) in handing down judgments. As others have argued, analysis of this type of judicial decision making has been somewhat neglected in studies of international law (Ginsberg 2005). We argue that in the quest to advance human rights and ensure the legacy of international law is understood and applied at the tribunals, the judges have seized opportunities to act in an entrepreneurial fashion. They seek to provide justice that not only accomplishes of the tribunals – to render verdicts – but which also speaks to people of the world beyond the narrow confines of the international legal community that will ensure the impact of the international tribunals for decades to come.

2

A Theory of International Tribunal Judges as Judicial Entrepreneurs

INTRODUCTION

Judges must navigate a judicial and political balancing act throughout the performance of their duties at the international criminal tribunals. On the one hand, they are independent decision makers who must reach verdicts and assess punishment for the guilty using their own judgment and interpretation of the evidence and the law. On the other hand, they are not entirely unfettered agents free to act within their cloistered environment in the manner they find most fit and proper for their roles. Rather, they are agents of an international community that sets boundaries and limitations on their authority, even if these boundaries are often difficult to precisely identify and may change over time. Our conception and theory of judicial decision making at the international criminal tribunals is rooted in this understanding of the dual roles judges perform. We make the argument in this chapter that judges are entrepreneurial decision makers as they strike this balance between independence and constraint. They will reach decisions that remain mostly within the legal and political parameters established in their founding documents by the international community and their own rules of procedure and evidence as necessary and appropriate. When, however, the opportunity or political/legal demand arises to forge beyond these parameters to progressively develop the law – to fill in or expand its protection of human rights – or use their expressive capacity to speak to the law's intrinsic value and aspirations for society, judges will utilize if not seize these opportunities.

In this chapter we develop our theory of judges as entrepreneurial decision makers that we will subsequently apply to demonstrate how and when judges push at the formal and informal boundaries that guide their work. We conceive of judges as agents of both the political decision makers who have created their institutions and institutional framework, whether it is the UN Security Council, nation-states or some combination thereof, and the international legal community within which they operate as professionals. These institutions and communities will typically expect an adherence to international law and the written rules contained in UN resolutions and formal statutes specifying their powers, as well as a certain degree of predictability and consistency in the judges' discharge of their duties. Judges, however, must grapple with many novel, situational circumstances and much uncharted, legal terrain as they act upon and interpret these founding documents and the relevant international law. The need to reach judgments on such matters both as a practical necessity to arrive at verdicts and punishments, and to carve out a pathway to guide their future decisions makes it problematic to strictly adhere to these guidelines. Instead, we contend that judges act as entrepreneurs using their independent judgment and power to bend or break these parameters as they believe is necessary and appropriate.

This chapter seeks to answer two questions that result from this two-part assumption. First, how and why do judges go beyond these statutory and political parameters? What immediate aims and what broader purposes are they seeking to realize when they act as judicial entrepreneurs? And second, under what conditions are judges willing to exceed these parameters? What case situations and questions of law might arise that would lead judges to perceive the need and possess the desire to push the parameters? We begin first with the development of our theory of judicial entrepreneurialism. We build from research on public policy entrepreneurs, and a more limited body of knowledge on entrepreneurial judges. From this research we extract insights into the political and policy conditions that give rise to judicial entrepreneurship – the types of activities they undertake in furtherance of their policy objectives, and their prospects for success. These theoretical antecedents help lay the groundwork for our theory of international judicial entrepreneurialism. The most important portion of our chapter then follows – our theory regarding why judges go beyond the bounds of the legal and political parameters to progressively develop international law and utilize its expressive capacity and the conditions under which they will do so.

We then describe the statutory and political parameters that create the environments in which judges make decisions. We discuss the influence exerted by both the formal, written rules judges are charged with implementing and the more informal pressures and political constraints that shape the world of the international criminal justice system. While these written and unwritten rules play a powerful role in this world, we also elucidate how the incomplete and sometimes conflicting guidance emanating from these rules provide judges with opportunities to fill in legal gaps and expand our interpretation of international law. Thus, we also review the manner in which ambiguous, incomplete and open-ended political and legal parameters provide many opportunities for judges to exercise discretion in the discharge of their duties. We conclude by discussing just how justices strike a balance between adherence to the limitations on and opportunities for entrepreneurial decision making. In Chapters Three and Four we test the theory of judicial entrepreneurship, while

Chapter Five focuses on the ultimate product of judgment day, the verdicts and sentences.

UNDERSTANDING ENTREPRENEURSHIP IN POLITICS AND JUDICIAL DECISION MAKING

We contend that judges at the international criminal tribunals act as judicial entrepreneurs in utilizing, if not seizing, opportunities to progressively develop the law. As entrepreneurs in the realm of international justice, we argue that judges act in ways analogous to policy entrepreneurs in the domestic setting. Therefore, it is to this literature on policy entrepreneurs that we turn to better inform our understanding of judicial entrepreneurs at the international level.

The analysis of the role of policy entrepreneurs has intellectual roots in a variety of studies of domestic and international politics. Kingdon's dynamic view of policymaking has domestic policy entrepreneurs – persons who recognize policy problems and solutions and compete for attention – working in issue-based networks to achieve their policy goals. These entrepreneurs use windows of opportunity to expend resources (time, energy, reputation, money) in the hopes of a potential return in the form of a policy gain – either in the short-term, but also in the long-term policy process (Kingdon 1995, 179). Such individuals exercise important influence in producing policy change (Costain and Majstorovic 1994; Haider-Markel, Joslyn and Kniss 2000; Sharp 1994). As Blavoukos and Bourantonis (2011, 655) write, "Policy entrepreneurs are actors who help propel dynamic policy change in their respective political environment, be it local, national or international. With their actions, they create or exploit new opportunities to push forward their ideas or policy options, thus having transformative effects on politics, policies, or institutions."

What exactly is it that entrepreneurs do? Mintrom has extensively analyzed the role and work of policy entrepreneurs and provides the following depiction. First, he suggests (2000, 36) policy entrepreneurs "... are individuals who, through their creativity, strategy, networking, and persuasive argumentation, bring ideas for policy innovation into common currency and thus promote policy change." He subsequently describes their behavior and contends "Among the activities that policy entrepreneurs engage in, the most important include identifying problems, networking in policy circles, shaping the terms of policy debates, and building coalitions to support policy change" (Mintrom 2000, 57).

Policy entrepreneurs must be alert to possibilities to advance an agenda or policy innovation. This, in turn, is aided considerably by an ability to perceive information and opportunities to advance these goals that may not be noticed by others – what Mintrom and Norman (2009, 652) refer to as "social acuity." Successful policy entrepreneurs have a finely honed sense of the policy space and the avenues open for the achievement of their goals. This is particularly the case for entrepreneurs in the domestic policy environment in which there is a complex political and policy environment populated by bureaucrats, politicians, interest groups and others all seeking to advance their preferences. They perceive policy vacuums in the environment or a need (preference) for a policy correction and seek to reformulate and revise policy choices (Carter, Scott and Rowling 2004, 278; Carter and Scott 2010). Such individuals and organizations may work in concert or competition with the entrepreneur in this very dynamic environment. According to Mintrom (2000) policy entrepreneurs must also possess excellent communication skills as they must use the written word as well as other forms of persuasion to advocate their ideas. Even entrepreneurs with excellent skills in all facets of their work, however, must contend with a policy-making environment, or milieu as Mintrom describes it, that sets the opportunity and participation parameters. When the milieu is open and conducive to participation, such as when the pace of change in a policy area is rapid and many governmental actors are engaged in policy reform, the opportunities for entrepreneurs are substantial. By contrast, when the pace of change is slow and the avenues for participation are limited, the milieu is not nearly as open to policy entrepreneurs. While often research focuses on the individual, crusading policy entrepreneur, Crow (2010, 301) points out that groups or collectives can also promote policy change.

Mintrom's work contains many critical insights that will inform our understanding and theory of international judicial entrepreneurs. While certainly judicial policy entrepreneurs and international judges are an altogether different breed of advocates, there are key similarities. The most critical work done by judges is carried out through writing well-substantiated and well-reasoned arguments – written communication resides at the center of both policy formation and legal judgments. Judges must be able to convince their audiences, especially when they seek to progressively develop international law and when they employ its expressive capacity, that their innovations are appropriate and necessary, as well as reflective of emerging normative and legal norms. The policy environment in which judges operate is also a key determinant of their ability to act as policy entrepreneurs. As we described earlier, the current international law milieu is ripe with opportunity for judges to explore the definitions of novel types of crimes, modes of liability and other policy matters that, at times, almost demand an answer if the international tribunals are to carry out their business. It is also a very dynamic environment in which, despite the length of the trials, judgments must be rendered within a comparatively short period of time. Decisions cannot wait but must be reached expeditiously given the calendar of trials and the need to keep the judicial enterprise moving forward. As the oft-repeated cliché goes, "justice delayed is justice denied." In short, judges at the international tribunals are exceptionally well-positioned because of their excellent communication skills and policy milieu to act as judicial entrepreneurs.

While an extensive body of literature examines entrepreneurial theories within interest groups and legislatures, research has begun to examine judiciaries as well. Judges act as policy advocates when they expand upon the issues presented in cases to raise other concerns (McGuire and Palmer 1996). As McIntosh and Cates (1997, xiv) note, however, "With rare exceptions, the notion of judicial entrepreneurship is conspicuously absent in the legal and political science literature." Their research describes the manner in which prominent jurists used their opinions and legal reasoning to advance a particular conceptualization of the law that changed people's understanding of powers, rights and responsibilities in the United States. They write that, "Our definition of an entrepreneurial judge . . . is *one who is alert to the opportunity for innovation, who is willing to invest the resources and assume the risks necessary to offer and develop a genuinely unique legal concept, and who must strategically employ the written word to undertake change*" (McIntosh and Cates 1997, 5; emphasis in the original). Their view of judicial entrepreneurs is congruent with Mintrom (1997) and Schneider, Teske and Mintrom's (1995) in which policy entrepreneurs invest resources and utilize communication to advance a policy preference.

Along the same lines, more recent scholarship has suggested that the "staff of international courts may act as [. . .] transnational norms entrepreneurs" (Danner 2006, 51) or that judges may see themselves as activists facing ambiguous laws (Jodoin 2010). While, in setting up the two ad hoc tribunals, the United Nations Security Council clearly stated that judges could not create law, the situations presented to the benches of the tribunals were so novel compared to the governing international legal system that judges had few realistic options but to innovate and educate future generations of jurists on the developing international legal order. In addition, as Danner (2006) suggests, the temporary and geographical limited jurisdiction of the ICTY, ICTR and SCSL might have helped the acceptance by the international community of some international judicial lawmaking, which is more extensively delimited by the ICC Statute, Rules of Procedure and Evidence and a separate document called the Elements of Crimes.

Why would judges seek to become policy entrepreneurs? As George and Berger (2005, 7) write, "Entrepreneurship may further a judge's policy goals, reinforce her legal perspective, satisfy professional objectives, or offer public recognition." As we argue below, judges at the international level no doubt possess multiple motivations in crafting their opinions. They seek to achieve instrumental ends, such as delivering a verdict and, if necessary, a sentence. They seek to clarify, fill in and expand international law. And they may view the law as a vehicle for advancing a particular policy goal, such as the protection of human rights. Cassese nicely summarizes the opportunities and motivations inherent in judicial decision making to act entrepreneurially in the context of the ICC when he writes, "The International Criminal Court is destined to flesh out and bring into effect those peremptory norms of international law which safeguard such fundamental values as human dignity, the respect for life and limb of innocent persons, and the protection of ethnic, religious or racial groups." Studies of policy entrepreneurs within the international tribunals, however, have been noticeably lacking.

At the international level, researchers have investigated the role played by epis-temic communities – networks of knowledge-based experts – in their realm of expertise (Haas 1992). Increasingly scholars recognize that broader communities and coalitions shape the policy process and that these coalitions help to shift pol-icy priorities and norms (Gamble and Ku 2000; Ku 1996).[1] Policy entrepreneurs within these communities and human rights organizations in particular promote humanitarian issues and help change ideas regarding norms of state sovereignty, the applicability of international law to emerging forms of conflict and the rights of victims and the innocent (Sikkink 1993). These players, working within domestic or transnational institutions, contribute to regime change (Evangelista 1995; Checkel 1993), and ultimately even the resolution of conflict and the de-escalation of vio-lence (Rasler 2000). Over time as these entrepreneurs play an agenda-setting role in international organizations, the institutions develop increasing levels of delegated authority and exhibit greater autonomy (Pollack 1997).

Closely related to our notion of judicial entrepreneurship is the term "judicial activism" that has been employed in the study of particularly US courts (e.g., Gins-berg 2005; Jodoin 2010; Kmiec 2004; Lindquist and Cross 2009; Roosevelt 2006; Rosenberg 1991; Segal and Spaeth 1993), although there is also significant work building on this concept in courts cross-nationally (e.g., Cepeda-Espinosa 2004; Smithey and Ishiyama 2002; Tezcur 2009). There is even some use of the termi-nology with respect to international courts. Schabas (2008, 758) characterizes the behavior of the ICTY judges as advancing "radical interpretations in a dramatic expression of judicial activism." He notes, however, that while most states seem to have supported the results of much of the ICTY's early judicial "activism," the framers of the ICC statute deliberately circumscribed that court's ability to act in such an unfettered manner.[2]

Conjoined to this scholarly debate about the meaning, utility and prevalence of judicial activism, there is also an ideological battle not only over its meaning, but more importantly over whether it is desirable and appropriate activity. Assessments by scholars and practitioners over whether a judicial ruling is "activist" have been heavily influenced by ideology. A conservative interpretation of the law may char-acterize liberal rulings as activist for expanding the law from the bench, while a liberal view of activism would suggest the same is true of rulings that provide novel interpretations of the law that prioritize conservative values. In short, there is a great deal of ideological baggage that is attached to the term which frequently taints its more scholarly and objective usage.

---

[1] See the special issue of the journal *International Organization* (1992, volume 46, issue 1) that was devoted to this topic.

[2] Interestingly, Schabas (2008) also notes that the appeals chambers of the ICC have often refused to intervene in prosecutorial appeals on interlocutory decisions in the interest of letting the pre-trial and trial chambers exercise their best judgment on such matters without interference from on high, which might suggest a tacit condoning of judicial activism.

Despite the politicized nature of the debate, Kmiec (2004) argues that there is utility in the concept and that when properly delineated it can provide a useful perspective on judicial decision making. According to Kmiec (2004), the concept of judicial activism has been employed with reference to five core meanings or attributes. First, its usage has frequently referenced activism as the judicial invalidation of "arguably constitutional actions of other branches" (2004, 1444), or more broadly, counter-majoritarianism (Lindquist and Cross 2009). Second, it can refer to a failure to adhere to precedent. Third, it can imply judicial legislating. As Ginsburg (2005) argues in the context of international law, judges do engage in some degree of lawmaking in the performance of their work. Fourth, the terminology suggests, " . . . departures from accepted interpretative methodology" (Kmiec 2004, 1444). And fifth, it implies a "results oriented judging" (Kmiec 2004, 1444). Lindquist and Cross (2009) would include the accumulation of power in the judiciary as another element in the meaning of judicial activism. These meanings and interpretations of judicial activism are also relevant at the international level, but especially the notions of judicial legislation and results-oriented judging. We agree with Wessel (2006) that while there are problems in transposing this concept to the international level, there are also insights from the extensive analysis of judicial activism that can shed light on decision making by international judges.

Some observers have argued that international judges have indeed engaged in such judicial activism. Schabas (2008) argues that the judges have creatively expanded the reach of international law, while Wessel (2006, 386) describes such efforts as "delegated policy-making" or "judicial policymaking" (see also Ginsberg 2005). Certainly, in the absence of executive and legislative oversight of their interpretation of the law and such activities as the development of the rules of procedure and evidence by the ad hoc tribunals, one could argue that the tribunal judges have stepped into this vacuum and taken "legislative" type action on some occasions (e.g., the rules of procedure and evidence), while refraining in other instances (e.g., declining to develop a sentencing schedule). In fact, Wessel (2006, 387) contends that the notion of "progressive development" of the law is a hallmark of judicial activism that is applicable at the international level.

Therefore, we believe that there is significant support in the literatures on policy entrepreneurship and judicial activism to suggest that judges engage in this activity at the international level. We contend that judges are most explicitly entrepreneurial when they progressively develop the law and use its power to give voice to more expressive concerns. Their entrepreneurialism is less in evidence in matters of the application of punishment and the development of sentencing criteria, but mostly because of their substantial and independent powers in this area. Given the role of policy entrepreneurs and activists within organizations and institutions at the domestic and international level of analysis, how might we conceptualize international criminal trial and appellate judges as policy entrepreneurs?

Based upon our understanding of the significant legal opportunities inherent in international law at this stage in its development, the ambiguities present in the tribunals' founding documents and the ever-evolving nature of customary international law, we contend that international tribunal judges have significant opportunity to act as policy entrepreneurs. Given the similarities in the environments within which policy entrepreneurs work at the domestic level and the international level, we can understand when conditions are ripe for entrepreneurial activity. Opportunity alone, however, does not create motivation. We must next explain why the judges of the international criminal tribunals would act as judicial entrepreneurs in the performance of their duties.

A THEORY OF JUDICIAL ENTREPRENEURSHIP

Human Rights Concerns and Judicial Entrepreneurship

We contend that first and foremost judges of the international tribunals will act as entrepreneurs in order to protect and advance human rights. Second, they will act as entrepreneurs and progressively develop the law and utilize its expressive capacity to strengthen a professional legacy for the tribunals and as jurists in their own right. As we outlined in Chapter One, we conceive of the progressive development of the law as that which, in general, expands the range of protection of human rights to encompass a wider range of crimes and liability for violation of human rights and punishment of such crimes. It is to the rationales for entrepreneurship that we now turn. *We must emphasize, however, that while we develop a rationale to explain what may motivate judges to work in an entrepreneurial manner, we do not test these specific motivations.* The personal and professional reasons that might provide the spark for judicial entrepreneurship are important to understand (George and Berger 2005), but we ultimately locate the circumstances and opportunities that arise in cases as the factors that predict when entrepreneurial behavior will occur. We also note that the object of our study – the judgments – are products of the collective efforts of judges in the trial and appeals chambers.

We do recognize that judges quite likely have opinions regarding their role and the mandates established for them that can shape their behavior. Some judges openly claim the need for and righteousness of judicial activism, while others pledge their loyalty to the existent legal order. Judgments in a way speak to us about specific positions. For example, Judge Shahabuddeen wrote "the principle of legality "does not prevent [the] court from interpreting and clarifying the elements of a particular crime [. . .] but [it] does prevent a court from creating new law or from interpreting existing law beyond the reasonable limits of acceptable clarification."[3]

---

[3] Prosecutor v. Milutinovic, Decision on Motion Challenging Jurisdiction, No. IT-99–37-AR72, para 38 (May 21, 2003). See also Meron (2005) commenting on the same passage: "Customary law evolves

Other judges have been more open about the need of judicial activism while facing insurmountable obstacles in creating novel judicial institutions. In one interview with Hazan (2004, 50) Cassese, commenting on the initial difficulties in establishing the tribunal, stated "either I accepted the facts as they were and, thus, the asphyxiation and the slow death of the tribunal or I launched myself into judicial activism, even to excess. Obviously, I chose the second solution."

From other perspectives, scholars have tried to narrow down the rationale behind such judicial activism or entrepreneurialism by attributing it to individual attitudes and interests (Jodoin 2010) or to the type of institutional appointment (Voeten 2007). However, international criminal tribunals represent a case sui generis, characterized by heightened tension among contrasting interests of justice, of defendants' rights, and of an elusive goal of peace and reconciliation for the affected societies. The international tribunals operate within novel political, legal and institutional environments that may encourage judges toward activism or conservatism collide with personal and professional preferences that motivate individual judges. We do not, however, seek to trace the origin of specific instances of judicial entrepreneurialism to the goals and influence of any particular, individual judges.

Advancing the Cause of Human Rights

The international criminal tribunals are responsible for providing justice to the victims and those responsible for violations of international humanitarian law, but in their opinions, the judges have also referred frequently to the need to protect the innocent and advance the cause of human rights. Indeed, that is the primary purpose of most of the legislative instruments judges use in reaching their decisions, including the international Convention on Genocide as well as international jurisprudence on crimes against humanity, large portions of the Geneva Conventions and the laws and customs of war. The Rome Statute refers to the need for ICC judges to not deviate from the emerging human rights norms and trends in their decisions. Whether we view judges as individual decision makers with their own normative preferences regarding human rights or as agents of the tribunals charged with protecting human rights, human rights values permeate the tribunals' efforts. Indeed, as Judge McDonald has written, "By ensuring this accounting[4], the Tribunals concretely show that the international instruments guaranteeing basic human rights are more than merely an aspiration" (2000, 480).

Many of the judges at the tribunals come from a human rights background (whether academic or activist), such as Theodor Meron, Fausto Pocar (ICTY); Sanji Mmasenono Monageng, Christine Van Den Wyngaert, Kuniko Ozaki (ICC),

---

through interpretation and application. Here the science of the law blends with the judicial culture of caution and restraint" (p. 826).

[4] Accounting meaning the prosecution of violations of international law.

to name but a few. Indeed, former ICTR President Navanethem Pillay went on to become United Nations High Commissioner for Human Rights. Therefore, we argue that judges will seek to progressively develop international law and utilize its expressive capacity as their principal vehicles for protecting and advancing human rights. To be sure, the judges must be ever mindful of the rights of the accused and the necessity of providing justice that is not just fair, but perceived to be fair. Nonetheless, this goal pertains to the mechanics by which they carry out their judicial enterprise, not the very purposes of it. Whether through the use of the Martens Clause or through a careful balancing act of conflicting objectives, judges have demonstrated a strong preference for protecting human rights.

The Martens Clause

The importance of human rights considerations can be seen in the consistent appeal to and application of the Martens Clause by the tribunals to the many cases in which deliberate and violent attacks on civilians were perpetrated. Although the Martens Clause was not intended to include principles of human rights protections, scholars and practitioners have clearly stated that the "principles of humanity" and "public conscience" to which the Clause refers are the mirror of principles common to humanitarian law and human rights laws. Where legal principles of protection of the rights of civilians cannot be found in humanitarian law, human rights law becomes the source of those principles (Meron 2000; Oberleitner 2015). Over time, the Martens Clause has become the ground upon which considerations of human rights and humanitarian law have found common application.[5] The Clause, as first introduced in the Preamble to the 1899 Hague Convention, is a minimum benchmark for the protection of civilians even in the absence of any international treaty. It establishes: "Until a more complete code of the laws of war is issued, the High Contracting Parties think it right to declare that in cases not included in the Regulations adopted by them, populations and belligerents remain under the protection and empire of the principles of international law, as they result from the usages established between civilized nations, from the laws of humanity and the requirements of the public conscience." It describes a norm of deference to human rights that can be referenced in those situations where the law has not caught up to new and emerging human rights violations.

However, the Clause also represents an additional opportunity for judges to expand international human rights law specifically for the interpretation of norms of international humanitarian and criminal law. As Wessel (2006, 390) writes, "The Martens Clause promotes judicial policy-making by codifying the role of judges to bridge the

---

[5] As reported by Meron (2000), in the 1996 case in front of the ICJ about the "Legality of the Threat or Use of Nuclear Weapons" Judge Weeramantry made a compelling argument that the landscape of international law has changed considerably after the adoption of the United Nations Declaration of Human Rights, such that considerations of public conscience must refer to human rights principles every time humanitarian concerns arise.

gap between the 'dictates of public conscience,' which they are instructed to define, and the more concrete *lex lata* – [namely the existent law as] articulated in treaties, customary international law and general principles." The definition of the Clause itself, which refers to the "empire of the principles of international law," has offered the judges the opportunity to "humanize" international law (Meron 2000; Swart 2010) and make sure that crimes that are not specifically prohibited by international treaties can still fall under the scrutiny of international justice. In several cases judges have taken the value-laden statements included in the Martens Clause such as the "laws of humanity and public conscience" and introduced novel interpretations of the law and the development of customary international law. As Wessel (2006, 390) writes, the Martens Clause provides judges with opportunities to define the concept of "public conscience" and in doing so gives judges a considerable amount of power in developing international law (Wessel 2006, 390; Zahnd 2000). Judges that have served at the ICTY have indicated how the Clause enables a progressive interpretation of international humanitarian law. Meron (2000, 88) writes, "When there already is some legal basis for adopting a more humanitarian position, the Martens Clause enables decision makers to take the extra step forward" in expanding the law to consider human rights concerns.

The ad hoc tribunals' jurisprudence is replete with cases that refer to the Martens Clause and its principles. Since their establishment the ICTY and ICTR have been instrumental in the implementation of basic rules for the respect of humanity as mentioned in the Martens Clause. For example, the jurisprudence of the ICTR and the development of the definition of crimes against humanity have strengthened considerably the protection of human rights of the civilian population regardless of the type of conflict taking place (internal vs. international). In the *Martic* case at the ICTY the Trial Chamber found that the use of war-fighting methods is not unlimited and that the basic respect of humanity "constitutes the foundation[s] of the entire body of international humanitarian law applicable to all armed conflict."[6] A more progressive interpretation of the application of human rights concerns through the interpretation of the Martens Clause can be found in *Kupreskic*. The Trial Chamber established that the "[Martens] Clause clearly shows that principles of international humanitarian law may emerge through a customary process under the pressure of the demands of humanity or the dictates of public conscience, even where State practice is scant or inconsistent."[7] Thus, human rights and humanitarian concerns have been at the center of international judicial reasoning. This concern, we contend, is a principal impetus for the need to expand the law and employ its language to speak to the law's higher moral purposes.

---

[6] The Prosecutor v. Milan Martic, Case No. IT-95–11-R61, Decision under Rule 61 of the ICTY Rules of Procedure and Evidence, March 8, 1996, para 13. See also, Meron (2000) and Cassese (2000) discussing the evolution and relevance of the Martens clause.

[7] The Prosecutor v. Kupreskic, Case No. IT-95–16-T, Trial Judgment, January 14, 2000, para 527.

Human Rights and Conflicting Norms

Another method by which we can demonstrate the importance of human rights to the judges is to assess the power of this goal in comparison to other tribunal objectives. That is, we should look for the difficult cases and issues where the promotion of human rights is advanced despite the cost to the achievement of other goals pursued by international tribunals. For example, there have been several cases at the tribunals in which judges have had to weigh the value and feasibility of protecting human rights against other military and political objectives. They have frequently come down on the side of protecting human rights.

One of the most vexing issues involving such judgments occurred in the very first case in which an individual was found guilty at the ICTY. In fact, the decisions in the case of Drazen Erdemovic, a Bosnian Serb soldier who pled guilty to taking part in the Srebrenica massacre and provided substantial cooperation with the OTP at the ICTY, are among the most far-reaching defenses of the primacy of the human rights of victims against the mitigating factors claimed by the accused in international law. The question of interest here concerns how and to what extent Erdemovic's defense of superior orders and duress in the commission of his crimes should factor into the Tribunal's verdict and punishment. Erdemovic claimed, and the ICTY judges who had taken part in his trial and appellate hearings accepted, that he was given an order by a superior to take part in mass executions of Bosnian Muslim men, and that he was threatened with execution himself if he did not take part. As well, Erdemovic's superiors threatened his family. The judges at the ICTY were presented with a novel opportunity to weigh a compelling defensive argument against the deliverance of justice to the victims. Could Erdemovic be acquitted on the basis of these defenses? The judges in his first trial opined that: "With regard to a crime against humanity, the Trial Chamber considers that the life of the accused and that of the victim are not fully equivalent. As opposed to ordinary law, the violation here is no longer directed at the physical welfare of the victim alone but at humanity as a whole."[8] Protection of the innocent is the greater good. Further, the Appeals Chamber addressed the issue of duress even more directly and succinctly by ruling that, "duress does not afford a complete defence to a soldier charged with a crime against humanity and/or a war crime involving the killing of innocent human beings." The economy of words should not disguise a strong defense of human rights. In the moral calculus of individuals weighing the consequences of committing violations of international law versus following a superior's orders, the threat of retaliation for disobedience is to be the lesser valued. The human rights of the innocent take precedence. Although duress has now been accepted as a legitimate defense for the accused at the ICC, the priority accorded to the defense of human rights for the innocent demonstrates the importance judges give this objective.

[8] The Prosecutor v. Drazen Erdemovic, Case No. IT-96–22-T, November 29, 1996, para 19.

Another area of international law where there is an emerging consensus on the primacy of protecting the innocent and advancing human rights can be seen in the application of the concept of military necessity. As Schmitt (2010, 796) writes, "military necessity exists in equipoise with the principle of humanity, which seeks to limit the suffering and destruction incident to warfare." The jurisprudence of the tribunals has slowly but steadily tipped the balance in favor of the safeguard of human rights. In *Blaskic* and in *Kordic and Cerkez* the ICTY Trial Chambers found that targeting civilians is prohibited under international law when not justified by military necessity.[9] In subsequent cases ICTY judges showed even greater consideration for the protection of civilians and civilian property than for the possible justifications of such attacks. In the *Galic* case involving the siege of Sarajevo by Bosnian Serbs, the ICTY Trial Chamber ruled that the deliberate targeting of civilians and the deliberate infliction of terror on civilians is illegal regardless of any consideration about military necessity.[10] In *Strugar*, the ICTY found that any attack against a non-military objective was illegal under international law. More generally, the ICTY has found that a "State sovereignty-oriented approach has been gradually supplanted by a human-being-oriented approach."[11] In *Kupreskic*, the ICTY found that reprisals – retaliation against one's enemy for actions taken by that adversary against one's own side – were forbidden as a matter of customary international law. The Trial Chamber argued that, "a slow but profound transformation of humanitarian law under the pervasive influence of human rights has occurred," in which "belligerent reprisals against civilians and fundamental rights of human beings are absolutely inconsistent legal concepts." Human rights were to take primacy over these types of military action.

More general reasons abound as to why human rights concerns would motivate judges to behave as judicial entrepreneurs. Judges have consistently used the human rights discourse in handing down their decisions to establish a set of norms and rules that define certain behaviors not only as unacceptable, but most importantly as criminal. In *Celebici*, the Appeal Chamber, referring to the applicable rules to internal and international conflicts, wrote "Both human rights and humanitarian law focus on respect for human values and the dignity of the human person. Both bodies of law take as their starting point the concern for human dignity, which forms the basis of a list of fundamental minimum standards of humanity." In *Jokic* the Trial Chamber referred to the core human rights treaties in condemning the terrorization of civilians as violating a fundamental right to security contained in the International Covenant on Civil and Political Rights and in the European Convention of Human Rights. Human rights norms carry a universal value that international criminal law

---

[9] The Prosecutor v. Blaskic, Case No. IT-95–10-T, Judgment, March 3, 2000, para 180 and the Prosecutor v. Kordic and Cerkez, Case No. IT-95–14/2-T, Judgment, February 26, 2001, para 328.

[10] The Prosecutor v. Galic, Case No. IT-98–29-T, Judgment, December 5, 2003, para 44.

[11] The Prosecutor v. Strugar, Case No. IT-01–42-T, Judgment, January 31, 2005, paras 293–94.

does not possess. The same reference to concepts such as "dignity" and "humanity" is reminiscent of ethical and moral claims to be protected by wrongdoings regardless of race, ethnicity, and religion. It is because of this type of universality that we suggest that judges refer to the primacy of human rights to send a broader message to the larger global community of law and to the societies that are rebuilding their social and political systems. As the ICTR ruled in the *Musema* case, quoting from the Furndzija judgment:

> The essence of the whole corpus of international humanitarian law as well as human rights law lies in the protection of the human dignity of every person, whatever his or her gender. The general principle of respect for human dignity is the basic underpinning and indeed the very *raison d'être* of international humanitarian law and human rights law, indeed in modern times it has become of such paramount importance as to permeate the whole body of international law.[12]

The very origins of the tribunals lie in the international community's horror at the unspeakable atrocities occurring throughout the world and the need to do something to help put an end to such tragedies and take steps to prevent their reoccurrence. The suffering of the innocent has always been at the forefront of these efforts of accountability. That is why we believe that the judges will remain committed to expanding the acceptance of international jurisprudence into post conflict states, as well as others at risk for such violence. Indeed, now after several years of jurisprudential development, we note that Article 21, section 3 of the Rome Statute states quite plainly that, "The application and interpretation of law pursuant to this article must be consistent with internationally recognised human rights." It is this concern for the human rights impact of their judgments that we contend provides a deep and enduring rationale to progressively develop the law; to utilize its expressive capacity; and, to a lesser degree, ensure behavior that violates human rights under international law is punished appropriately. We argue that the concern for human rights as reflected in the statutes and decisions of the tribunals, and amongst the judges themselves, provides a compelling rationale that motivates judicial entrepreneurship when the need and opportunity arise.

Judicial Legacy

Judges affect not just the outcome of the immediate case at hand, but the development of the broader field of international law. The impact of their decisions lives on in the creation of new standards for defining crimes, assessing responsibility, and a myriad of other elements of international law that will shape future jurisprudence. The judges are acutely aware of the legacy their decisions will have for future generations. As former ICTY President Meron has stated (2004, 525):

---

[12] The Prosecutor v. Musema, Case No. ICTR-96-13-A, Judgment and Punishment, January 27, 2000, para 225.

I do not pretend that the ICTY has been free from error or from inefficiency in its history, but its work in building a model of international criminal adjudication will serve as a basis for future prosecutions of serious violations of humanitarian law, whether conducted by the International Criminal Court or by domestic judicial entities.

Indeed, as the ICTY and ICTR wind down their operations they are working on their legacy projects.[13] We contend that among the many reasons why judges are keenly aware of the importance of their work for future generations, first and foremost they wish to leave a legacy of expanding upon and improving international law. If the tribunals did nothing more than merely weigh facts and allocate blame, fundamental as they are to their specific purposes, we believe that judges will have fallen short of their aspirations for advancing the cause of international criminal law as the instrument challenging impunity and furthering the cause of human rights. Especially in the case of the ad hoc tribunals, with their finite life span coupled with the novelty of their creation as the first tribunals after a long drought in the development of international jurisprudence, we should find great emphasis attached to the development of legacies. Even if the tribunals themselves do not live on as active institutions, their jurisprudence and the legacy of their efforts to protect human rights can. Thus, we should find that concerns for their legacy encourage judicial entrepreneurship. Indeed, the testimonies given over the years by the presidents of the tribunals are replete with references to this legacy.

In his June 20, 2000, address to the United Nations Security Council, ICTY President Claude Jorda opined:

> Lastly, and not the least important, the place the Tribunal now occupies within the mechanism of humanitarian international law, especially in view of the establishment and implementation of the International Criminal Court, places a degree of responsibility on our shoulders. There is no question that much of what is being done in The Hague will, at best, serve as an example of what to do, and, at worst, as an example of what should not be done.[14]

President Theodor Meron proclaimed in his presentation to the Security Council on December 7, 2011:

> With respect to legal doctrine, the greatest achievement of the Tribunal, and its sister court, the ICTR, has been their contribution to developing substantive, procedural, and evidentiary international criminal law. This corpus of jurisprudence outweighs by far that of Nuremberg.[15]

---

[13] See, for example, http://www.icty.org/en/outreach/legacy-conferences.

[14] As found at http://www.icty.org/sid/7842/en on December 7, 2012.

[15] As found at http://www.icty.org/x/file/Press/Statements%20and%20Speeches/President/111207_pdt_meron_un_sc_en.pdf.

International Criminal Court President, Judge Sang-Hyun Song, described the purposes of the ICC in particular, but all tribunals in general:

> Finally, I come to norm-setting. This I see as the ICC's greatest potential – to have a significant preventive effect by entrenching a system of norms that outlaw atrocities. I do not mean only a layer of international laws that make certain crimes punishable. What we need to achieve is a system of fully internalised legal and moral norms that make the Rome Statute crimes not only punishable but also simply unacceptable in modern societies. Naturally, the Rome Statute must be seen as part of the wider international movement aimed at protecting fundamental human rights and dignity.[16]

We contend that the great concern for and pride in their legacy regarding international law evinces a desire to move international law forward. As Justice Wald (2001, 89) wrote, the task of the tribunals lies in, " . . . performing three functions: adjudicating international crimes, developing international humanitarian law, and memorializing important, albeit horrible, events of modern history." The judges are the principal custodians of international law in whose care the law will progress or remain in a state of embryonic development. As Wessel argues (2006, 443), judges come from an international legal community in which "the professional norms of the community" produce judges who are committed to the progressive expansion of the law. We contend that the judges strongly prefer the former and thus will work to ensure that the legacy they pass on to future generations of jurists and the larger international community is a favorable and progressive one that advances human rights under international law. This is a major spur to judicial entrepreneurship. That the judges seized this opportunity to shape the future of international law is evidenced in this 2004 remark by former ICTY President, Judge Gabrielle Kirk McDonald (2004, 568): "The Tribunal has contributed more to the jurisprudence of international humanitarian law in 10 years than had been developed in the entire half-century since the Nuremberg and Tokyo trials."

HOW, WHERE AND WHEN DOES JUDICIAL ENTREPRENEURSHIP OCCUR?

Having described the underlying forces that should inspire judicial entrepreneurship, we turn next to analyzing when such behavior occurs. There are multiple avenues through which judges can find opportunities for entrepreneurship to develop international law and utilize its expressive capacity. We describe the most

---

[16] Judge Sang-Hyun Song. "From Punishment to Prevention Reflections on the Future of International Criminal Justice." Wallace Wurth Memorial Lecture. February 14, 2012. As found at http://www.icc-cpi.int/NR/rdonlyres/29D0B2A7-71D4-457A-B9A3-9AC4E78DD968/284266/120214ICCPresidentUNSWWallaceWurthmemoriallecture.pdf.

important situations in which opportunities for judicial entrepreneurship are most likely to arise.

The Development of Customary International Law

The progressive development of the law can take place through the utilization of the principles of customary international law. Although judges spend a considerable amount of time interpreting *usus*[17] and *opinio juris*[18] as the fundamental legal tenants of their decisions, they have done so by pushing the boundaries of customs. Scholars and practitioners (Swart 2010; Mettraux 2005; Nollkaemper 2001; Mundis 2001) have noted that international judges have been rather quick to assign the rank of custom to the legal reasoning of their decisions, by loosely interpreting the principles on which customary law is based – that is, *opinio juris* and *usus* – and applying principles of law as customary even in the absence of a generally accepted *opinio juris* or in the presence of a persistent objector – namely a state objection to an imposition of the custom.[19] By applying customary international law, judges must walk a fine line between respect for the principle of legality and excessively liberal interpretation of the laws. The language of the documents establishing these international courts has left considerable room for interpretation regarding their subject matter jurisdiction in the application of the principles informing customary international law. In particular, while the ICC has explicitly referred to the principle of legality in Article 22 of its Statute, the ICTY, ICTR and SCSL do not have a similar disposition in their founding documents. The ICTY has extensively used customary international law as a vehicle through which to develop international humanitarian and criminal law and has done so, not only by focusing on one constitutive element of customary law, namely *opinio iuris*, more than *usus*, but also by qualifying crimes with additional elements to fit criminal behavior within a specific framework of a crime. Although such extensive interpretation has led to criticism by international scholars and some members of the international community (Mettraux 2005), who had wished that judges had remained more faithful to the principle of legality, others have praised the creation of an "evolutionary" customary international law as indispensable for the prosecution of novel crimes (Schabas 2006b). Judge Meron (1996) highlighted the innovative use of customary international law by the Appeals Chamber of the ICTY in the *Tadic* case, emphasizing specifically that the contribution to the definition of crimes within non-international armed conflicts would be beneficial to the

[17] Usus is one of the two elements contributing to the establishment of customs as law. It specifically refers to a consistent state practice or behavior. Usus is usually tested against the presence of a "peristent objector," namely the presence of states objecting to the application of custom to themselves.
[18] Opinio iuris is the second component of customary international law and it refers to the understanding or subjective interpretation by a state that the behavior is intended to binding as a law.
[19] The principle of the "persistent objector" is elaborated in the ICJ decision on the Anglo Norwegian Fisheries Case (UK vs. Norway), December 18, 1951.

future application of international law by other courts and in particular by the ICTR. The application and interpretation of international customary law in the *Tadic* case were also revolutionary since it clearly indicated how judges would proceed to determine whether the criminal responsibility of an individual could be assessed within customary law. It became clear that faced with the difficulty of determining whether states conformed with general rules during times of conflict (*usus*), the essence of criminal responsibility had to be found in the "consistency and cogency of the case law and treaties [. . .] (in) general principles of international law and national legislation"[20] thereby warranting the conclusion that such crimes were violations of customary rules of international criminal law. The Appeals Chamber of the ICTY further established a general framework for the respect of the principle of legality in *Milutinovic et al.* establishing that the general principle of *nullum crimen sine lege* "does not prevent a court from interpreting and clarifying the elements of particular crime. Nor does it preclude the progressive development of the law by the court."[21]

The ICTR Chambers have also used customary international law as the platform upon which to define new circumstances and actions that amount to crimes against humanity. Notably, the ICTR offered one of the first extensive definitions of the crime of rape as a crime against humanity under customary international law. In the first sentence handed down by the ICTR in the case of the *Prosecutor v. Akayesu*, the judges established that rape was a coercive physical and sexual invasion, which humiliates and undermines the dignity of the victim. The importance of the decision handed down in *Akayesu* is twofold. By specifically indicating elements of the crime of rape as a crime against humanity (as well as genocide), the ICTR Trial Chamber elevated the responsibility of criminals to one of the gravest crimes that can be committed as a governmental policy during conflict as well as in times of peace. In addition, the definition of the crime of rape by the Trial Chamber in *Akayesu* represented an opportunity for the development of international humanitarian law through a creative application of customary international law. The development of the crime of rape as a crime under international human rights law was quite rapid. Judges at the ICTY further specified concepts of "coercion"[22] and qualified acts within the graver concept of rape rather than sexual assault.[23] The cumulative decisions of the ICTY and ICTR gave momentum to the development of substantive international human rights law and its application by the ICC. Several elements of

---

[20] The Prosecutor v. Duško Tadic, Case No.: IT-94–1-A, Appeal Judgment, July 15, 1999, para 226.

[21] Decision on Dragoljub Ojdanic's Motion Challenging Jurisdiction – Joint Criminal Enterprise, para 38. See also the Prosecutor v. Aleksovski, Case No. IT-95–14/1-A, Appeal Judgment, March 24, 2000, paras 126–127; the Prosecutor v. Delalic, Case No. IT-96–21-A, Appeal Judgment, February 20, 2001, para 173.

[22] The Prosecutor v. Delalic, Case No. IT-96–21-T, Trial Judgment, November 16, 1998; the Prosecutor v. Kunarac et al, Case No. IT-96–23T, Trial Judgment, February 22, 2001.

[23] In the *Prosecutor v. Furundzija*, the Trial Chamber qualified as rape, thus a crime against humanity and not sexual assault, forced oral penetration.

the crimes as defined by the chambers of the ad hoc tribunals have been included in the statute of the ICC. Indeed, as former ICTY President Meron (2006, 567) has opined, "the ICTY and the ICTR have been groundbreaking in this area. The tribunals made a major contribution in grounding the prohibition of rape in customary international law."

In its relatively brief history the SCSL has also made several contributions to the development of international human rights and humanitarian law through the application of international customary law. In a landmark decision handed down by the SCSL Appeals Chamber on February 22, 2008 in the case of the *Prosecutor v. Brima, Kamara and Kanu*, the judges recognized forced marriage as a crime against humanity under customary international law in the category of "other inhumane acts." The Appeals Chamber also took the opportunity to further define the crime of child soldiers' enlistment and conscription, and shed light on the practice used by guerrillas to rape young girls and force them into their army. All these had been considered elements of a new form of criminal activity that could be categorized as crimes against humanity.

The ICC is bound to benefit considerably from the development and extensive interpretation of customary international law performed by these courts. The drafters of the Rome Statute must have been particularly aware that most of the challenges faced by international judges at the ad hoc tribunals were due to the need to extrapolate rules and laws from an existing system of customary international law and apply them to novel circumstances. Thus, the statute of the ICC is the result of a learning process; some of its articles indicate that the drafters of the Rome Statute have learned from the experiences, difficulties, and criticisms that the ad hoc tribunals have faced in applying an interpretative system of customary international law, as in the extensive delineation of the elements of crimes and the complementarity norm (Wessel 2006). Some of the articles of the ICC Statute give judges considerable liberty in taking into consideration behaviors that although not fitting the description of the crimes listed in Article 5 of the Statute are nonetheless international crimes. In particular, Articles 10 and 22 of the ICC statute, respectively, establish that the explicit list of crimes in the first part of the statute shall not be interpreted as "limiting or prejudicing in any way existing or developing rules of international law for purposes other than this Statute" or "the characterization of any conduct as criminal under international law independently of this Statute" (Article 22.3). Indeed, Wessel (2006) argues that the Rome Statute ultimately leaves judges with considerable discretion in interpreting and applying the elements of the crimes given the conflicting guidance of the Statute regarding whether judges are required or exhorted to apply these elements.

International judges have shown a considerable respect for legal certainty *and* a notable commitment to renew the life and ability of customary international law in developing international humanitarian law. They have not hesitated to use general principles of customary international law to buttress their path breaking decisions. Indeed, the broad parameters of customary international law provide an ideal setting and opportunity for judges to engage in judicial entrepreneurship. Ultimately, as we demonstrate in the next chapter, despite the numerous restrictions and limitations placed on judicial decision making, considerable room exists for the exercise of judicial discretion. And while the ad hoc tribunals clearly enjoy a greater quantity and quality of opportunity for judicial entrepreneurship and are the principal objects of inquiry here (given the small number of judgments from the ICC), we should not overlook the extent to which such opportunities exist at the ICC and the ability of those judges to creatively find the occasional window of opportunity left open.

Embryonic International Law

Judges also enjoy considerable discretion in their work because of the embryonic nature of international law, which has created opportunities to develop legal definitions and understandings where such are lacking, imprecise or evolving. It has developed in fits and starts over the last one hundred plus years, but much of the most important work has taken place in the last twenty years as the ad hoc tribunals have interpreted and applied many of these treaties and elements of international humanitarian and human rights law for the first time. There are definitional issues with key terms of such treaties, such as "protected groups" within the Genocide Convention and "military necessity" that have aroused considerable debate among judges and scholars alike. The judges have also confronted gaps in international law, such as the disparity in protections offered for civilians during international wars versus internal wars. They have moved assertively to advance the cause of human rights by extending such protections even if, at times, such law development may not comport with UNSC guidance. They have also dealt with emerging issues in international law, such as those involving child soldiers. Where emerging norms suggest that such rights exist, but where the international criminal and humanitarian law has not caught up, judges have not feared to tread. Again, we find instances where judges have, in the name of advancing human rights, showed little reluctance in developing the law.

They have dealt with the many ambiguities in international law. For example, they have advanced international jurisprudence regarding the liability of states for the actions of their agents in international wars, as in the *Tadic* decision at the ICTY.[24] As ICTY President Claude Jorda said in his address to the UNSC in June 2000, "This justice must conform to the highest standards of humanitarian international law in respect of both the victims and the accused. In short, it must move that law forward, that law which is constantly being born anew." We discuss several of the

[24] The Prosecutor v. Duško Tadic, Case No. IT-94-1-A, Appeal Judgment, July 15, 1999.

most prominent areas in which the embryonic state of international law has created opportunities for the exercise of judicial entrepreneurship.

Ambiguous Language

Given that judges are now applying many heretofore untested areas of international law, many key definitional issues have arisen as judges grapple with international law language that is often out-of-date or unclear. For example, one of the more prominent, definitional issues that have sparked a good deal of innovative judicial interpretation and scholarly debate has concerned the operationalization of the "protected groups" term in the language of the tribunals' statutes governing genocide. The language, which was lifted directly from the Genocide Convention, refers to the protected groups as defined by their "national, ethnical, racial or religious" character. No international judges had ever before been forced to confront this language and define it in practice. The unique characteristics of the groups targeted in both the Rwandan and Yugoslav conflict made the task of applying the Genocide Convention all the more complicated. The old and ambiguous language of the Convention, coupled with the sociodemographic peculiarities of the populations at issue, led to a great deal of judicial creativity. And while some of the jurisprudence on the subject, such as the ICTR's attempt to define the protected groups by their stable and permanent character, may have been definitional dead ends (Schabas 2007), the overall effort to grapple with these definitions has led to healthy and productive debates. Many such opportunities continue to arise as international tribunal judges must take the lofty ambitions of human rights laws coupled with their often undefined terminology, and apply them in new and novel situations. Opportunities for judicial entrepreneurship and the advancement of human rights abound.

Gaps in International Law

Among the three areas that form the issue jurisdiction of all the tribunals – crimes against humanity, war crimes and genocide – only the last two have even been codified in international treaties and conventions. Indeed, the Geneva Conventions and the Genocide Convention are over sixty years old. In the absence of further elaboration in the law on the types of actions they criminalize, the threshold requirements that make such actions international rather than merely domestic crimes, and the groups for whom their protections are extended, there are a plethora of issues that will continue to give rise to judicial creativity in the development of the law. For example, the distinction in international law on war crimes over the protections offered for civilians and non-combatants during internal wars versus international conflicts has been a fairly controversial topic, especially for the ICTY. Despite the fact that the ICTY was instructed to confine itself to judgments that did not stray beyond extant, customary international law, the *Tadic* judges found that international criminal responsibility did attach to the offenses committed in civil wars.

Schabas (2007, 115) described this ruling as, "broad and innovative" and even went so far as to suggest that the interpretation, ". . . was open to criticism as a form of retroactive legislation." But while such progressive development of international law was considered rather extraordinary at the ICTY given its UNSC mandate, the breakdown in the distinctions between war crimes for international versus internal wars continued apace at the ICTR and the ICC. Seen in retrospect, it would appear the ICTY judges were exploiting a problematic division in international law whose lines were becoming blurred.

Judicial entrepreneurship and expansive interpretation of crimes can also be seen in the definition of some elements of the crime of genocide. The first conviction entered for the crime of genocide that took place in Srebrenica, the *Krstic* Judgment, has been very controversially analyzed by the judicial legal community. In assessing whether "destruction" of a group (Bosnian Muslim men) was the real intent of the accused, the Appeals Chamber went as far as to refer to the International Law Commission preparatory work of the International Criminal Court and its interpretation of the *travaux préparatoires* of the Genocide Convention. The Appeals Chamber, while correctly asserting that "the destruction in question is the material destruction of a group either by physical or by biological means",[25] interpreted the removal of Bosnian Muslim men as the specific intent of destruction, which is required to classify a crime as genocide. In this case it seems that judges were moved by the desire to punish a new form of conduct that did not strictly align with the old definition and interpretation of the crime. Rather, the law had to be adapted to the novel situations upon which judges were required to decide. Just as nature abhors a vacuum, so too do international jurists. Such opportunities arise continually as the skeletal framework of international law meets the complex nature of modern warfare. As Casses (2004, 590) has argued:

> the absence of an international law-maker and an international court with compul-
> sory universal jurisdiction entails that many rules are not clear, particularly when
> they are of customary origin, and are thus open to differing interpretations-hence
> the need for courts gradually to spell out the contents of those rules, if need be
> through *obiter dicta*.

Emerging Crimes

Closely related to the legal need to fill in these gaps in international law is the equally compelling pressure for the law to catch up with emerging crimes. The use of child soldiers, while not necessarily a new practice in war, has rapidly become a major concern in conflict resolution and demobilization, and an issue that has posed vexing challenges for the ad hoc tribunals. One of the signature tactics of the wars in Sierra Leone was the use of young children to lead the fighting, but it was not readily

---

[25] The Prosecutor v. Krstic, Case No. IT-98-33-A, Judgment, April 19, 2004, footnote 39.

obvious that such tactics had been criminalized at the time they were committed. Despite differing opinions as to whether all acts pertaining to the use of child soldiers (e.g., recruitment, conscription, abduction, employment) were criminalized at the time, the SCSL judges went ahead and asserted that such actions were offenses, even if they took place prior to the adoption of the Rome Treaty in July 1998 (Schabas 2007, 129).[26] Similarly, ICTY judges have confronted political and military tactics, most especially ethnic cleansing, that while old in many respects, had not yet been expressly defined as such. Indeed, whether the crimes are new and novel, or have a long-standing, if ignored history, judges have struggled to deploy the law to keep up with the ever-expanding boundaries of human cruelty. While international law in this area will not remain embryonic forever, it continues to undergo a phase of development and codification that will continue to provide ample opportunity for judicial entrepreneurship.

Gaps and Ambiguity in Statutory Guidance on Judgments

Judges also enjoy significant opportunities to engage in judicial entrepreneurship because of gaps and ambiguities in their founding documents (Ginsberg 2005; Shapiro 1994). Judges are given rather general and ambitious expectations regarding the tribunals' ultimate objectives, which in turn empower the judges to reference these goals as needed and give meaning to them as they see fit. As Wessel (2006, 384) writes, "greater amounts of judicial discretion create the *potential* for greater amounts of judicial policymaking" (see also Eskridge 1994). For example, the United Nations Security Council resolutions that created the ICTY and ICTR are noteworthy less for the explicit guidance they provide the tribunals regarding judgments and punishments than for the rationales that led to the establishment of the tribunals. Statements such as the Security Council is, "*Convinced* that in the particular circumstances of Rwanda, the prosecution of persons responsible for serious violations of international humanitarian law would enable this aim to be achieved and would contribute to the process of national reconciliation and to the restoration and maintenance of peace," and that it is "Determined to put an end to such crimes and to take effective measures to bring to justice the persons who are responsible for them" hint at the Security Council's expectation that the tribunals contribute to advancing peace, reconciliation and ending impunity for violations of international law. The agreement between the United Nations and Sierra Leone establishing the Special Court references a concern regarding the "prevailing situation of impunity," while the SCSL statute declares the Court will prosecute those most responsible for the

---

[26] In the Case of Lubanga Dyillo at the ICC, the judges took an additional step forward in defining the criminal acts pertaining to the use of child soldiers and determined that conscripting and enlisting children under the age of fifteen are continuous crimes in nature and they only "ends when the child reaches the age of 15 or leaves the force or group." The Prosecutor v. Thomas Lubanga Dyilo, Case No. ICC-01/04-01/06, Trial Judgment, March 14, 2012, para 618.

atrocities and who, "have threatened the establishment of and implementation of the peace process in Sierra Leone." The Preamble of the International Criminal Court Statute states:

> **Recognizing** that such grave crimes threaten the peace, security and well-being of the world,
>
> **Affirming** that the most serious crimes of concern to the international community as a whole must not go unpunished and that their effective prosecution must be ensured by taking measures at the national level and by enhancing international cooperation,
>
> **Determined** to put an end to impunity for the perpetrators of these crimes and thus to contribute to the prevention of such crimes (emphasis in the original).[27]

Given that these founding resolutions, most especially in the case of the three ad hoc tribunals, are long on statements of recognition about the past and expressions of hope for the future, and largely bereft of explicit guidance regarding judicial decision making (as in the issue of punishment), they provide ample discretion for judges to define and clarify the law and justify progressive development of jurisprudence on such general goals. For example, the articulation of punishment rationales (e.g., retribution, deterrence) and the identification of sentencing determinants (e.g., gravity of the crime, abuse of power, expressions of remorse) have been largely left to the judges to develop as needed. Judges have been given certain broad parameters within which they are to operate, but they are also given tremendous discretion, most especially in determining how verdicts and punishments will serve the aims of peace, justice, and the end of impunity. The method and extent to which justice, retribution, deterrence, and reconciliation might be achieved through the punishment of the guilty and the relative prioritization of these goals was largely entrusted to the judges. Hence, substantial opportunity exists for entrepreneurial judicial decision making to realize the ambitions of the founding documents.[28]

---

[27] As found at http://www.icc-cpi.int/NR/rdonlyres/ADD16852-AEE9-4757-ABE7-9CDC7CF02886/283503/RomeStatutEng1.pdf.

[28] The statutes and Rules of Procedure and Evidence of all the international tribunals are more explicit in their language, if equally as brief. Within the ICTY Statute, Articles 23 and 24 concern the issuing of verdicts and sentences. Judgments must be delivered in public by a majority of the judges in the Trial Chamber and include a justification for the decision. The Chamber can sanction only with imprisonment, although restoration of property is possible. Judges are empowered to have recourse to the general sentencing practices of the former Yugoslavia and the "gravity of the offence" and the individual circumstances of the defendant when sentencing. Articles 27 and 28 concern incarceration and the authority for commutation of sentences. The ICTR Statute contains largely identical language. The Special Court for Sierra Leone is also to take cognizance of the gravity of the offense, the individual circumstances of the accused, and the sentencing practices of Sierra Leone (as well as those of the ICTR). The SCSL may also "order the forfeiture of the property, proceeds and any assets acquired unlawfully or by criminal conduct, and their return to their rightful owner or to the State of Sierra Leone." Compared to the statutory provisions of the three, preceding tribunals, the rules governing penalties in the Rome Treaty for the International Criminal Court are more extensive. First, the judges

There are numerous other elements of the ad hoc tribunal statutes that are ambiguous but pertain to just one issue, such as the reference made to the need for judges to refer to the sentencing practices of the national courts when handing down punishments. The judges are left to determine the weight to be attached to such practices. Their statutes also stipulate that, "All persons shall be equal before the International Tribunal," but leave the judges to determine just how an equality of arms is to be defined and determined. Other portions of the statutes provide the judges with considerable power to determine a wide range of policies at their discretion, such as this language from the ICTR statute:

> The Judges of the International Tribunal for Rwanda shall adopt, for the purpose of proceedings before the International Tribunal for Rwanda, the Rules of Procedure and Evidence for the conduct of the pre-trial phase of the proceedings, trials and appeals, the admission of evidence, the protection of victims and witnesses and other appropriate matters of the International Tribunal for the former Yugoslavia with such changes as they deem necessary.

As noted by Ginsburg (2005),[29] the UNSC delegated a legislative power to the judges of the ICTY and ICTR when assigning the creation of the Rules of Procedure and Evidence to the same judges dispensing justice at the tribunals. As the principal the UNSC delegated authority to the tribunals. As Danner writes:

> Because of concerns about accountability, states simply do not want to acknowledge that international courts make international law-even as the vague treaties they provide to these courts effectively act as a delegation of lawmaking authority. International judges, in turn, understand and reinforce the political slight-of-hand by denying that they make law. (2006, 47)

We note that the ICTY and ICTR in particular have enjoyed a degree of discretion the other international courts do always not possess. Indeed, one noteworthy testament to the considerable powers the ad hoc tribunals have enjoyed to give meaning to their founding documents can be found in the length and detail of the ICC

---

are to generally sentence individuals to no more than thirty years in prison, although life sentences may be given in exceptional cases. The Court may also impose a fine and forfeiture of proceeds, property and assets of any ill-gotten gains. Like the other tribunals ICC judges are to consider the gravity of the crime and the individual circumstances of the accused when determining the appropriate sentence. For individuals convicted of multiple offenses the judges are to provide a sentence for each guilty count as well as a global sentence. While the Rome Treaty provides more detail regarding the general factors that should inform the determination of the sentence, such as the damage and harm caused by the criminal conduct, its elaboration of the mitigating and aggravating circumstances is particularly detailed. Ultimately, however, there are few provisions in Rule 145 that have not already been extensively referenced and utilized in the judgments of the ad hoc tribunals. As such, Rule 145 is more reflective of emerging norms and perhaps even customary international law with regard to sentencing determinants.

[29] Ginsburg, Tom. "Bounded Discretion in International Judicial Lawmaking." *Virginia Journal of International Law* (2005) 45: 631–673.

Statute (seventy-four pages) as compared to the ICTY Statute (ten pages). It seeks to fill in those very areas left open for jurisprudential development at the ICTY and ICTR.

Despite these limitations on the judicial discretion of ICC justices, there are some passages in the Rome Statute that suggest judges do have some opportunities for the progressive development of international law. The Statute provides that, "Nothing in this Part [of the Statute] shall be interpreted as limiting or prejudicing in any way existing or developing rules of international law for purposes other than this Statute."[30] As well, the Statute's admonition that the Court's work not deviate from "internationally recognized human rights" gives it implicit power to ensure its decisions keep pace with developments in the law, perhaps when its own Rules of Procedure and Evidence and possibly even the Rome Statute itself do not keep pace with developments in human rights. As others have pointed out (e.g., Wessel 2006, 437), the decentralization of international law in general means that ample room exists for progressive development of the law as well as eventual acceptance of the expansion of the law.

Therefore, we contend that incentives and opportunities exist in abundance at the international criminal tribunals for the progressive development of the law and the utilization of its expressive capacity, and to a lesser degree the allocation of punishment. This, in turn, creates ample opportunity for judicial entrepreneurship. Lest we leave the reader with the impression that judges enjoy unfettered discretion to exercise their judgment, however, we take note here of the constraints that serve as the ultimate check on judicial lawmaking.

CONSTRAINTS ON JUDICIAL DECISION MAKING IN INTERNATIONAL CRIMINAL LAW

We contend that judges are independent decision makers who reach decisions assessing the evidence and arguments submitted to their attention. However, we also observe that judges are also constrained by the founding documents and their own rules of procedure and evidence that provide guidance in the dispensation of international justice, even though at times they may raise more questions than they answer (Wessel 2006). In the following section we set to explore these legal, procedural and social parameters and how judges are constrained by them.

Statutes of the ICTY, ICTR and SCSL and the Rome Treaty

The statutes passed by the United Nations Security Council (ICTY and ICTR) and the United Nations General Assembly (SCSL) provide the most explicit and extensive rules and guidelines for the ad hoc international tribunals. The Rome Statute for

---

[30] Rome Statute, Article 10.

the International Criminal Court serves the same purpose. Of all the formal, written language that gives effect to the wishes of those who created these courts, these founding documents provide the most explicit guidance. First, the statutes specify the competence of the courts. The ICTY is responsible for crimes that occurred in the former Yugoslavia since 1991, while the ICTR exercises jurisdiction over crimes committed in Rwanda in 1994. For the SCSL these are crimes committed in Sierra Leone since November 30, 1996. The competence of the ICC is significantly more complex. It hears cases that involve crimes committed since July 1, 2002, when the Rome Statute entered into force where these crimes occur in the territory of states that are parties to the Treaty or involve nationals of the states parties. The Office of the Prosecutor may undertake investigations with respect to those states on her own motion, or may do so at the request of a state party. The United Nations Security Council can also refer cases involving any state to the ICC for investigation by the OTP.

The jurisdiction of the tribunals limits which conflicts these courts can wade into, while their substantive jurisdiction provides some limits on the types of crime that can be prosecuted. For example, neither the ICTR nor the SCSL Statute reference grave breaches of the Geneva Conventions as the ICTY and ICC Statutes do, although in practice this has not prevented the former tribunals from prosecuting the types of violations of international law that characterized the conflicts in Rwanda and Sierra Leone. The articles of their statutes that pertain to the types of war crime, crimes against humanity and genocidal crimes also, in theory, limit the discretion of the tribunals. At the same time, however, the statutes create generic categories of crime, such as "other inhumane acts" as crimes against humanity. They also provide language that indicates that the enumeration of types of crime is not exhaustive lists, such as this language from Article 3 of the ICTY Statute regarding violations of the laws and customs of war, "Such violations shall include, but not be limited to." Thus, in general we find that while the tribunal statutes provide general guidance and create some restrictions on the scope of judicial decision making, their sparse language provides ample opportunity for judicial entrepreneurialism. To be sure, ICC judges are more circumscribed than their counterparts at the ad hoc tribunals, but we must await the development of a significant jurisprudential record to determine the degree to which these judges have been limited in their judicial activism.

Rules of Procedure and Evidence

We begin by calling attention to the important role played by the Rules of Procedure and Evidence (RPE) that guide the day-to-day and more specific operations of all the international criminal courts. The various RPE provide extensive guidance regarding, inter alia, pre-trial proceedings, investigations, rights of defendants, court decisions and orders, production of evidence, depositions, motions, case presentations, judgments and sentences. Judges at the ad hoc tribunals have the power to develop and revise their RPE largely as they see fit. In fact, in the cases of the ICTY, ICTR and SCSL their RPE have been amended forty-nine, twenty and thirteen times, respectively. The ICC possesses an RPE, but all such rules and regulations must be approved by the Assembly of States Parties and not the judges on their own authority. The ICC is constrained by additional guidance in the form of policies on elements of crimes, regulations of the court, the prosecutor and the registry, financial regulations, codes of ethics and similar rules.[31] The RPE do constrain judges in many ways, as do all bureaucratic rules and regulations. Nonetheless their primary purpose and benefit is rather to streamline the work of the tribunals so that their work is consistent, efficient, and not subject to reinvention with each new case. To that extent they do, in part, relieve the judges from much of the day-to-day work of managing complex cases and allow them to focus on more critical issues of legal interpretation and judgment. Thus, while the RPE constrain the judges, they are self-imposed constraints that work to the benefit of the administration of the tribunals.

Stare Decisis

The system described in the previous section creates an image of international judges who have interpreted their role within their mandate and rules. However, as we have also argued, judges have interpreted their role as a balancing act, in which legal principles have been respected and innovations have been legally justified through the interpretation and application of domestic law, national jurisprudence, treaties and customary international law. Judges do not render final decisions and create new crimes completely unconstrained – they have been mindful of the limits on their decisional power. In addition to paying respect to their mandate and customary international law generally recognized by nations, international judges have developed a lengthy and consistent international jurisprudence by frequently referring to prior decisions handed down by other judges within the same tribunal and others. The system of constant reference and citations of prior cases is somewhat surprising although not unexpected in international criminal law. They are not always wedded to prior decisions, as the continuing debate over the notion of "specific direction" in the context of the crime of aiding and abetting has played out over a series of ICTY, ICTR and SCSL decisions demonstrates (see Ventura 2013). It is surprising because international law has no equivalent of the common law system and thus judges are not bound by decisions handed in previous cases. As correctly pointed out by other scholars (Danner 2001), however, the respect that the Appeals Chamber in particular shows to prior decisions is not to be interpreted

---

[31] As found at https://www.icc-cpi.int/en_menus/icc/legal%20texts%20and%20tools/Pages/legal%20tools .aspx.

as the equivalent of the stare decisis in common law jurisdictions. As the ICTY Appeals Chamber found in the case of the *Prosecutor v. Aleksovski*, "[. . .] a proper construction of the Statute, taking due account of its text and purpose, yields the conclusion that in the interests of certainty and predictability, the Appeals Chamber should follow its previous decisions, but should be free to depart from them for cogent reasons in the interests of justice."[32]

In spite of the remarks made by the Appeals Chamber in *Aleksovski*, our analysis of judicial behavior shows that judges use a considerable degree of self-citation (that is to say citations of decisions handed down within the same court and sister international criminal tribunals), as well as citations of domestic courts in justifying the application of general principles and interpretations of international law (see also Fleming 2002; Guillaume 2011; Nerlich 2013). It seems as if they have established praxis according to which past decisions are treated as somewhat akin to precedents for new ones, even if these earlier decisions are intended to influence not determine current decisions. It is our contention that judges believe that innovative stances undertaken in prior decisions will be readily accepted by the international community if they demonstrate a certain consistency, as well as a compelling rationale. However, the question we must address is: why do judges create for themselves a system similar in some respects to the common law doctrine of *stare decisis?* We contend that the considerable amount of citations that judges use to support their decisions is an internal validity check in which judges, recognizing that application and interpretation of international law has evolved into something like lawmaking behavior, seek to ensure consistency in the development and application of such laws. Ultimately, international judges know that the legacy they will leave is the result of a collective effort to promote a coherent system of international criminal justice.

We also contend that the logic behind the extensive use of citations may be different between a trial chamber and the appeals chamber of a given international court. Judges in trial chambers know that their decisions are scrutinized by the international community and by the appeals chambers for consistency, legitimacy and validity. As indicated in nearly every appeal judgment "the Appeals Chamber has the power to 'affirm, reverse or revise' a judgment imposed by a Trial Chamber. The Appeals Chamber considers that it should not exercise that power except where it believes that a trial chamber has committed an error in exercising its discretion, or has failed to follow applicable law."[33] The internal review to which trial chamber decisions are subjected prompts judges to rely on a substantial body of case law when interpreting legal criteria and crimes. The greater the degree of consistency that judges show in applying criteria previously developed in other decisions, most

---

[32] The Prosecutor v. Aleksovski, Case No. IT-95–14/1-A, Appeal Judgment, March 24, 2000, para 107.

[33] Most all Appeals Chamber decisions contain similar statements to the one quoted from the case Omar Serushago v. the Prosecutor, ICTR-98–39-A, Appeal Judgment, April 6, 2000, para 32.

importantly by the appeals chambers of the same or other courts, the greater the chance that those criteria will gain legitimacy. This is especially important when novel situations, crimes and circumstances are present in a case, forcing judges to find a logical and consistent foundation for their decisions. We contend as well that judges are paying close attention to the legacy they will leave for the future generations of international judges and tribunals. Thus, judges have indeed created a system in which prior decisions help inform and guide future ones. However, they have done so to validate the work of their own institutions, to show consistency and legitimacy, and increase the likelihood that their work will be valued as a historical stepping stone for the modernization of international humanitarian and criminal law. Indeed, as Judge Orie (himself a critic of the Alexsovski rule) has stated (2012, 640–641):

> This so-called "Aleksovski rule" was adopted by the Appeals Chamber itself on the basis of: first, the hierarchical structure established in Article 25 of the ICTY Statute, where the Appeals Chamber is tasked with settling definitively disputes on matters of law and fact; secondly, the need for an assurance of certainty and predictability in the application of the law; and thirdly, the avoidance of a chaotic structure in which each of the chambers could develop its own construction of the law. The Aleksovski rule very much resembles what is known in domestic jurisdictions as vertical stare decisis: the inferior court is bound by the precedents established by the superior court.

Hence, such reference to past decisions does serve as an important constraint on the ability and willingness of judges to depart dramatically from their own precedents.

International Socialization

In addition to the legal and political constraints imposed upon judges by the institutions that have created international criminal tribunals and their own RPE, there is an additional factor playing a role on judicial behavior. International judges have become very much socialized in a system of international political and legal norms that constrains judicial decision making (Wessel 2006). The proliferation of international criminal courts in the last two decades has created a considerable net of interactions among international tribunals and international judges (Helfer and Slaughter, 2005). International judges have operated within this system by increasingly engaging in a "global communication" (Ginsburg 2005) of rules, procedures, and values destined to shape the international legal landscape for many decades to come. As Helfer and Slaughter (2005, 9) point out, judges participate in a "global community of law "defined as a community of interests and ideals shielded by legal language and practice in which participants understand themselves to be linked through their participation in, comprehension of, and responsibility for legal discourse." International judges use this global community of law as a reference point to guide their decisions, procedures, and legal interpretation of novel situations with a goal of creating a practicable and legitimate system of international law.

Today international judges are actors in a global system of rules that they have created and by which they tailor their decisions in a consistent manner. We suggest that international judges have gone through a process of *"acculturation"* (Goodman and Jinks 2004). Over the years they have identified themselves with a specific group (the international criminal legal community) charged with a mandate (prosecuting violations of humanitarian and human rights law) and in pursuit of a similar interest (leaving a lasting legacy broadly accepted by the international community, states, and political actors to advance human rights). As such, judges have become strategic actors recognizing that in order to follow their mandate and realize their interests they must adopt procedures and values that are the expression of a coherent system of rules that will make their work more readily acceptable by the international community at large and by the political forces that are "masters of their fate." Why might judges constrain themselves to ideological and legal norms developed by the larger legal community? Specifically we contend that the reason why judges prefer to follow international legal norms is twofold and is the result of the web of relations within which international judges operate. International judges communicate their work through two different structures. "Horizontally," international judges speak to the international legal and political community which scrutinizes their work. They are very much aware that the more coherent the international jurisprudence they create, the greater the likelihood that their work will be recognized and praised for shaping a consistent international legal community of common values, ideals and procedures. As Judge Kwon (2007, 376) has written, testifying to the common bonds that link judges together and have furthered the cause of international justice:

> We come from diverse domestic jurisdictions with many different methods of running criminal trials, and somehow we have managed to blend these methods together to successfully adjudicate crimes on a scale never attempted or even fathomed in domestic jurisdictions. This is a testament to our vision, our cooperativeness and our empathy. The continued evolution and expansion of international criminal justice demands that we always maintain these three virtues.

More importantly, we contend that international judges constrain their decisions to common patterns of legal and procedural norms to reach more effectively the local community. One goal international judges have sought to realize is the development of jurisprudence that is accepted by the local communities in the relevant states. We suggest that international judges speak "vertically" to national judges and courts. In particular, we contend that with their decisions judges have considerably restructured the social understanding of international crimes. The development of international criminal law and the creation of new crimes have challenged the impunity of political leaders and the idea that war excuses crimes. We suggest that domestic courts and local constituencies, which will ultimately grapple with the legal and political legacy of the tribunals, will more readily accept the new ideological and legal norms created by international judges the greater the consensus of the international legal community. For example, the ICTY and ICTR have reached out to national judges who will be administering justice in national prosecutions for violations of international law. Several cases, whose defendants were initially brought in front of the ICTY, have been transferred to local courts in Bosnia and Herzegovina, Croatia and Serbia according to Rule 11bis of the Rules of Procedures and Evidence. While there have been some concerns as per the readiness of local judiciaries to administer justice for international crimes, judges, the OTP, and the various outreach programs have contributed considerably to the capacity building of local courts as to guarantee the effective prosecution of war crimes. Collectively, all of these forces constrain judges from advancing too far beyond the degree of change that is feasible and acceptable within the domain of international justice.

THE BALANCING ACT: JUDICIAL ACTIVISM AND JUDICIAL RESTRAINT

International tribunal judges recognize that there is some form of law development and lawmaking activity in their decision making (Cassese 2001, 119). At the same time, judges are not entirely free agents in these activities. They must navigate the guidelines offered by their mandates and statutes while remaining mostly faithful to the principle of legal certainty (Ginsberg 2005). Nonetheless, as we have demonstrated above substantial opportunity exists for the exercise of judicial discretion and entrepreneurial activity. In conclusion we describe three different broad strategies or methods by which judges strike a balance between the needs of the law and the demands of their principals; between the exercise of independence and discretion, and the application of restraint.

First, judges adhere to the desires and demands of their principals – the key actors of the international community – by advancing the goals (justice, human rights, peace, reconciliation) set forth in the founding resolutions and statutes. They do so, however, by utilizing (some might say, "exploiting") the ambiguities and gaps in these documents to progressively interpret the law in a manner that is both faithful in spirit to these goals, but reflective of emerging human rights norms at the same time. If the overall goal is justice and the protection of human rights, while the founding documents are ambiguous, judges have not hesitated to develop new interpretations of the law that give priority to justice and human rights, even if, occasionally there is, arguably, a cost to the rights of the accused. The ICTY, ICTR and SCSL have grappled with this issue, but all have developed significant jurisprudence in this regard that has advanced human rights, even if at times they have strayed beyond the borders of the written law.

We also contend that within the founding documents' main principles, international judges follow the prescription to apply international customary law, but do so in a fairly liberal fashion when it is appropriate or necessary to develop the law. Although judges are supposed to generally apply international customary law recognized by the vast majority of states, judges have often sacrificed the principle of legal certainty in favor of liberal interpretation of customary law. Customary international law has represented a ground over which judges have at times justified and constrained their judicial independence, and other times liberally interpreted customary international law principles by weighing differently the importance of the *"usus"* or *"opinio"* in assessing the applicable law. They have, in effect, sought to have their cake and eat it too with respect to international customary law.

In particular, international judges have weighed less *"usus"* than *"opinio juris"* and have often justified their decision because of the nature of the crimes committed. In *Krstic*, the Trial Chamber heavily relied on the general *opinio juris* of states with regard to the acts of genocide[34] and in *Kupreskic* it detailed why relying on *opinio juris* is something of a necessary step when the blatant violation of human rights and humanitarian law by states deprive customary international of one of its components, namely *usus* and the absence of an "objector." In *Kupreskic* the judges stated:

> Admittedly, there does not seem to have emerged recently a body of State practice consistently supporting the proposition that one of the elements of custom, namely *usus* or *diuturnitas* has taken shape. This is however an area where *opinio iuris sive necessitatis* may play a much greater role than *usus*, as a result of the aforementioned Martens Clause. In the light of the way States and courts have implemented it, this Clause clearly shows that principles of international humanitarian law may emerge through a customary process under the pressure of the demands of humanity or the dictates of public conscience, even where State practice is scant or inconsistent. The other element, in the form of *opinio necessitatis*, crystallising as a result of the imperatives of humanity or public conscience, may turn out to be the decisive element heralding the emergence of a general rule or principle of humanitarian law.[35]

Third, we contend that judges have developed something of a system of "stare decisis" in order to further balance judicial independence and restraint. In particular, we suggest that judges have created a system of "internal validity checks" by implementing a mechanism of judicial references to the decisions handed down by other judges in other cases within their own court. It is our understanding that judges rely heavily on internal decisions for two different reasons. Trial chamber judges know that they are subject to an internal review and want to increase the likelihood that their reasoning is validated by other decisions, while the Appeal Chamber is mindful of the legal and historical legacy they will leave to future international courts. Consistency of decisions and logical evolution of international criminal law

---

[34] The Prosecutor v. Radislav Krstic, IT-98–33-T, August 2, 2001, para 541.
[35] The Prosecutor v. Kupreskic, Case No. IT-95–16-T, Trial Judgment, January 14, 2000, para 527.

throughout the years leave a strong international jurisprudence that will inform considerably the decisions of other judges. To the extent judges can ground the progressive development of the law in particular, but also utilize its expressive capacity in a structured and consistent jurisprudence rooted in protection of human rights and supported by customary international law, the legitimacy and influence of their legacy is made more firm. As Judge Cassese (2004, 590) has argued, "As long as the rights of the accused are respected and the *nullum crimen sine lege* principle is complied with, international judges may contribute to the gradual clarification of existing law."

While this discussion focuses principally upon the notion of judicial entrepreneurialism in the context of the progressive development of the law, we must not overlook its importance in judicial expressivism and in sentencing. Judicial expressivism may not represent a radical departure from the use and practice of international law as it pertains to the moral weight and value of the act of judgment. Nonetheless, it is a means of going beyond the guidance in the tribunals' founding documents to claim a role in the moral adjudication of international crime. Judges act independently to choose to include language that is not essential to perform their judicial functions. Words of condemnation and expressions of shock and outrage are not necessary to find a defendant guilty and sentence him. But they are a tool by which the judges can speak to a wider audience to advance human rights and to solidify the legacy of the tribunals. Thus, judges not only advance beyond what is necessary to reach legal decisions in their case to progressively expand international law, they also seek to strike out beyond the legal realm to the moral universe through their expressive language.

The third judicial role we examine is the punishment of the guilty. In contrast to the limitations regarding interpretation of international law in the tribunals' founding documents, these same statutes provide judges with ample authority to sentence the guilty as they find most proper. But if the founding documents are short on detail regarding sentencing, the international legal community has often sought to encourage judges to curb their independent powers of sentencing in favor of more explicit criteria and sentencing guidelines, which they have consistently declined to do. Therefore, in matters of sentencing, judges have less call to engage in entrepreneurial activity as they are already furnished with significant power.

In the case of the progressive expansion of the law, the use of expressive language and in sentencing, judges ultimately are concerned with preserving their powers and asserting judicial prerogative. Whether this entails proactive, entrepreneurial activity or more reactive assertions of judicial power, the judges have engaged in institution building in the service of human rights and their legacy. In the next chapter we introduce the hypotheses we derive from this theory of judicial entrepreneurialism, and conduct our qualitative and quantitative analyses to assess their validity.

3

Analyzing the Progressive Development of International Law

INTRODUCTION

In Chapter Two, we developed our theory of entrepreneurial decision making by judges at the international criminal tribunals. In general we argued that because international law is embryonic and replete with gaps and ambiguities, there are significant demands, and thus opportunities for judges to develop the law. We argued further that judges will utilize such opportunities to develop international law because they generally share a common concern for the protection of human rights, and seek to leave an influential legacy. Having explained when and why the progressive development of international law is likely to occur, we turn next to explaining where in the broad field of international law such entrepreneurialism is most likely to take place, while in Chapter Four we focus on when judges utilize the expressive capacity of the law. Based on this theory we develop several specific hypotheses regarding the conditions under which these judges will seek to progressively develop international law.

While the scope of our analysis is not the investigation of the legal doctrines developed by the ICTY, we believe that the novel relationship in the realm of international criminal institutions between the trial chambers and appeals chambers, the introduction of new crimes charged by the prosecutors, such as the crime of rape, and the new forms of criminal perpetration, such as the creation of the Joint Criminal Enterprise (JCE) doctrine, have offered judges an extensive opportunity to develop and address some of the most vexing legal and procedural uncertainties affecting international criminal law. We suggest that these circumstances represent the perfect opportunity for the judges to progressively develop international criminal law and expand doctrines supporting new forms of criminal liability, while at the same time empowering the protection of human rights. Not surprisingly groundbreaking decisions of the appellate chambers of the ad hoc tribunals deciding controversial legal and procedural circumstances have been consistently cited in multiple cases and used as benchmark decisions for the further development of the jurisprudence of the tribunals.

Our plan for this chapter begins with the articulation of these hypotheses. Our underlying assumption is that where international laws on war crimes, crimes against humanity and genocide are relatively underdeveloped and/or are characterized by ambiguities or gaps in their application, definitions and criminal elements, judges will have substantial opportunities to resolve such problems. Our hypotheses concern more precisely just where and when judges will utilize these opportunities. We argue that international criminal tribunal judges will be most likely to advance international law to address (1) issues regarding a problem or gap in international jurisprudence on the attribution of liability for these crimes; (2) cases involving crimes of special intent, in particular, persecution and genocide; and (3) issues regarding the determination of punishment.

HYPOTHESES

Superior and Individual Liability for International Crimes

One of the most fundamental issues for all actors participating in the trials of suspected war criminals is the determination of the individual's responsibility for the crimes (Bantekas 1999; Danner and Martinez 2005). The nature of the individual liability for such crimes must be specified and proven alongside the determination that such crimes actually took place. There are several types of liability that have been utilized at the international tribunals. The most straightforward legal variant of liability is that which links a specific individual directly to the commission of a specific crime – direct perpetration. Given evidence that the individual physically took part in, for example, acts of torture, destroyed property for no legitimate military rationale or murdered innocent civilians, there are few legal controversies involved in attributing liability to such principal perpetrators. While there have been a number of cases, especially in the early years of the ICTY that involved trials of lower ranking military officials who physically carried out such abuses, more often cases at the tribunals involve mid-ranking and especially high level officials whose hands are not always so dirty. In these cases the prosecution must prove and the judges must determine whether the individuals can be held liable for crimes committed by subordinates or partners. For many such accused the judges must determine which among a number of legal theories of liability is applicable and has been correctly proven beyond a reasonable doubt. These types of liability for individuals who play an active role in the organization of crimes, but are not typically the principal perpetrator include doctrines such as "joint criminal enterprise" (also known as "common design" or "common purpose") and "co-perpetration." Additionally, there are other critical concepts and elements of crimes, such as "aiding and abetting." For individuals charged as responsible for crimes because of their superior liability, there are also theories and elements of liability such as "strict liability," "effective control," "duty to prevent," "duty to punish" and others. We briefly survey some of the more prominent controversies and developments in the law to highlight why we contend that liability issues will tend to attract judicial entrepreneurship and the progressive development of the law.

Superior Liability

International jurisprudence on superior liability for crimes against humanity, war crimes and genocide has changed significantly since the Nuremberg and Tokyo tribunals. Where once a doctrine of strict liability could be applied to Japanese generals who were held accountable for actions taken by their forces, about which they "should have known," the strict liability theory has been overtaken by competing theories of superior liability. Other constructions of superior liability, such as "effective control" propounded most notably in the *Celebici* case, have been developed in numerous judgments at the ICTY and ICTR. At the same time judges have been forced, by virtue of the individuals on trial and the facts of cases, to address other elements of superior liability such as the responsibility of the superior to remain apprised of the movement and behavior of the forces under his command; his duty to prevent these forces from taking part in criminal activity and his responsibility to punish those who have committed such crimes. These have become prominent issues not simply because of the superior liability of political and military leaders who have been put on trial and the types of large-scale crime they stand accused of planning, but also because many, if not most, such individuals have offered their own theories regarding why liability could not be attributed to them, such as alleging parallel chains of command that circumvented their authority. Still others have contended that they did not possess the requisite intent to carry out such crimes. Thus, there is reason to expect that issues of superior liability will figure prominently in the progressive development of international law given the evolution of standards over time.

Joint Criminal Enterprise

There has also been a great deal of jurisprudential ferment regarding liability for those taking part in criminal activities that do not fall neatly into either direct, principal perpetration or superior liability. Many cases at the tribunals have involved individuals who have played prominent, but not always leading roles in the activities of groups carrying out criminal activities. Judges, as well as many commentators, have argued over the merits of the doctrine of "joint criminal enterprise" in particular as a relatively recent and novel development in such liability (Boas 2013). The three types of joint criminal enterprise include (1) "common design plans" where an individual enters into an agreement with others to commit criminal actions; (2) "systems of ill-treatment," primarily detention camps where there is organized repression in which the accused takes part; and (3) criminal acts that are not part of a common design, "if such acts are a natural and foreseeable consequence of the effecting of that common purpose" (Bassiouni 2008, 485). For example, in the course of a forcible expulsion of people from their homes individuals may engage in acts of criminal violence, which may not be planned but which are likely to occur under such fraught circumstances. This extended form of JCE allows those who took part in the planned action to be held liable for the criminal acts committed by others in their group, which were not part of the original plan of action, but were nonetheless a foreseeable consequence of that. While the JCE theory of liability has been used repeatedly at the ad hoc tribunals to hold individuals accountable for the actions of the groups of which they are a member, there has also been a fair amount of discomfit over this doctrine, which is not so popular in many national, criminal justice systems. Indeed, as Danner and Martinez (2005, 104) write in their analysis of JCE, "Joint criminal enterprise . . . has largely been created by the judges and prosecutors of the Yugoslav Tribunal." The concept of aiding and abetting has also been a prominent aspect of liability theories where evidence of direct involvement in perpetration or a JCE has been lacking and where intent is also absent. Judges have sought to specify a legal standard of the quantity and quality of such assistance to determine what the OTP must prove in such cases. Therefore, we believe that because of legal controversies, ambiguities in the law and definitional issues, judges possess ample opportunity and reason to progressively develop international jurisprudence regarding liability.

Case Facts

The nature of the conflicts over which the tribunals exercise jurisdiction is also critically relevant in encouraging judicial entrepreneurship on issues of liability. These conflicts have been characterized by inchoate and shifting lines of political and military authority over individuals in various states of (dis)organization. For example, in the former Yugoslavia many prominent militias took part in crimes (e.g., White Eagles, Arkan's Tigers, Seselj's Men, Scorpions) as well as even more informal groups of individuals involved in torture, rape and killings in detention facilities. Establishing the liability of superiors for these crimes that may not always have been coordinated with military assaults has proven vexing. Further, a number of high ranking officials (e.g., Blaskic, Krstic) have argued that there have been parallel and secret chains of command, devised by scheming and secretive politicians to carry out crimes and evade responsibility. Others have argued that they exercised little authority over those who committed such crimes (e.g., Musema, Krajisnik) and that their authority existed in name only. Hence, given these blurred lines of authority and the typical lack of "smoking gun" evidence linking leaders to such crimes, the development of legal theories of liability has been all the more important in the adjudication of these conflicts. Evolving and ambiguous law applied in factual situations that may be equally as inchoate create a perfect recipe for judicial entrepreneurialism and the progressive development of the law.

Human Rights Concerns

While it is a difficult endeavor proving with certainty that judges have undertaken the entrepreneurial exercise of expanding individual liability to further human rights projections, the results achieved by the judges might speak of this very judicial intent. Attributing responsibility to commanders for criminal actions perpetrated by subordinates, finding criminally liable those who participated in the design of a common criminal plan or otherwise aided and abetted the perpetration of crimes allow judges to expand the protection of human rights for victims who otherwise would see those most responsible for these violations go unpunished. Most importantly judges have pushed the boundaries of individual criminal liability to protect the human rights of innocent individuals under the changed political and legal context within which crimes have been adjudicated, in which more and more indictees are not those directly responsible for the perpetration of the crimes but the master-minders behind them. In their critical analysis of the tendency of ICTY judges of forging new modes of criminal liability Danner and Martinez (2005) state that "The history of JCE at the ICTY, therefore, may be seen not only as an example of the victim-oriented cast of human rights law but also as borrowing some of human rights law's most important, and expansive, interpretive methodologies. As a practical matter, in the chaotic conditions in which war-time violations occur, and due to the post-war dislocation experienced by many victims, it is often very difficult to locate specific evidence proving that defendants have committed particular crimes. Joint criminal enterprise helps prosecutors secure convictions when such proof may be lacking" (Danner and Martinez 2005, 133).

We also suggest that the rationale behind the extensive interpretation of individual criminal liability is to be found in the general principles of humanity dictated by the Martens Clause and used by the judges of the international tribunals as a remedy to the silence of the law when those principles of humanity have indeed been violated. Under the pressure of human rights violations, judges have reshaped international humanitarian law so that where the principles of protection of civilians were not provided by the extant law, whether written or customary, judges could resort to the "principles of humanity" and "dictates of public conscience" as provided for in the *Martens* Clause."[1] In the interlocutory decision in the *Hadzihasanovic et al.* case, Judge Hunt dissented with the majority on the definition of responsibility of a commander for violations of humanitarian law committed by his subordinates before he became their superior and claimed that in the absence of the law such a responsibility finds its reason in the protection of humanity as whole. More recently, Judge Picard made a very compassionate appeal to the need for expanding the responsibility of superiors for aiding and abetting in order to extend the protection

---

[1] Separate and Partially Dissenting Opinion of Judge Hunt on Command Responsibility Appeal in the case of the Prosecutor v. Enver Hadzihasanovic, Mehmed Alagic and Amir Kubura, Case No. IT-01–47, July 16, 2003, para 40.

of victims. In her dissenting opinion in the case of *Stanisic and Simatovic* she stated that "If we cannot find that the Accused aided and abetted those crimes, I would say we have come to a dark place in international law indeed. It is a place, in the words spoken by the Honorable Judge Robert H. Jackson in 1949, where "law has terrors only for little men and takes note only of little wrongs."[2]

Our purpose here is not to dissect these legal doctrines to support our argument that superior liability issues will be associated with the progressive development of international law. Rather, we seek to demonstrate that these issues are ripe for an expansion of international jurisprudence. While there exist many areas of international law where the judges would find potential for progressive development, we argue that because of (1) the fundamental importance of liability doctrine in holding individuals responsible for international crimes; (2) the nature of the conflicts over which the tribunals exercise jurisdiction and in which lines of authority were often, and deliberately, kept ambiguous and dynamic; and (3) the presence of various, emerging theories of liability, judges will be significantly likely to develop the laws in this area.

Hypothesis 1: *Appeals judgments that involve issues regarding individual and superior liability will be more likely to influence tribunal judges to progressively develop international law.*

Crimes with Special Intent

Of all the embryonic areas of international law, few are as lacking in prior jurisprudence as those pertaining to bias crimes. Never before has an international tribunal prosecuted individuals for taking part in criminal behavior that is characterized by a special intent – *dolus specialis* – to target a protected population. The crime of genocide was not charged as such at the Nuremberg Tribunal and the crime of persecution came into existence only during the Nuremberg trials (Fournet and Pegorier 210, 714). The crimes of genocide and persecution, which is a crime against humanity, pertain to criminal actions that are specifically directed at individuals by virtue of their membership in protected groups. For genocide, individuals are protected by virtue of their membership in national, ethnical, racial or religious groups. The crime of persecution targets people on political, racial or religious grounds. The criminal actions that are specifically banned with regard to genocide are:

(a) killing members of the group;
(b) causing serious bodily or mental harm to members of the group;
(c) deliberately inflicting on the group conditions of life calculated to bring about its physical destruction in whole or in part;

---

[2] Dissenting Opinion of Judge Michele Picard in the case of the Prosecutor v. Jovica Stanisic and Franko Simatovic, Case No. IT-03-69-T, May 30, 2013, para 867.

(d) imposing measures intended to prevent births within the group;

(e) forcibly transferring children of the group to another group.[3]

While the core list of actions classified as genocide has remained stable over time, judges at the ad hoc tribunals have expanded the criminal acts that could amount to genocide, such as rape.[4] Persecution encompasses all criminal actions that fall under the heading of crimes against humanity, such as deportation, torture, rape, in which there is bias against individuals on the basis of their political, racial or religious background.[5] We contend that adjudication of these crimes will necessitate progressive development of international law both because the special intent element has rarely arisen in international criminal law, and because the specific populations targeted for these crimes (e.g., Tutsis in Rwanda and Bosnian Muslims in the former Yugoslavia, thus far) present unique, factual characteristics that further complicate jurisprudence. Whether it is because their membership in one of the protected populations is not readily apparent (e.g., Tutsi in Rwanda as a distinct group from Hutus), or the limited geographical targeting of these groups (e.g., the Muslims of eastern Bosnia) calls into issue the "in whole or in part" clause of the crime of genocide, these fact patterns have forced the judges to consider deeply the definitional elements of these crimes.

The fact patterns of the adjudicated genocide cases have highlighted the necessity of the development of workable definitions of the relevant terms and provisions. The language of the Genocide Convention, while direct and succinct, contains numerous terms and clauses that have begged for further definition and explication (Schabas 2006a). The tribunals have struggled with developing a more accurate and relevant understanding of what is meant by the terms, "national, ethnical, racial and religious groups," and with the "in whole or in part" portion of the crime of genocide given the factual characteristics of the Tutsi and Bosnian Muslim populations. In Rwanda the Hutus and Tutsi are of one "nation," are very similar in their racial and ethnic characteristics, and mostly share the same religious affiliations. The ICTR judges have argued that Article 2 of their statute is nonetheless applicable because the language of the Genocide Convention was intended to protect all "stable and permanent" groups, such as the Tutsis, although this particular application has not gained wide acceptance.[6] ICTR and ICTY judges have also proffered an understanding of the "protected groups" element that would accord such status if the individuals are characterized and treated by their persecutors as belonging to such groups.[7] This definition is also not without defect as it appears to rely on

---

[3] As found in the ICTY Statute, for example, in Article 4.2.

[4] The Prosecutor v. Jean-Paul Akayesu, Case No. ICTR-96-4-T, September 2, 1998, e.g., paras 507–508.

[5] As found in the ICTY Statute, for example, in Article 5.

[6] The Prosecutor v. Jean-Paul Akayesu, Case No. ICTR-96-4-T, September 2, 1998, para 516.

[7] The Prosecutor v. Georges Rutaganda, Case No. ICTR-96-3-T, December 6, 1999, paras 55–58 and The Prosecutor v. Ignace Bagilishema, Case No. ICTR-95-1A, July 3, 2002, para 65.

the subjective and changing perceptions of the perpetrator rather than fixed and objective criteria. Such difficulties in applying this terminology, we believe, will necessitate progressive development of the law as both a legal necessity and because the judges will, given their concern for ensuring the human rights of the victims, seek to ensure that they are afforded protection under the law.

As well, in the case of the Muslims of eastern Bosnia, who were singled out for genocide by Bosnian Serb military forces, judges have addressed both whether the limited geographic focus of the campaign (i.e., the Srebrenica massacre) and the targeting of just military age Bosnian men made Article 4 of the ICTY Statute applicable. In *Krstic* the judges debated whether the removal of the able bodied men from safe areas and the separation of the women and children[8] demonstrated a specific intent of "destroying in whole or in part a national, ethnic, racial or religious group."[9] Given the typical absence of direct evidence of the perpetrator's special intent, the need to demonstrate that the populations are protected has become even more important in proving intent. Furthermore, in the *Prosecutor v. Jelisic* case the Trial Chamber addressed another of the lacunae of the Genocide Convention; namely whether genocide can be committed in a limited geographical area. The Trial Chamber recalled the prior decision of the ICTY pursuant to Rule 61 (review of the indictment) in the *Dragan Nikolic* case and concluded that:

> [t]he Trial Chamber adopted a similar position in its Review of the Indictment Pursuant to Article 61 filed in the Nikolic case. In this case, the Trial Chamber deemed that it was possible to base the charge of genocide on events which occurred only in the region of Vlasenica. In view of the object and goal of the Convention and the subsequent interpretation thereof, the Trial Chamber thus finds that international custom admits the characterisation of genocide even when the exterminatory intent only extends to a limited geographic zone.[10]

In the absence of hard evidence demonstrating that a campaign of genocide had been deliberately organized from which intent could be inferred, judges have been forced to determine whether the intent to commit genocide could be determined by the quantitative and qualitative characteristics of those targeted for murder. The unique factual characteristics of the Tutsi and Bosnian Muslim populations forced the judges to determine whether their persecutors possessed the requisite special intent of targeting these individuals for their membership in the protected populations. In addition to the aforementioned ambiguity regarding the meaning and measurement of the protected groups and the "in whole or in part" clause, there have also been issues surrounding the crime of incitement to commit genocide and the attribution of intent to those who are accomplices in genocide.[11] Therefore, we contend that these

---

8 The Prosecutor v. Radislav Krstic, Case No. IT-98–33-T, Trial Judgment, August 2, 2001, para 48.
9 The Prosecutor v. Radislav Krstic, Case No. IT-98–33-T, Trial Judgment, August 2, 2001, paras 541–550.
10 The Prosecutor v. Goran Jelisic, Case No. IT-95–10-T, Judgment, July 5, 2001, para 83.
11 The Prosecutor v. Radislav Krstic, Case No. IT-98–33-A, April 19, 2004, para 238.

fact patterns have also necessitated the progressive development of international law regarding the crimes of genocide and persecution.

The crime of persecution is of very recent origin in international law, and like genocide has presented several, critical conceptual problems in its application (Danner 2001; Nilsson 2011). Nilsson (2011, 219) writes, "... the crime of persecution was hardly applied in international or national law before the start of the ICTY proceedings." The most recent issue regarding the crime of persecution pertains to the legal framework under which the crime should be located. Must crimes of persecution be a part of customary international law? Should such crimes be based on international treaty law? Or should crimes that are characterized by persecution be equal in gravity to crimes against humanity? These debates have played out over a series of decisions, including *Blaskic*, *Kupreskic* and *Kvocka*, which we believe indicates an area of law that is underdeveloped and in flux (Nilsson 2011). As Fournet and Pegorier (2010, 714) argue, "The crime of persecutions thus remains an ill-defined concept, artificially located between crimes against humanity and genocide and confusingly overlapping with war crimes." In effect, it is primed for progressive expansion of the law.

Stating that judges have proceeded to expand the definition of crimes such as genocide and persecution moved by concerns for the furtherance of the human rights cause is a quasi-redundant statement. The creative interpretation of protected groups, the novel inclusion of criminal acts amounting to international law violations, and the expansive interpretation of the criminals' mens rea has contributed to increasing the effective protection of individuals' human rights. The particularly relevant consideration is to note that for the crime of persecution as a crime against humanity the weakening of the link of the crime with the presence of an international conflict, established by the jurisprudence of the ICTY in *Tadic* and the absence of such link in the ICTR statute has reinforced the idea that the crime relies more on principles of international human rights law than on international humanitarian law. The aim of the criminalization of persecution under such conditions has been indeed that of protecting individuals in the more extensive way possible.

As noted by scholars (Akhavan 2008, citing Ambos and Wirth 2002) the broader category of the crimes against humanity, under whose rubric persecution is located, are "no longer linked to the laws of war but rather to human rights law"(Akhavan 2008, 37). In addition, Akhavan (2008) notes that "In the Blaskic case, for instance, the Appeals Chamber considered 'charges of killing and causing serious injury' as persecutions in light of 'the inherent right to life and to be free from cruel, inhuman or degrading treatment or punishment... recognized in customary international law and... embodied in Articles 6 and 7 of the ICCPR, and Articles 2 and 3 of the ECHR'." Similarly in the case of *Kristic* the Trial Chamber found that "persecutory acts are not limited to those acts enumerated in other sub-clauses of Article 5 or elsewhere in the Statute, but also include the denial of other fundamental human rights."[12]

---

[12] The Prosecutor v. Radislav Krsitic, Case No. IT-98–33-T, August 2, 2001, para 535.

Likewise, in the identification of the "national, ethnical, racial or religious group" as possible target of the crime of genocide the Trial Chamber in the *Kristic* case proceeded to analyze several instruments of international and regional human rights agreements. More precisely, the Trial Chamber considered "European instruments on human rights," the work of the Sub-commission on Prevention of Discrimination and Protection of Minorities, and the International Convention on the Elimination of all forms of Racial Discrimination.[13] Lastly in *Jelisic* the Trial Chamber reaffirmed the importance of the Convention on the Prevention and Punishment of the Crime of Genocide as one of the "most widely accepted international instruments relating to human rights."[14]

> **Hypothesis 2:** *Appeals judgments that involve issues regarding genocide and persecution will be more likely to lead tribunal judges to progressively develop international law.*

Sentencing

The sentences for those convicted of war crimes, crimes against humanity and genocide are the culmination of the lengthy, legally complex and politically fraught process that is international criminal justice. Punishment is heavy with meaning designed to communicate to the offender the depth of the debt he owes society. It must speak to the victims to express the measure of justice they are to be afforded for their sufferings. And it must demonstrate to the international community condemnation for the crimes that threaten its values and its peace. Because of the multiple goals pursued by sentencing, the process is likely to be heavily contested and produce substantial jurisprudence.

Those convicted of international crimes are unlikely to ever accept their punishment, unless their sentence reflects the recommendation of a plea bargain arrangement concluded with the Office of the Prosecutor, and accepted by the Trial Chamber. And there are few, if any, disincentives to discourage individuals from seeking a reduction in their sentence using every conceivable avenue of legal appeal. The defendants have one big bite at the apple and thus the tendency has been to plead multiple legal errors in sentence determination, and improper assessment of sentencing determinants (e.g., mitigating and aggravating circumstances). Indeed, the peculiar aspects of sentencing by the international tribunals would seem to encourage many and diverse legal challenges. For example, the ICTY and ICTR have long operated without formal sentencing phases of the trial but combine both the verdict and the punishment into one decision-making process. Thus, during the course of their trials, defendants must raise reasonable doubts regarding the prosecutor's case and argue any mitigating factors germane to punishment, should they be found guilty.

---

[13] The Prosecutor v. Radislav Krsitic, Case No. IT-98–33-T, August 2, 2001, para 555.
[14] The Prosecutor v. Goran Jelisic, Case No. IT-95–10-T, July 5, 2001, para 60.

Another element of sentencing that has raised legal challenges has been the practice of cumulative convictions. Cumulative convictions can be entered for the same criminal actions if it can be proven that there are materially distinct elements present in one conviction that are not present in another. For example, in the *Akayesu* case the ICTR Trial Chamber found that genocide, crimes against humanity, and violations of Article 3 common to the Geneva Conventions and of Additional Protocol II have different elements and are intended to protect different interests." The Trial Chamber established that it does not violate the principle of legality if cumulative charges are brought against individuals even if descending from the same conduct. The Trial Chamber concluded that "it is legitimate to charge these crimes in relation to the same set of facts. It may also, additionally, depending on the case, be necessary to record a conviction for more than one of these offences in order to reflect what crimes an accused committed."[15] The Appeals Chamber in *Celebici* came to the same conclusion relying on their reasoning on the prior conviction in *Tadic* and referring to *Akayesu*. The Appeals Chamber stated, "Cumulative charging is to be allowed in light of the fact that, prior to the presentation of all of the evidence, it is not possible to determine to a certainty which of the charges brought against an accused will be proven. The Trial Chamber is better poised, after the parties' presentation of the evidence, to evaluate which of the charges may be retained, based upon the sufficiency of the evidence. In addition, cumulative charging constitutes the usual practice of both this Tribunal and the ICTR."[16] The Office of the Prosecutor can also appeal against sentences it considers too light given the severity of the defendant's conduct, or because the sentence was the product of faulty legal reasoning (e.g., the defendant was convicted of a lesser degree of liability than was appropriate and thus attracted a lighter sentence). For these reasons, we contend that the unique qualities of the international sentencing regime and the high stakes of the outcome, particularly for those convicted, should give rise to substantial expansion of the jurisprudence on the subject.

As we have argued previously, judges have been granted significant discretion in the manner in which they interpret the goals of the tribunals as they pertain to punishment, as well as the specific determinants of sentencing (Drumbl 2007a; Ewald 2010; Harmon and Gaynor 2007; Hola, Smeulers and Bijleveld 2011; Meernik 2011; Sloane 2007a, 2007b). Given the lofty aims of the tribunals to advance peace, justice, reconciliation and other such national level goals, it is not surprising that judicial interpretation of the importance of these goals gives rise to controversy in the application of such abstract ambitions to individual cases. For example, while

---

[15] The Prosecutor v. Jean-Paul Akayesu, Case No. ICTR-96-4-T, Judgment, September 2, 1998, para 469.

[16] The Prosecutor v. Zejnil Delalic, Zdravko Mucic, Hazim Delic and Esad Landzo, Case No. IT-96-21-A, February 20, 2001, para 400.

some judges may wish to accord prominence to the goal of general deterrence by sentencing an individual to many years in prison, the defendant is likely to challenge the use of *his* judgment to communicate to a global audience of potential war criminals. In general, anchoring punishment to the subjective values and goals of international justice may well lead to disparate legal and factual justifications of sentences that can create doctrinal confusion and disparate outcomes, both of which are likely to encourage appeals. Similarly, the wide variety of sentencing determinants utilized by the judges (e.g., type of liability, extent of the crimes, mitigating circumstances), may also give rise to perceptions of unequal and unfair treatment as it allows judges to choose, as they see fit, which criteria to apply. This, in turn, creates incentives to appeal against sentences contending, for example that excessive or improper weight was given to aggravating circumstances or insufficient attention was accorded to mitigating factors. In general, operationalization of the few, subjective and internationally-oriented goals (e.g., deterrence) in individual cases, coupled with the diverse, specific criteria on which sentences are informed are likely to generate perceptions of comparative unfairness. No one is likely to be satisfied with their punishment, but the degree of dissatisfaction can be expected to increase with the perception that one's peers are being accorded better treatment. Such legal controversies are likely to encourage judicial efforts at doctrinal development, and thus, the progressive development of the law.

Hypothesis 3: *Appeals Judgments that involve issues regarding sentencing will be more likely to lead tribunal judges to progressively develop international law.*

METHODOLOGY

To test these hypotheses we must determine where and when judges progressively develop international law. One might arrive at such conclusions through either subjective or objective means. Subjectively, we can look to the assessments by the judges themselves as well as scholars and legal commentators to identify rulings that have expanded the definition of a particular crime, such as the decision that rape is a genocidal crime, or have expanded the reach of the law, such as the decoupling of crimes against humanity from the existence of armed conflict. Indeed, much legal commentary concerns whether judges have broken new legal ground and the wisdom of such developments. Thus, one could, through a somewhat subjective analysis of such other, subjective assessments identify the most likely instances of progressive development of the law.

We utilize a more subjective approach (explained in greater detail later in this chapter) and a more objective and data-driven strategy for testing our hypotheses. To conduct our objective and data-driven method, we look to determine the prevalence of particular rulings in the jurisprudence of the tribunals to identify when the judges are likely to be progressively developing the law. We examined every appeals chamber judgment from the ICTY, ICTR and SCSL to determine which cases they cite. That is, we examined all appeals judgments to identify all the specific decisions (e.g., *Akayesu, Tadic*) and paragraphs from within these decisions (e.g., *Akayesu*, paragraph 10) that were cited to determine which judgments were receiving the most attention – that is the most citations. Just as scholars determine the impact of their work by determining how many times a specific article has been cited, so too can we determine which appeals chamber judgments are the most important for the development of international criminal law through examination of the frequency with which their rulings are cited in subsequent cases. Then, we undertake a doctrinal analysis of particular issues and cases where our hypotheses are supported to explain why particular judgments represent a progressive development of the law and what elements of these judgments justify their characterization as landmark decisions. We also analyze other frequently referenced jurisprudence that we did not expect would generate as much citation to determine what contributions these rulings may have had on international jurisprudence.

To do this we read through every Appeals Chamber judgment from the three ad hoc tribunals and identified every instance where a citation was made to an earlier judgment. We identified the case name, case number, tribunal name, paragraph number and whether the reference was made in the judgment or dissenting opinion for each and every such citation. Using this substantial database, we then aggregated all references to the same case paragraph across all the Appeals Chamber judgments to arrive at a frequency of the number of times each instance of Appeals Chamber jurisprudence was cited. The key unit of analysis is the case paragraph. We contend that the greater the number of times a case paragraph is cited, the greater the likelihood that the opinion in that paragraph is important and thus likely to represent a progressive development of the law. We rely on the Appeals Judgments rather than on the first tier decisions because Appeals Chambers' decisions are those which crystallize the jurisprudence of international tribunals and, if undisputed and therefore cited as supportive arguments, represent the final word on the development of international law.

We rely on this methodology of citation counts to measure the importance of a particular ruling for several reasons. First, while there has been a vigorous academic debate over the meaning and importance of citations, most especially US Supreme Court cases, this debate has not been conclusively resolved. Those who contend precedent exercises little influence on judicial decision making (e.g., Segal and Spaeth 1993) argue that given the plethora of potential cases and the central role of ideological preferences in their decisions, judges use citations instrumentally to support their pre-determined conclusions. Scholars have, however, challenged such arguments and emphasize the legal and textual import of precedent in US Supreme Court jurisprudence and have found evidence to the contrary (Cross, Spriggs Jr, Johnson and Wahlbeck 2010). Rather, these scholars stress that citation to precedent is neither meaningless nor determinative of judicial decision making. Thus, with the notable exception of those devoted to the attitudinal model, significant academic work has argued and found that citations to precedent are an important element of jurisprudence. Indeed, as Cross et al. (2010, 490) write, "Citations function something like the currency of the legal system. An opinion's references to authoritative legal materials, most often the Court's own prior decisions, form the fundamental justification for a judicial decision."

Second, there is a growing literature assessing the importance of judicial decisions with reference to the frequency with which subsequent opinions cite these cases (Cross, Spriggs Jr, Johnson and Wahlbeck 2010; Fowler, Johnson, Spriggs, Jeon, Wahlbeck 2007). As Fowler et al. (2007, 329) write, "At the most basic level the number of citations from other cases (inward citations) can be used to measure the importance of a given court decision." Thus, we contend that the number of citations that a given Appeals Chamber case paragraph produces is a key indicator of its importance in the jurisprudence of the international criminal tribunals. We believe that the judges cite prior judgments not because they wish to buttress preconceived notions of their desired outcomes, but because citation reference helps ground current decisions in precedent, protects the legitimacy of the court and provides guidance for prosecution and defense attorneys regarding the current and correct legal reasoning.

We also coded the issues at stake in these paragraphs for all those paragraphs that were cited at least five times. This represents approximately 50 percent of all such citations. We concluded that those judgment paragraphs cited four or fewer times were not likely to be of particular import.

ANALYSIS

We begin with a very straightforward exercise – identifying the cases and the paragraphs in those cases that are cited most often in subsequent Appeals Chamber decisions. We provide in Table 3.1 a list of all those case paragraphs that were cited at least twenty-five times in subsequent trial and appellate judgments. Including in this table those case paragraphs cited less than twenty-five times would create an impossibly large table.

We see first and most clearly that a number of case paragraphs from the ICTY have been extensively cited. Portions of the *Tadic, Furundzija, Alexsovski, Blaskic, Vasiljevic and Kvocka* cases, among others, have been cited more than sixty times. A paragraph from the *Tadic* case regarding the standard of review on appeals cases is the most cited paragraph (ninety-six times) of all the appeals judgments from the ICTY, ICTR and SCSL. In fact, this same topic is also at issue in six of the top ten most frequently cited case paragraphs. We found through the course of our analysis that the Appeals Chamber typically begins every judgment with a description of the function of an Appeals Chamber Judgment and the circumstances under which the Appeals Chamber will consider reversing a decision by a trial chamber. We quote,

TABLE 3.1. *Case Paragraphs Cited at Least Twenty-Five Times by ICTY, ICTR and SCSL Appeals Chambers*

Cited Case	Cited Paragraph	Issue	Number of Times Cited
Tadic	64	appellate standard of review	96
Furundzija	37	appellate standard of review	85
Kvocka et al.	23	appellate standard of review	85
Aleksovski	63	assessment of witness	84
Tadic	227	definition of common design or purpose	76
Blaskic	13	appellate standard of review	68
Vasiljevic	12	appellate standard of review	62
Musema	18	appellate standard of review	61
Brdanin	430	elements and definition of JCE	56
Celebici	458	assessment of circumstantial evidence	55
Tadic	229	aiding and abetting	55
Kupreskic et al.	30	appellate standard of review	54
Kunarac et al.	43	appellant responsibility to follow appeals procedures	51
Kunarac et al.	48	legal sufficiency of evidence	51
Kupreskic et al.	89	indictment challenges/issues	51
Kupreskic et al.	114	indictment challenges/issues	47
Stakic	219	appellate standard of review	46
Kupreskic et al.	32	appellate standard of review	45
Celebici	717	sentences are individualized	43
Tadic	220	definition of common design or purpose	43
Vasiljevic	102	aiding and abetting	43
Kupreskic et al.	88	indictment challenges/issues	42
Celebici	725	standard of review for sentences	41
Nahimana et al.	194	assessment of witness	41
Tadic	228	definition of common design or purpose	41
Kunarac et al.	47	legal sufficiency of evidence	40
Kupreskic et al.	31	legal sufficiency of evidence	40
Aleksovski	187	standard of review for sentences	37
Celebici	412	cumulative convictions	37
Celebici	434	legal sufficiency of evidence	37
Gacumbitsi	10	appellant responsibility to follow appeals procedures	37
Gacumbitsi	49	legal sufficiency of evidence	37
Kupreskic et al.	39	legal sufficiency of evidence	37
Vasiljevic	100	elements and definition of JCE	37
Aleksovski	182	role of gravity in sentencing	36
Brdanin	413	elements and definition of JCE	36
Kunarac et al.	39	appellate standard of review	36
Kunarac et al.	41	right to reasonable opinion	36
Kupreskic et al.	29	appellate standard of review	36
Celebici	435	legal sufficiency of evidence	35

TABLE 3.1. (*cont.*)

Cited Case	Cited Paragraph	Issue	Number of Times Cited
Celebici	481	legal sufficiency of evidence	35
Musema	20	assessment of witness	35
Simic et al.	85	aiding and abetting	35
Celebici	498	legal sufficiency of evidence	34
Rutaganda	19	appellate standard of review	34
Tadic	196	definition of common design or purpose	34
Tadic	204	definition of common design or purpose	34
Blagojevic and Jokic	127	aiding and abetting	33
Brdanin	24	appellate standard of review	33
Furundzija	40	appellate standard of review	33
Tadic	65	assessment of witness	33
Celebici	506	assessment of witness	32
Vasiljevic	11	appellate standard of review	32
Blaskic	680	standard of review for sentences	31
Niyitegeka	10	appellant responsibility to follow appeals procedures	31
Niyitegeka	200	equality of arms	31
Vasiljevic	6	appellate standard of review	31
Aleksovski	62	legal sufficiency of evidence	30
Blaskic	15	power of AC to articulate correct legal standard	30
Blaskic	48	aiding and abetting	30
Kajelijeli	6	appellate standard of review	30
Krajisnik	139	right to clear but not detailed response	30
Krstic	40	appellate standard of review	30
Rutaganda	18	appellate standard of review	30
Simba	103	legal sufficiency of evidence	30
Gacumbitsi	9	appellate standard of review	29
Kajelijeli	7	appellant responsibility to follow appeals procedures	29
Kunarac et al.	44	appellant responsibility to follow appeals procedures	29
Nchamihigo	47	assessment of witness	29
Simic et al.	86	aiding and abetting	29
Brdanin	411	definition of common design or purpose	28
Kvocka et al.	33	indictment challenges/issues	28
Tadic	202	definition of common design or purpose	28
Akayesu	178	appellate standard of review	27
Celebici	413	cumulative convictions	27
Furundzija	35	appellate standard of review	27
Kunarac et al.	40	appellate standard of review	27
Nahimana et al.	428	assessment of witness	27
Ntagerura et al.	28	indictment challenges/issues	27

(*cont.*)

TABLE 3.1. (*cont.*)

Cited Case	Cited Paragraph	Issue	Number of Times Cited
Vasiljevic	8	appellate standard of review	27
Blagojevic and Jokic	11	appellant responsibility to follow appeals procedures	26
Kvocka et al.	83	JCE mens rea	26
Semanza	361	liability through ordering	26
Tadic	188	definition of common design or purpose	26
Tadic	203	definition of common design or purpose	26
Blagojevic and Jokic	189	aiding and abetting	25
Blaskic	69	effective control/de facto authority	25
Boskoski and Tarculovski	17	appellant responsibility to follow appeals procedures	25
Brdanin	16	appellate standard of review	25
Brdanin	410	elements and definition of JCE	25
Gacumbitsi	60	actus reus genocide	25
Kordic and Cerkez	28	liability through ordering	25
Krnojelac	10	appellate standard of review	25
Krnojelac	11	appellate standard of review	25
Martic	168	elements and definition of JCE	25
Mrksic et al.	12	power of AC to articulate correct legal standard	25
Muvunyi	18	legal sufficiency of evidence	25
Rutaganda	29	assessment of witness	25

in its entirety, the *Tadic* appellate judgment, paragraph 64, which is the most cited paragraph of any appellate judgment:

> The two parties agree that the standard to be used when determining whether the Trial Chamber's factual finding should stand is that of unreasonableness, that is, a conclusion which no reasonable person could have reached. The task of hearing, assessing and weighing the evidence presented at trial is left to the Judges sitting in a Trial Chamber. Therefore, the Appeals Chamber must give a margin of deference to a finding of fact reached by a Trial Chamber. It is only where the evidence relied on by the Trial Chamber could not reasonably have been accepted by any reasonable person that the Appeals Chamber can substitute its own finding for that of the Trial Chamber. It is important to note that two judges, both acting reasonably, can come to different conclusions on the basis of the same evidence.

In fact, we found the following language, in this case from the *Kupreskic* decision (paragraph 30), repeated quite often in many cases, with slight variations and replete with references to other judgments that used this same, basic language on the nature of the appeals process:

TABLE 3.2. *Top Twenty-Five Most Cited Appeals Chamber Judgments*

Cited Case	Number of Times Cited
Celebici	2,012
Tadic	1,847
Blaskic	1,077
Galic	1,029
Rutaganda	969
Kupreskic et al.	925
Simic et al.	921
Brdanin	808
Stakic	771
Kunarac et al.	759
Kvocka et al.	742
Kordic and Cerkez	727
Krajisnik	671
Vasiljevic	650
Nahimana et al.	595
Semanza	593
Krstic	583
Aleksovski	509
Furundzija	487
Krnojelac	485
Martic	457
Gacumbitsi	437
Ntagerura et al.	424
Galic	423
Musema	412

Pursuant to the jurisprudence of the Tribunal, the task of hearing, assessing and weighing the evidence presented at trial is left primarily to the Trial Chamber. Thus, the Appeals Chamber must give a margin of deference to a finding of fact reached by a Trial Chamber. Only where the evidence relied on by the Trial Chamber could not have been accepted by any reasonable tribunal of fact or where the evaluation of the evidence is "wholly erroneous" may the Appeals Chamber substitute its own finding for that of the Trial Chamber.

Thus, the issues of most concern to judges are those involving the ground rules of the appeals process. Before the judges even begin to discuss the substantive appeals lodged by the prosecution and the defense, they are compelled to note the nature of the rules that are applied in appeals judgments. Once these preliminary matters are dealt with, judges delve into more substantive matters of the law. We also find judges have made continual reference to the need for appellants to follow the correct appeals procedures and provide accurate documentation. Judges make frequent reference to issues involving how they will assess the credibility and import of particular witnesses and the evidence.

That the Appeals Chambers would refer to these fundamental, procedural issues to inaugurate each new judgment is not surprising. To a large degree these references to fundamental, preliminary matters seem to be almost reflexively inserted into judgments. Yet, these references to standards of review, assessment of witness testimony, the need for appellants to provide clear and supportive briefs, and the like also seem to be serving an educative function. Given the large number of counsel on both sides who have practiced before the tribunals, the judges have been at pains to make sure that they and the defendants clearly understand how the judges make their more substantive judgments. Regardless, these most cited paragraphs on standards of review are an essential element of all judgments.

While we would not diminish the importance of these preliminary matters, we must note that because all judgments take note of these review and evidentiary standards, the numbers of such citations are inflated. And while these are essential elements of the opinions that set the stage for the Chambers' substantive rulings, we should not necessarily conclude at the outset that these are the most important issues facing the ad hoc tribunals.

Once we move beyond the citations to judgments regarding appellate review and evidentiary standards, we find a variety of more substantive issues addressed in the most frequently cited portions of judgments. Among the other issues we see in Table 3.1 that have been the focus of those cases cited at least twenty-five times, we find: definition of a common design or purpose from *Tadic*, paragraph 227, which has been cited seventy-six times; *Brdanin* paragraph 430 regarding elements and definition of JCE, which has been cited fifty-six times; *Tadic* paragraph 229 regarding aiding and abetting, which has been cited fifty-five times; *Kupreskic* paragraphs 89, 114 and 88 on issues and problems with indictments, which have been cited fifty-one, forty-seven and forty-two times, respectively; *Vasiljevic* paragraph 102 on aiding and abetting, which has been cited forty-three times; paragraphs 717 and 725 on sentencing from the *Celebici* decision, which have been cited forty-three and forty-one times, respectively; and *Tadic*, paragraphs 220 and 228 on the definition of a common design or purpose, which have been cited forty-three and forty-one times.

These represent a majority of the issues where we had expected to find judges behaving as entrepreneurs and progressively developing international law. In particular, we find that matters relating to individual liability, as evaluated through the lens of a definition of a "common design" or "purpose"; "aiding and abetting"; and the elements of a "joint criminal enterprise" are the issues most frequently cited (with the exception of the appellate standards of review). We also see that issues pertaining to sentencing are raised quite frequently in the judgment paragraphs cited most often. Not surprisingly, a paragraph regarding the standard of review for sentencing ranks as the most frequently cited paragraph on sentencing (from *Celebici*), while another paragraph from *Celebici* on the principle of individualized sentencing is the second most cited paragraph on this topic. There were no case paragraphs that were so frequently cited and that dealt with bias crimes. So while the appeals procedures references are by far the most cited and prevalent of all the issues involved in these top cited paragraphs, the other issues that do rise to the top are two of those we had hypothesized would be most likely to lead to progressive development of the law. We will go into significantly more depth on these particular paragraphs, the issues involved and their impact on international jurisprudence in the next section.

When we shift our focus from the most cited paragraphs to the most cited cases we find what most tribunal observers would predict, but which are still very revealing in their illustration of the landmark decisions. As we might expect, two ICTY cases stand out above all the rest – *Celebici* (cited 2,012 times) and *Tadic* (cited 1,847 times). These cases have attracted a great deal of legal and scholarly attention because of their role in establishing appellate standards of review, the legitimacy of the ICTY and the definition of internal versus international armed conflict (*Tadic*), as well as their jurisprudence on superior liability and sentencing (*Celebici*). The next most oft cited case is the *Blaskic* decision (1,077 times), which is known for setting precedent on command control. The *Blaskic* case is also notable for the variety of issue rulings that are cited in subsequent decisions. In addition to frequent references to its jurisprudence on command and control issues, it is also cited for rulings on appellate review standards, crimes against humanity issues, sentencing jurisprudence and bias crimes. The *Galic* case was cited 1,029 times, principally for issues involving the targeting of civilians during military campaigns – in this case the shelling of Sarajevo. The ICTR case cited most often is *Rutaganda*, which is the seventh most cited case (969 times). It was cited in a variety of contexts, but especially concerning appellate review standards and issues involving trial fairness. While this brief exposition on the top cited cases is useful in identifying which cases attract the most attention, to better understand what is at stake we turn to the most important piece of this part of the analysis – the issues.

We present our results on the most cited issues in Tables 3.3 and 3.4. Table 3.3 breaks the issues down into fairly distinct and specific categories, and lists them in order of the frequency with which they have been cited in paragraphs of tribunal judgments. Table 3.4 groups many related issues together into broader categories. Because we coded the issues germane to the case paragraphs in a fairly specific manner, there are many similar topics pertaining to each of the broader issue types. In order to determine just how often these general issue categories were cited, we combine the various specific issue categories into eight groupings: (1) Appeals Chamber standards regarding the appeals process and outcomes (e.g., appellate standard of review, legal sufficiency of evidence, etc.); (2) issues pertaining to the fairness of the trial (e.g., equality of arms, accusations of judicial bias); (3) other issues pertaining to the appeals and trial processes; (4) sentencing issues; (5) issues pertaining to superior and individual liability; (6) issues pertaining to bias crimes – persecution and genocide; (7) issues pertaining to crimes against humanity (excluding persecution); and (8) issues pertaining to war crimes. Table 3.4 lists these general categories of crimes in order of how many times they were cited.

TABLE 3.3. *Issues Cited in Appeals Chamber Judgments*

Issue	Number of Times Cited
appellate standard of review	2,919
definition of common design or purpose	794
aiding and abetting	749
legal sufficiency of evidence	601
assessment of witness	521
standard of review for sentences	477
appellant responsibility to follow appeals procedures	463
elements and definition of JCE	406
power of AC to articulate correct legal standard	289
indictment challenges/issues	280
liability through failing to stop	273
cumulative convictions	231
forced transfer	196
right to clear but not detailed response	173
procedural/nonsubstantive reference to record	165
consistency in sentencing	146
assessment/definition of mitigating factors	144
role of gravity in sentencing	143
equality of arms	119
intent for persecution	112
liability through ordering	108
individual liability	104
assessment of circumstantial evidence	103
definition of crime of persecution	101
superior liability – had reason to know standard	100

Appeals Chamber judges first and foremost assert Appeals Chamber procedures and standards. As the reader will see in Table 3.3, we found 2,919 case paragraphs that pertained to the basic standards of appellate review. In addition, there are several other issues involving the appellate review process that are repeatedly arising in cases, such as the legal sufficiency of evidence (601 paragraphs on that topic have been cited); assessments of witness veracity and credibility (cited 521 times); defendant's responsibility to follow correct procedures (cited 463 times); the power of the Appeals Chamber to articulate the correct legal standard (when the Trial Chamber has erroneously applied the wrong standard, which has been cited as at issue in 289 case paragraphs). The prevalence of these "meta" issues in tribunal jurisprudence makes clear that the administration of international justice is a fundamental object of the judges' work. Unless the parties understand the criteria by which judges make decisions and follow the procedures set forth in making their appeals, the "real work" of international justice cannot proceed. That so much attention is accorded this subject demonstrates that the institutionalization of international

TABLE 3.4. *General Issues Cited by Appeals Chambers*

General Issue	Number of Times Cited
Appeals Standards	5,501
Superior & Individual Liability Issues	1,590
Sentencing Issues	1,312
JCE	1,278
Fairness Issues	720
Crimes Against Humanity Issues	563
Bias Crime Issues	266
War Crimes Issues	256
Evidentiary and Defense Issues	87

justice is proceeding apace. As we see in Table 3.4, the total number of references to all such issues is 5,501 – more than three times the next most frequently cited general issue.

Nonetheless, we find significant support for two of our three hypotheses. There are a plethora of issues regarding modes of liability that are raised in appeals decisions. We see in Table 3.3 that "definition of a common design or purpose" is the second most frequently mentioned issue in case paragraphs, and has been cited 794 times. It is closely followed by cites regarding the issue of aiding and abetting, which have been cited 749 times. The tribunals have also repeatedly made reference to the elements and definition of the JCE standard (cited 406 times) and liability through failing to stop individuals from carrying out illegal activities (cited 273 times). When we examine the prevalence of all issues regarding superior and individual liability in Table 3.4 we see that such matters arise in 1,590 case paragraphs. This is the second most frequently cited issue. We also see in Table 3.4 that all of the various JCE issues have been cited a total of 1,278 times.

In Table 3.4 the data show that sentencing is the third most frequently referenced general issue for a grand total of 1,312 citations. The issue of the appropriate standard for reviewing sentences that are being appealed has been at issue in 477 case paragraphs. Jurisprudence involving such penal matters as cumulative convictions (231 citations); consistency in sentencing (146 citations); the assessment of mitigating and aggravating factors (144 citations) and the importance of gravity in determining sentences (143 citations) are also frequently cited.

However, we find that bias crimes do not seem to have attracted a great deal of attention at the tribunals. While issues pertaining to crimes against humanity that do not involve bias or persecution are frequently at issue in the jurisprudence of the ad hoc tribunals, those issues pertaining more directly to persecution and genocide do not seem to have led to as much legal ferment as many of the other contentious issues. We caution against rejection of this hypothesis, however, until we have analyzed the jurisprudence on bias crimes itself to determine if the real legal impact of these rulings is not reflected in the relative infrequency with which judges refer to such matters.

What does all of this mean, and how exactly do we infer what these results portend for entrepreneurial judicial decision making and the progressive development of international law? It is a truism that increasing numbers of citations to a particular case or specific part of a case do not automatically mean that new legal ground has been broken. Nonetheless, scholars are increasingly counting citations as a quantitative measure of impact of Supreme Court opinions (Cross, Spriggs Jr, Johnson and Wahlbeck 2010; Fowler, Johnson, Spriggs, Jeon, Wahlbeck 2007). We saw that the most frequently cited issues by far were those references to the basic standards and procedures of the appellate process. Before Appeals Chamber judges consider the merits of the case they typically lay out the background and these standards to set the stage for their analysis of the grounds of appeals. Such continual reference to these basic rules of the game is important. At the same time we also see that while our hypothesis predicted that bias crimes issues would result in significant citations to the relevant jurisprudence we did not find evidence of such in our data. Thus, we have one example where we see the tribunals making frequent reference to an issue that is important, but may not be as important as we might expect given the substantial number of citations. And we have another example where there is a lack of citations to a potentially important issue. To resolve these issues and engage our hypotheses further we next examine the jurisprudential record to develop a better understanding of what judgments and what issues have inspired the most progressive development of the law. Increasing numbers of citations to a case are, in effect, a necessary, but not sufficient condition for identifying where international law has been progressively expanded. Therefore, our next step must be to utilize this information to determine which of the most cited case paragraphs represent a progressive development of international law.

ASSESSING THE PROGRESSIVE DEVELOPMENT OF THE LAW

Superior Liability, Command and Control and Joint Criminal Enterprise

Matters involving individual liability for the violation of international law – whether as a consequence of direct involvement (e.g., ICTY Statute Article 7(1)), or acting as a superior (e.g., ICTY Article 7(3)) are among the most cited issues in the jurisprudence emanating from the appeals chambers of all the ad hoc tribunals. These concerns have been the subject of some 1,590 citations, as seen in Table 3.4. This is the second highest issue category – second only to matters of appellate review standards and questions. Additionally, the reader will note that when examining the more specifically coded issues among these questions of liability, the topic of "aiding and abetting" is the third most frequently cited more specific issue in Table 3.4 – cited 749 times. Among the other frequently cited specific issues listed in Table 3.3

concerning liability are issues of responsibility involving a failure to prevent crimes (273 citations); issues pertaining to ordering the commission of crimes (108 citations); general issues of individual liability (104 citations); and the "had reason to know" standard for superior liability (100 citations).

Aiding and Abetting

We look first to the matters involving aiding and abetting. Not only is this the single most cited specific issue pertaining to liability, it is also the subject of one of the most oft-cited paragraphs in the jurisprudence of the ad hoc tribunals. We begin by reproducing below the relevant language from the ICTY Statute Article 7 as it has featured so prominently in a series of early rulings and a more recent controversy that saw one prominent accused acquitted on appeal over differences in interpretation of aiding and abetting:

> 1. A person who planned, instigated, ordered, committed or otherwise aided and abetted in the planning, preparation or execution of a crime referred to in articles 2 to 5 of the present Statute, shall be individually responsible for the crime.

The most cited paragraph on aiding and abetting, as well as the most cited paragraph in general addressing individual and superior liability issues arises from the *Tadic* Appeals Chamber judgment, paragraph 229, which has been cited fifty-five times.[17] A persuasive argument can be made that the aiding and abetting issue herein pertains more to joint criminal enterprise jurisprudence, but the focal point of contention here and in subsequent rulings concerns the argument that there is a specific direction requirement embedded within liability for aiding and abetting. That is, must the prosecution prove that the accused not only gave the perpetrators material assistance that had a substantial effect on the commission of a crime, but that he also gave specific instructions for the perpetrators to carry out these crimes? The *Tadic* case discusses this issue in light of and in contrast to aiding and abetting in the context of a JCE, but subsequent rulings have differed on whether the specific direction requirement allegedly established in *Tadic* governs other forms of liability. We begin by quoting the *Tadic* appellate judgment paragraph 229:

> 229. In light of the preceding propositions it is now appropriate to distinguish between acting in pursuance of a common purpose or design to commit a crime, and aiding and abetting.
> 1. The aider and abettor is always an accessory to a crime perpetrated by another person, the principal.
> 2. In the case of aiding and abetting no proof is required of the existence of a common concerted plan, let alone of the pre-existence of such a plan. No plan or agreement is required: indeed, the principal may not even know about the accomplice's contribution.

[17] The Prosecutor v. Dusko Tadic, Case No. IT-94-1-A, July 15, 1999, para 229.

3. The aider and abettor carries out acts specifically directed to assist, encourage or lend moral support to the perpetration of a certain specific crime (murder, extermination, rape, torture, wanton destruction of civilian property, etc.), and this support has a substantial effect upon the perpetration of the crime. By contrast, in the case of acting in pursuance of a common purpose or design, it is sufficient for the participant to perform acts that in some way are directed to the furthering of the common plan or purpose.

4. In the case of aiding and abetting, the requisite mental element is knowledge that the acts performed by the aider and abettor assist the commission of a specific crime by the principal. By contrast, in the case of common purpose or design more is required (i.e., either intent to perpetrate the crime or intent to pursue the common criminal design plus foresight that those crimes outside the criminal common purpose were likely to be committed), as stated above.

The key passage is found in part 3, which has indicated to some Appeals Chambers that specific direction is a necessary element of aiding and abetting, while to others it is intended to distinguish the elements of aiding and abetting from JCE, which is the principal focus of an extended discussion regarding Tadic's liability (Coco and Gal 2014; Ventura 2013). Indeed, not only have scholars argued that the *Tadic* language was simply designed to contrast JCE aiding and abetting with aiding and abetting behaviors in other types of liability, but the appeals chambers in *Taylor*[18] and *Sainovic*[19] argued as much.

The specific direction requirement in *Tadic* paragraph 259 was frequently cited thereafter, although as Ventura (2013) points out, neither the *Tadic* paragraph nor subsequent references to it bothered to conduct a thorough review of national and international jurisprudence to determine whether there was evidence that this requirement had become part of customary international law. Thus, while the *Tadic* language has proven popular, any differences of opinion regarding its meaning and status did not generate controversy until the *Perisic* appeals judgment.[20] Until that decision there is little evidence that such a specific direction standard had been applied in other cases. In *Perisic*, the Appeals Chamber ruled that specific direction was a necessary element of aiding and abetting, which subsequently became the focal point of a series of contrasting appellate chamber outcomes at the ICTY and the Sierra Leone tribunal, as described by Ventura (2013).

Ventura provides an excellent analysis of these cases, so we will provide just a brief summary here. A trial chamber of the ICTY sitting in judgment in the *Perisic* case found the accused – the highest ranking general of the Yugoslav Army – guilty of aiding and abetting the work and criminal actions of the Bosnian Serb army (VRS) through the provision of material, payment of salaries and benefits,

---

[18] The Prosecutor v. Charles Taylor, Case No. SCSL-03-01-A, September 26, 2013.
[19] The Prosecutor v. Sainovic et al., Case No. IT-05-87-A, January 23, 2014.
[20] The Prosecutor v. Momcilo Perisic, Case No. IT-04-81-A, February 28, 2013.

and assistance with some operations. The ICTY Appeals Chamber overturned all of Perisic's convictions, and most especially that for aiding and abetting by arguing that there was a requirement that the accused give specific direction to the VRS. Simply providing aid, which might be used for any number of purposes, was not sufficient to prove this type of collaboration unless the accused had directed the aid to be used for criminal purposes, especially in light of the physical distance between the accused and the perpetrators. Subsequently, the Appeals Chamber of the SCSL in the *Taylor* case[21] and the ICTY Appeals Chamber hearing the appeal of Nikola Sainovic in the *Milutinovic*[22] case rejected that reasoning and after surveying national and international jurisprudence since World War II could find very little evidence that specific direction was part of customary international law.

As Ventura (2013) indicates, the back-to-back defeats of the specific direction requirement in aiding and abetting would seem to have dealt that notion a fatal blow. However, because the language in the Rome Statute – Article 23 (c)(3) – would seem to leave open the possibility that specific direction is a necessary element of aiding and abetting, the issue has not entirely been settled, but must await further rulings at the ICC, and perhaps the ICTY as well. Thus, while the specific direction element has not featured prominently in the paragraphs we find cited most often (with the quite notable exception of the *Tadic* and *Blagojevic and Jokic* appellate judgments), the likelihood that any of the aforementioned cases, along with others on the subject such as *Mrksic and Sljivancanin*,[23] will be cited frequently in the future would seem to be quite high.

In a related and frequently cited case on the matter of aiding and abetting, *Blagojevic and Jokic* (paragraph 189, cited twenty-five times), Jokic pleads that individuals should not be held liable for aiding and abetting when, as Jokic claims, the actus reus is part of what the defendant claims is the normal course of his duties and job performance. Dragan Jokic commanded the Zvornik Engineering Brigade of the VRS and was charged with providing assistance to those Bosnian Serb forces that carried out the Srebrenica genocide. As part of his plea, Jokic argued that rather than holding him responsible for "merely" performing his job, the OTP must prove that he gave "specific direction" to those he is accused of aiding and abetting in the commission of crimes. The judges, however, note that while the liability of some, especially low-ranking individuals may be lessened because their actions did not have a "substantial effect upon the perpetration of the crime" (discussed later in this chapter) and may well be characterized as routine job functions, this did not describe Jokic's actions, who was a higher ranking officer who actively took part in the planning of the operations that aided and abetted the genocide. After discussing the extent of Jokic's involvement in the Srebrenica genocide and concluding

---

[21] The Prosecutor v. Charles Taylor, Case No. SCSL-03–01-A, September 26, 2013.
[22] The Prosecutor v. Sainovic et al., Case No. IT-05–87-A, January 23, 2014.
[23] Prosecutor v. Mrksic and Sljivancanin, Case No. IT-95–13/1-A, May 5, 2009, para 159.

that his actions went beyond normal job performance, the Appeals Chamber notes that:

> 189. The Appeals Chamber observes that while the *Tadic* definition has not been explicitly departed from, specific direction has not always been included as an element of the *actus reus* of aiding and abetting.[498] This may be explained by the fact that such a finding will often be implicit in the finding that the accused has provided practical assistance to the principal perpetrator which had a substantial effect on the commission of the crime. The Appeals Chamber also considers that, to the extent specific direction forms an implicit part of the *actus reus* of aiding and abetting, where the accused knowingly participated in the commission of an offence and his or her participation substantially affected the commission of that offence, the fact that his or her participation amounted to no more than his or her "routine duties" will not exculpate the accused.

Thus, while the "routine duties" aspect of Jokic's appeal is conjoined with his argument regarding the necessity of proof of "specific direction," the latter subject has become a much more controversial topic in the jurisprudence of the ad hoc tribunals. Interestingly, the *Blagojevic and Jokic* Appeals Chamber does not approach the specific direction issue as though there were any significant deficiencies in ICTY jurisprudence in need of clarification. Rather, the judges argue in a somewhat matter-of-fact manner that *Tadic* was not intended to be a complete definition of aiding and abetting and that its language should be understood as an attempt to define aiding and abetting in the context of JCE.

Another oft-cited piece of jurisprudence that describes the elements of aiding and abetting in the context of JCE (not unlike *Tadic*) comes from the *Vasiljevic* appellate judgment. Paragraph 102 is the second most frequently cited paragraph within jurisprudence regarding liability (cited forty-three times).

> 102. Participation in a joint criminal enterprise is a form of "commission" under Article 7(1) of the Statute. The participant therein is liable as a co-perpetrator of the crime(s). Aiding and abetting the commission of a crime is usually considered to incur a lesser degree of individual criminal responsibility than committing a crime. In the context of a crime committed by several co-perpetrators in a joint criminal enterprise, the aider and abettor is always an accessory to these co-perpetrators, although the co-perpetrators may not even know of the aider and abettor's contribution. Differences exist in relation to the *actus reus* as well as to the *mens rea* requirements between both forms of individual criminal responsibility:
>
> (i) The aider and abettor carries out acts specifically directed to assist, encourage or lend moral support to the perpetration of a certain specific crime (murder, extermination, rape, torture, wanton destruction of civilian property, etc.), and this support has a substantial effect upon the perpetration of the crime. By contrast, it is sufficient for a participant in a joint criminal enterprise to perform acts that in some way are directed to the furtherance of the common design.

(ii) In the case of aiding and abetting, the requisite mental element is knowledge that the acts performed by the aider and abettor assist the commission of the specific crime of the principal. By contrast, in the case of participation in a joint criminal enterprise, i.e. as a co-perpetrator, the requisite *mens rea* is intent to pursue a common purpose.

The primary intent, like *Tadic*, is to distinguish aiding and abetting within and outside of the context of JCE. The above passage like much of language preceding it is descriptive and does not break any new legal ground. Indeed, it provides few supporting references for what had largely become accepted understandings of the various forms of JCE, mens rea, actus reus and the particularities of aiding and abetting in JCE. At the same time, however, we see once again that the judges have, in the course of contrasting two different types of aiding and abetting, made use of language that would seem to suggest specific direction is a required element of aiding and abetting outside of JCE. The controversy would lie dormant until the *Perisic* judgment and *Sainovic et al.*

Definition of Aiding and Abetting

Often the most cited and most important jurisprudence that arises from the tribunals pertains to defining crimes and modes of liability that the tribunals' founding documents left open to interpretation. The *Simic et al.* case has been cited numerous times for its clear and succinct definitions of aiding and abetting, which are especially instructive in light of the controversy detailed above. Three paragraphs in particular have been particularly prominent. First is paragraph 127, which has been cited thirty-three times in subsequent tribunal jurisprudence and reads:

> 127. The Appeals Chamber has explained that an aider and abettor carries out acts specifically directed to assist, encourage, or lend moral support to the perpetration of a certain specific crime, which have a substantial effect on the perpetration of the crime.[342] The *actus reus* need not serve as condition precedent for the crime and may occur before, during, or after the principal crime has been perpetrated.[343] The Appeals Chamber has also determined that the *actus reus* of aiding and abetting may be satisfied by a commander permitting the use of resources under his or her control, including personnel, to facilitate the perpetration of a crime.[344] The requisite mental element of aiding and abetting is knowledge that the acts performed assist the commission of the specific crime of the principal perpetrator.[345] In cases of specific intent crimes such as persecutions or genocide, the aider and abettor must know of the principal perpetrator's specific intent.[346]

Paragraph 85 of *Simic et al.* has been cited thirty-five times at these tribunals. This paragraph further describes the actus reus and the mens rea of aiding and abetting. As well, the adjacent paragraph 86, which continues with this description is also one of the more cited pieces of jurisprudence (twenty-nine citations). We quote both paragraphs here:

85. The Appeals Chamber recalls that the *actus reus* of aiding and abetting consists of acts directed to assist, encourage or lend moral support to the perpetration of a certain specific crime, and which have a substantial effect upon the perpetration of the crime.[259] It is not required that a cause-effect relationship between the conduct of the aider and abettor and the commission of the crime be shown, or that such conduct served as a condition precedent to the commission of the crime.[260] The *actus reus* of aiding and abetting a crime may occur before, during, or after the principal crime has been perpetrated, and the location at which the *actus reus* takes place may be removed from the location of the principal crime.[261]

86. The requisite *mens rea* for aiding and abetting is knowledge that the acts performed by the aider and abettor assist in the commission of the specific crime of the principal perpetrator.[262] The aider and abettor must be aware of the essential elements of the crime which was ultimately committed by the principal.[263] In relation to the crime of persecutions, an offence with a specific intent, he must thus be aware not only of the crime whose perpetration he is facilitating but also of the discriminatory intent of the perpetrators of that crime. He need not share the intent but he must be aware of the discriminatory context in which the crime is to be committed and know that his support or encouragement has a substantial effect on its perpetration.[264] However, it is not necessary that the aider and abettor knows either the precise crime that was intended or the one that was, in the event, committed. If he is aware that one of a number of crimes will probably be committed, and one of those crimes is in fact committed, he has intended to facilitate the commission of that crime, and is guilty as an aider and abettor.[265]

These paragraphs are noteworthy for their clear articulation of the legal standard for establishing guilt through this more particular form of individual liability, and do not seem to have aroused significant controversy. Nonetheless, the jurisprudence on the definition of aiding and abetting that has come out of the ICTY has provided the international legal community with a succinct and powerful definition of these variants of individual liability. Where the statutes of all the ad hoc tribunals have been mostly quiet on some definitional issues, judges have articulated through analysis of national and international law the current status of customary international law.

Further clarification of the meaning of aiding and abetting is found in *Blaskic* and supports the argument that aiding and abetting does not require there to be a cause and effect relationship between the supportive acts of the aider and the commission of the crime. Paragraph 48 of the *Blaskic* Appellate Judgment has been cited thirty times on the matter of causation:

48. The Trial Chamber in this case went on to state:

Proof that the conduct of the aider and abettor had a causal effect on the act of the principal perpetrator is not required. Furthermore, participation may occur before, during or after the act is committed and be geographically separated there from.[91]

The Appeals Chamber reiterates that one of the requirements of the *actus reus* of aiding and abetting is that the support of the aider and abettor has a substantial effect upon the perpetration of the crime. In this regard, it agrees with the Trial Chamber that proof of a cause-effect relationship between the conduct of the aider and abettor and the commission of the crime, or proof that such conduct served as a condition precedent to the commission of the crime, is not required. It further agrees that the *actus reus* of aiding and abetting a crime may occur before, during, or after the principal crime has been perpetrated, and that the location at which the *actus reus* takes place may be removed from the location of the principal crime.

The jurisprudence on causation has been reproduced quite often and thus significantly advanced our contemporary understanding of this subject. It is also interesting to read such language in light of the later *Perisic* judgment's pronouncement of the specific direction requirement, which would have posed a rather formidable obstacle to proving aiding and abetting. The *Blaskic* ruling lowers the barrier to establishing guilt by dispensing with the notion that a direct linkage between the assistance and the act, while *Perisic* would have required a specific direction from the aider that would be tantamount to proving that the aider's assistance and direction led directly to the crime.

Superior and Subordinate Relationship

One ICTR case is included in the category of superior and individual liability jurisprudence that has been cited at least twenty-five times. In *Semanza* (paragraph 361, cited twenty-six times) the ICTR Appeals Chamber ruled on the nature of the superior-subordinate relationship:

> Thus, in its definition, the Trial Chamber did not require proof of a formal superior-subordinate relationship for the Appellant to be found responsible for ordering. All that it required was the implied existence of a superior-subordinate relationship. The Trial Chamber's approach in this case is consistent with recent jurisprudence of the Appeals Chamber. As recently clarified by the ICTY Appeals Chamber in *Kordic and Cerkez*, the *actus reus* of "ordering" is that a person in a position of authority instruct another person to commit an offence. No formal superior-subordinate relationship between the accused and the perpetrator is required.[765] It is sufficient that there is proof of some position of authority on the part of the accused that would compel another to commit a crime in following the accused's order.[766] The Trial Chamber thus committed no legal error in its enunciation of the elements of ordering.

The *Semanza* jurisprudence harkens back to the effective control standard established in the *Celebici* Trial Chamber judgment and confirmed on appeal. As becomes clear, however, in the language following the paragraph cited earlier the *Semanza* judgment notes that effective control may be a temporary phenomenon in the context of the commission of a crime where the accused asserts authority over the principal perpetrators for a limited time and in a situation where he exercises no formal leadership position. As conditions in the context of massive atrocities such as genocide and crimes against humanity are often dynamic and chaotic, such recognition of the transient nature of leadership and influence are necessary to encompass the actions of individuals who behave as conflict entrepreneurs exploiting their community influence for nefarious ends.

Lastly, the *Blaskic* (paragraph 69, cited twenty-five times) and *Kordic* (paragraph 28, cited twenty-five times) cases are cited for rulings on the nature of effective control. At issue in *Blaskic* is interpretation of Additional Protocol I to the Geneva Conventions and those specific factors that indicate military officers exercise effective control over subordinates. The Appeals Chamber found that while the *Blaskic* appeal argues that various indicators of effective control, such as issuing orders that are followed, should be a required condition for proving superior liability, such an indicator is better understood as one among multiple, potential measures of a superior relationship. In *Kordic* the language is succinct and clear:

> 28. The *actus reus* of "ordering" means that a person in a position of authority instructs another person to commit an offence.[22] A formal superior-subordinate relationship between the accused and the perpetrator is not required.[23]

The language stipulates what has been a widely accepted understanding of superior liability – that it may be characterized by either de jure or de facto powers. As was indicated in the earlier *Celebici* Trial Chamber decision, what matters is whether the superior exercised effective control over the individual(s) who committed the violation of international law. Thus, the *Kordic* language provides an early and clear statement of one key aspect of superior liability. Thus, we find it cited many times in subsequent jurisprudence to ensure that such individuals could be successfully prosecuted and human rights protected.

Questions of individual liability are the second most cited type of issue at the ad hoc tribunals, and the most cited substantive law issue. These tribunals have established many new precedents in international law that have ensured individuals who were involved, in one way or another, in gross violations of human rights can be held accountable for their actions. Given the many novel means by which these individuals, especially superiors, have engineered these abuses, convicting them has been no easy task. Loose and shifting lines of authority, parallel chains of command, puppeteers who obscured the strings attached to their marionettes, and de facto, almost causal command relationships have posed many legal challenges to both the prosecution and the judges. In particular, we find two, principal areas of jurisprudence where the judgments handed down by the Appeals Chambers represent a progressive development of international law.

First, we argue that the development of an accepted set of criteria for establishing effective control has not only clarified and streamlined the process of proving guilt, the criteria have also accounted for the myriad methods by which individuals have exercised such control. The *Celebici* Trial Chamber judgment was a landmark decision in this respect even though it has not been cited as often as we might have expected. Among the most cited cases that we have found through our data analysis, the *Simic et al.* and *Blaskic* cases are cited for their definitions of aiding and abetting, while the *Semanza* and *Kordic and Cerkez* judgments have been frequently cited for their explication of the nature of superior liability. By establishing these criteria and ensuring that the legal mechanisms were in place to establish the guilt of those who participated in the violation of international law, this body of jurisprudence represents a progressive development of international law.

Second and closely related is the issue of specific direction in aiding and abetting. Were it not for the *Perisic* decision, it is unlikely we would have commented on this topic. Yet, because the anomalous requirement that such direction is a necessary component of aiding and abetting resulted in the release of one of the most high-ranking individuals in the Yugoslav political and military establishment and threatened to derail efforts to prosecute other such individuals, like Charles Taylor, we must recognize the critical nature of jurisprudence on this subject. While the *Taylor* and *Sainovic* judgments have come too late in the history of the tribunals to have generated significant citations, their refutation of the specific direction requirement prevented a potentially regressive development in international law. Such a requirement would have made it extraordinarily difficult to prosecute the highest echelon of leaders who would have undoubtedly taken steps to further obscure their direction of forces they were assisting. For this reason, and under the assumption that the specific direction requirement is most likely in abeyance for now at least, the *Taylor* and *Sainovic* rulings represent a critical, progressive development in international law.

Joint Criminal Enterprise

While we do not find the term JCE in the Statutes of the ad hoc tribunals, the elaboration of the doctrine has been entirely developed by ICTY judges especially in the case of *Tadic*. Indeed, while article 7(1) of the Statute of the ICTY tribunal establishes that individual criminal liability for violations of international humanitarian law is not limited to those who directly commit the actus reus, but also to those who have "planned, instigated, ordered, committed or otherwise aided and abetted in the planning, preparation or execution of a crime," the term JCE does not appear in any part of the article. Thus, it is not surprising that some of the most cited paragraphs concerning this mode of liability are those that define the doctrine itself. The key paragraphs are those that identify the three categories of JCE in the appellate decision of the ICTY in the case of *Tadic*. The three categories of JCE are described in paragraphs 196, 203, and 204 which are cited thirty-four, twenty-six and thirty-four times, respectively. We reproduce the three relevant paragraphs of the Appeals Chamber here:

> 196. The first such category is represented by cases where all co-defendants, acting pursuant to a common design, possess the same criminal intention; for instance, the formulation of a plan among the co-perpetrators to kill, where, in effecting this

common design (and even if each co-perpetrator carries out a different role within it), they nevertheless all possess the intent to kill. The objective and subjective prerequisites for imputing criminal responsibility to a participant who did not, or cannot be proven to have, effected the killing are as follows: (i) the accused must voluntarily participate in one aspect of the common design (for instance, by inflicting non-fatal violence upon the victim, or by providing material assistance to or facilitating the activities of his co-perpetrators); and (ii) the accused, even if not personally effecting the killing, must nevertheless intend this result.

203. This category of cases (which obviously is not applicable to the facts of the present case) is really a variant of the first category, considered above. The accused, when they were found guilty, were regarded as co-perpetrators of the crimes of ill-treatment, because of their objective "position of authority" within the concentration camp system and because they had "the power to look after the inmates and make their life satisfactory" but failed to do so. It would seem that in these cases the required actus reus was the active participation in the enforcement of a system of repression, as it could be inferred from the position of authority and the specific functions held by each accused. The mens rea element comprised: (i) knowledge of the nature of the system and (ii) the intent to further the common concerted design to ill-treat inmates. It is important to note that, in these cases, the requisite intent could also be inferred from the position of authority held by the camp personnel. Indeed, it was scarcely necessary to prove intent where the individual's high rank or authority would have, in and of itself, indicated an awareness of the common design and an intent to participate therein. All those convicted were found guilty of the war crime of ill-treatment, although of course the penalty varied according to the degree of participation of each accused in the commission of the war crime.

204. The third category concerns cases involving a common design to pursue one course of conduct where one of the perpetrators commits an act which, while outside the common design, was nevertheless a natural and foreseeable consequence of the effecting of that common purpose. An example of this would be a common, shared intention on the part of a group to forcibly remove members of one ethnicity from their town, village or region (to effect "ethnic cleansing") with the consequence that, in the course of doing so, one or more of the victims is shot and killed. While murder may not have been explicitly acknowledged to be part of the common design, it was nevertheless foreseeable that the forcible removal of civilians at gunpoint might well result in the deaths of one or more of those civilians. Criminal responsibility may be imputed to all participants within the common enterprise where the risk of death occurring was both a predictable consequence of the execution of the common design and the accused was either reckless or indifferent to that risk. Another example is that of a common plan to forcibly evict civilians belonging to a particular ethnic group by burning their houses; if some of the participants in the plan, in carrying out this plan, kill civilians by setting their houses on fire, all the other participants in the plan are criminally responsible for the killing if these deaths were predictable.

The decision in *Tadic* represents one of the most important groundbreaking moments in the jurisprudence of international criminal tribunals, which has impacted greatly all subsequent cases in which JCE and other forms of complex, individual criminal liability were adjudicated. Specifically, key passages of the definition of the JCE doctrine, which have been the objects of extensive jurisprudential evolution, are (i) the establishment of the requirements to identify an individual as a member to the JCE and (ii) the responsibility for acts that "while outside the common design was nevertheless a natural and foreseeable consequence of the effecting of that common purpose" as indicated in the third JCE category.

Members to the JCE

Scholars and observers of the ICTY have commented on the complexities and inconsistencies in the judicial application of JCE and specifically in determining which individuals can be considered members of the JCE (Farhang 2010; Fiori 2007; Jain 2014; O'Rourke 2006). The issue has featured significantly in the paragraphs we find cited most often by the Appeals Chambers. Following a controversial finding by the Trial Chamber in the case of *Brdanin*, in which the judges established that to be considered a member of the JCE there must be an agreement or understanding between the physical perpetrator and the accused,[24] scholars have indicated that the Trial Chamber had considerably limited the ability of the JCE doctrine to hold superiors responsible for acts committed by criminal perpetrators that were located remotely (Jain 2010, 50). This aspect has become a controversial topic in the jurisprudence of the ICTY and the judges of the Appeals Chamber have since addressed the issue looking more closely at the rationale behind the definition of the JCE given in *Tadic*. In one of the most cited paragraphs of the ICTY jurisprudence, paragraph 430 of the *Brdanin* Appeals Chamber decision, cited fifty-seven times, the judges lowered the standard of proof of membership to the JCE, affirming that:

> Where the principal perpetrator is not shown to belong to the JCE, the trier of fact must further establish that the crime can be imputed to at least one of the members of the joint criminal enterprise, and that this member – when using a principal perpetrator – acted in accordance with the common plan.[25]

Thus, while formal agreement was not mentioned in *Brdanin*, the appellate judges further softened the burden of proof establishing that the prosecution is not required to prove "that the persons who carried out the actus reus of the crimes in questions were members of a joint criminal enterprise"[26] but rather they committed an act that can be imputed to at least one of the members of the JCE. This reversal in opinion by the Appeals Chamber in the case of *Brdanin* has been welcomed with

[24] The Prosecutor v. Radoslav Brdanin, Case No. IT-99–36-T, September 1, 2004, paras 344 and 347. For a complete analysis see also Fiori (2007) and Farhang (2010).
[25] The Prosecutor v. Radoslav Brdanin, Case No. IT-99–36-A, April 3, 2007, para 430.
[26] The Prosecutor v. Radoslav Brdanin, Case No. IT-99–36-A, April 3, 2007, para 414.

favor by scholars and judges alike, underlying the fact that the interpretation given by the Trial Chamber in *Brdanin* contradicted considerably the definition of JCE provided in *Tadic*.[27] In the words of Gustafson (2007, 134) the presence of an express agreement is "unpractical": "arguably in a 'system-criminality' context such as the one that developed in the former Yugoslavia during the time period in question, the organizers of criminal activity are unlikely to enter into express criminal agreements with those who physically carry out crimes, because existing organized hierarchies provide much more efficient mechanisms by which leaders are able to ensure the realization of their criminal plans."

Foreseeable Acts

Another often cited aspect of the jurisprudence on JCE regards the issue of responsibility for acts not included in the original plan but that are a foreseeable consequence of the criminal enterprise. Key passages on this issue are included in *Tadic* paragraph 228, cited forty-one times, *Brdanin* paragraph 411, cited twenty-nine times, and *Kvocka* paragraph 83, cited twenty-six times. The jurisprudential evolution provided by the Appeals Chamber of the ICTY in the above mentioned cases was meant to properly define the objective and subjective elements of this type of individual criminal responsibility for crimes. In *Tadic* the judges laid down one of the most often cited ground rules of "responsibility for crimes other than the agreed upon in the common plan" establishing that such responsibility arises if "(i) it was foreseeable that such a crime might be perpetrated by one or other members of the group and (ii) the accused willingly took that risk."[28] However, in *Kvocka* and in *Brdanin* the judges further qualified the definition of the 'foreseeable' requirement by specifying the subjective element of responsibility. In paragraph 83 of the *Kvocka* Appeal decision, the judged stated:

> In order to be held responsible for crimes which were not part of the common criminal purpose, but which were nevertheless a natural and foreseeable consequence of it, the accused must also *know that such crime might be perpetrated by a member of the group*, and willingly take the risk that the crime might occur by joining or continuing to participate in the enterprise. (emphasis added)[29]

Similarly in *Brdanin* the judges established that:

> When the accused, or any other member of the JCE, in order to further the common criminal purpose, uses persons who, in addition to (or instead of) carrying out the *actus reus* of the crimes forming part of the common purpose, commit crimes going beyond that purpose, the accused may be found responsible for such crimes

[27] The Prosecutor v. Radoslav Brdanin, Case No. IT-99–36-A, April 3, 2007, para 390. See also Farhang (2010) p. 150; Gustafson (2007).

[28] The Prosecutor v. Dusko Tadic, Case No. IT-94–1-A, July 15, 1999, para 228.

[29] The Prosecutor v. Kvocka et al., Case No. IT-98–30/1-A, February 28, 2005, para 83.

provided that he participated in the common criminal purpose with the requisite intent and that, in the circumstances of the case, (i) it was foreseeable that such a crime might be perpetrated by one or more of the persons used by him (or by any other member of the JCE) in order to carry out the *actus reus* of the crimes forming part of the common purpose; and (ii) the accused willingly took that risk – that is the accused, with the *awareness that such a crime was a possible consequence of the implementation of that enterprise, decided to participate in that enterprise.* (emphasis added)[30]

Thus, while not changing entirely the provisions established in *Tadic*, the judges in *Kvocka* and *Brdanin* qualified the link between the mens rea of the accused and perpetrators by speaking respectively of "knowledge" and "awareness" by the accused that the crime might be perpetrated by a member of the group. We note that the connection made between the mens rea of the accused and that of the physical perpetrator has been one of the most important developments in establishing the responsibility of individuals whose criminal acts present connotations that do not fit neatly into the original definition of the JCE doctrine.

Therefore, we believe the evidence assembled here and in the earlier quantitative data clearly demonstrates that issues involving superior liability, command and control and joint criminal enterprise are among the marquee advancements in international jurisprudence developed by the tribunals. Judges have both filled in gaps in these areas, such as their definitional elements, and expanded into new directions such as the development of JCE. Especially in an age where the nature of superior liability and the various mechanisms through which individuals participate in international crimes have grown more expansive at the same time they have grown more complex and dynamic, such a development should not be underestimated. By ensuring that superiors and other leaders can be effectively prosecuted and thereby further eroding the heretofore prevailing norm of impunity, the judges are able to advance the cause of human rights.

Bias Crimes

We hypothesized that the appeals chambers of the ad hoc tribunals would frequently cite jurisprudence from cases involving genocide and persecution, a crime against humanity. Because these crimes had never been adjudicated in an international criminal tribunal, and given that the conflicts in the former Yugoslavia and Rwanda involved unusual fact patterns, we argued that there would be a number of controversial issues to address that would presumably lead to frequent and important precedents. We do not, however, find this to be the case. In fact, there are no case paragraphs pertaining to genocide and persecution, which we term "bias crimes," that have been cited twenty-five times or more. A paragraph from the *Krstic* case

---

[30] The Prosecutor v. Radoslav Brdanin, Case No. IT-99–36-A, April 3, 2007, para 411.

(paragraph 140) from the ICTY Appeals Chamber concerning the notion of mens rea in the context of aiding and abetting genocide has been cited eighteen times. Overall, we see that bias crimes in general have been at issue in 256 cites. These citations include such specific issues as definition of the crime of persecution; the notion of intent in persecution; and the mens rea for genocide.

We had expected that jurisprudence surrounding the issue of protected groups in genocide would have been a particularly ripe issue that would have generated significant debate. But while such debate has been present in the literature (Akhavan 2005; Bettwy 2011; Danner 2001; Schabas 2008; Sloane 2007b; Szpak 2012), no particular ruling has apparently inspired subsequent citation on par with the other seminal rulings of the tribunal. The ICTY and ICTR have considered defining protected groups by their "stable and permanent" character[31]; perceptions of the perpetrators that such individuals belong to a distinct group[32]; and a mixed approach combining elements of both subjective perception and historical context.[33] Yet, despite the critical importance of the issue and its continuing relevance in the case of Darfur, no one ruling seems to have adequately captured a best practice of jurisprudence on protected groups.

More generally, we believe that the lack of oft-cited rulings on genocide and persecution may be the result of several factors. First, the very fact that both the ICTY and the ICTR have had to grapple with such unusual fact patterns given the groups targeted has made the development of jurisprudence rather difficult. It is a cliché that bad facts make bad law, but there is an element of truth to that notion in these cases. The key issue for the ICTR has been the blurring of ethnic, racial, national and religious lines between Hutu and Tutsi in Rwanda. While nearly all observers would agree that each comprises a distinct group, the factors that make each group unique are difficult to precisely identify and have been fraught with historical, social and psychological baggage. The key issue for the ICTY has been the limited geographic scope of the genocide in its key case involving Srebrenica. Again, few would dispute the notion that Bosnian Muslims are a distinct group that are entitled to protection under the genocide convention. The controversy has been the limited scope of the targeting that occurred – only men of a certain age in a specific part of Bosnia. Hence, while each tribunal has sought to understand and implement the concept of protected groups, each has done so as a result of fairly different situational characteristics.

Second, we also believe that because ICTY rulings in general receive greater mention in subsequent appeals chamber judgments, and because genocide has

---

[31] The Prosecutor v. Akayesu, Case No. ICTR-96-4-T, Trial Chamber Judgment, September 2, 1998, para 516.
[32] The Prosecutor v. Nchamihigo, Case No. ICTR-01-63, Trial Chamber Judgment, November 12, 2008, paras 329–338.
[33] The Prosecutor v. Krstic, Case No. ICTY ICTY-98-63, Trial Chamber Judgment, August 2, 2001, para 560.

been much more of an issue for the ICTR, the relative infrequency of case paragraphs involving genocide may be explained by the relative lack of attention given to ICTR judgments. Third, we are also puzzled by the lack of citations concerning the crime of persecution. Persecution is also a bias crime, albeit one with a somewhat broader range of protected groups that includes individuals singled out for their political beliefs. Given its rather inchoate nature, which encompasses crimes against humanity and other violations of fundamental rights that target individuals on the basis of their membership in the protected groups (the ICTY Statute lists political, racial and religious groups) while the ICTR statute includes ethnic and national groups as well and the SCSL Statute includes ethnic groups, although these distinctions have meant little in practice as the tribunals have essentially found that most groups would enjoy protection (Fournet and Pegorier 2010, 737), we had expected a significant level of attention. Yet, this same lack of clarity seems to have persisted in tribunal jurisprudence over the years and has created a certain amount of doctrinal confusion over the distinctions between persecution and all other crimes under the tribunals' jurisdictions (Fournet and Pegorier 2010). As well, because so many cases involving persecution at the ICTY have been settled in plea agreements in which the defendant pleads guilty to a single count of persecution, there have been fewer appeals. In sum, it would appear the bias crimes are still an evolving issue for international criminal justice for which no ruling has adequately conveyed a clear and convincing resolution.

Sentencing

Individualized Sentences

Citations to the most oft-cited portions of judgments regarding sentencing primarily concern a few key issues. First and foremost are those citations involving the individualized nature of punishments, and specifically, paragraph 717 of the *Celebici* appellate judgment. That paragraph has been cited forty-three times, which is the most referenced piece of jurisprudence regarding sentencing. It reads:

> Trial Chambers exercise a considerable amount of discretion (although it is not unlimited) in determining an appropriate sentencing. This is largely because of the overriding obligation to individualise a penalty to fit the individual circumstances of the accused and the gravity of the crime. To achieve this goal, Trial Chambers are obliged to consider both aggravating and mitigating circumstances relating to an individual accused. The many circumstances taken into account by the Trial Chambers to date are evident if one considers the sentencing judgements which have been rendered. As a result, the sentences imposed have varied, from the imposition of the maximum sentence of imprisonment for the remainder of life, to imprisonment for varying fixed terms (the lowest after appeal being five year). Although certain of these cases are now under appeal, the underlying principle is that the sentence imposed largely depended on the individual facts of the case and the individual circumstances of the convicted person.

This paragraph and the surrounding and related text arise from a request to the ICTY Appeals Chamber to develop sentencing guidelines that would aid both the prosecution and the defense by making sentencing criteria more transparent and objective. Yet, as all the tribunals had done before the *Celebici* judgment was handed down in February 2001, and as they have done since, the Appeals Chamber politely declined. Justifying the lack of more explicit sentencing criteria as necessary given the peculiar characteristics of each defendant's crimes, their level of involvement and background, the appeals chambers have been reluctant to tie the hands of the judges to either fixed sentencing determinants or a specific schedule of punishments. While acknowledging the principle that two defendants who commit similar crimes should receive roughly similar sentences, the judges have consistently argued that there are more differences than such similarities in any given case. Indeed, two paragraphs later, in another portion of the *Celebici* judgment that is one of the most frequently cited aspects of sentencing jurisprudence, the ICTY Appeals Chamber opines in paragraph 719 (cited twenty-five times):

> It is noted that, in their submissions, each party urges the Appeals Chamber to compare their case with others which have already been the subject of final determination, in an effort to persuade the Appeals Chamber to either increase or decrease the sentence.[1216] Although this will be considered further in the context of the individual submissions, the Appeals Chamber notes that as a general principle such comparison is often of limited assistance. While it does not disagree with a contention that it is to be expected that two accused convicted of similar crimes in similar circumstances should not in practice receive very different sentences, often the differences are more significant than the similarities, and the mitigating and aggravating factors dictate different results. They are therefore not reliable as the *sole* basis for sentencing an individual.

In such language we find the tribunals seeking not so much to forge substantively new ground in the broad purposes or the specific determinants of punishment but rather to preserve a key element of judicial decision making, namely the discretionary power of the judges to determine sentencing. When the tribunals are asked by both the prosecution and the defense (to say nothing of the substantial scholarly work that has sought greater consistency and clarity in sentencing [Bagaric and Morss 2006; Drumbl 2007a; Harmon and Gaynor 2007; Henham 2007; Olusanya 2005; Sloane 2007a]) to provide such guidance they are, in effect, being asked to make a choice between the principles of individualized punishment and consistent sentencing.

It should come as no surprise to students of the tribunals that the judges prefer the principle of individualization and the discretionary power it preserves. This criterion is explicitly mentioned in their founding documents (e.g., Article 24 of the ICTY Statute, which reads, "In imposing the sentences, the Trial Chambers should take into account such factors as the gravity of the offence and the *individual circumstances of the convicted person* [emphasis added]). Furthermore, adherence to this principle also preserves the discretionary power of judges on such matters. Given the wide variety of individuals and crimes at issue before the ad hoc tribunals, as well as their finite mandates, eschewing the enumeration of sentencing criteria makes legal and political sense. By the time the judges were sufficiently acquainted with the diversity of defendants and crimes, the development of sentencing guidelines might have been perceived as too late in the history of the tribunals as well as prejudicial to defendants whose cases had already concluded (and thus left the chambers open to charges of unfairness).

The key element in the progressive development of the law concerns this choice of fundamental principles regarding punishment. The appeals chambers of the ad hoc tribunals have chosen to fix their course and subsequent jurisprudence on this principle of individualized punishment. Thus, we find that since the specific articulation of this principle in *Celebici*, judges have continually cited this need to determine punishment based on the specific facts at hand rather than sentencing guidelines or tariffs that would tie their hands. Indeed, while the Treaty of Rome provides somewhat more guidance on the subject of punishment (such as the stipulation that sentences of life imprisonment should be rare and reserved for the truly most horrific of crimes) it too preserves substantial discretion for the judges. In its very first sentencing judgment in the case of the Congolese war criminal, Thomas Dyilo, the trial chamber judges were asked once again to develop a sentencing regime. They wrote:

> The prosecution argues that in order "to avoid inexplicable sentencing discrepancies," the sentencing policy of the Court should presume a "consistent baseline" for sentences, which should not be adjusted on the basis that some crimes are less serious than others. It is submitted that the appropriate "baseline" or starting point for all sentences should be set at approximately 80% of the statutory maximum, and this should then be adjusted in accordance with Rule 145 to take into account any aggravating and mitigating circumstances and other factors relevant to the convicted person and the circumstances of the crimes. No established principle of law or relevant jurisprudence under Article 21 of the Statute has been relied on in support of this suggested approach, which would bind the judges to a minimum starting point of 24 years in all cases. In the judgment of the Chamber, the sentence passed by a Trial Chamber should always be proportionate to the crime (see Article 81(2)(a)), and an automatic starting point – as proposed by the prosecution – that is the same for all offences would tend to undermine that fundamental principle.[34]

Even as international tribunals become increasingly institutionalized and international criminal laws become ever more refined and codified, judges are disinclined to subject this fundamental power and ultimate outcome of international justice to a fixed set of criteria. Continual adherence to such jurisprudence has been a hallmark of the judicial legacy of the tribunals, and the progressive development of the law.

---

[34] Dyilo judgment paras 92 and 93.

Standard of Review

The second most cited paragraph concerning sentencing regards the standard of review the Appeals Chamber judges use when asked to reconsider a sentence. It too comes from the ICTY Appeals Chamber and from the *Celebici* judgment:

> The test to be applied in relation to the issue as to whether a sentence should be revised is that most recently confirmed in the *Furundzija* Appeal Judgement. Accordingly, as a general rule, the Appeals Chamber will not substitute its sentence for that of a Trial Chamber unless "it believes that the Trial Chamber has committed an error in exercising its discretion, or has failed to follow applicable law."[1232] The Appeals Chamber will only intervene if it finds that the error was "discernible."[1233] As long as a Trial Chamber does not venture outside its "discretionary framework" in imposing sentence,[1234] the Appeals Chamber will not intervene. It therefore falls on each appellant, including the Prosecution in its appeal against Mucic's sentence, to demonstrate how the Trial Chamber ventured outside its discretionary framework in imposing the sentence it did.

Interestingly, the *Furundzija* opinion that is initially mentioned only garners twenty-three citations in subsequent jurisprudence while this *Celebici* ruling is cited forty-three times. The Appeals Chamber also cites several other cases, including *Serushago, Aleksovski* and *Tadic*. Thus, an appeals chamber will only substitute its judgment when there has been a discernible error or a trial chamber failed to follow applicable law. Even then, it is up to the appellant to demonstrate that such problems have arisen. The same issue arises in another case, *Galic*, which is cited frequently (twenty-five times):

> Appeals against sentence, as appeals from a trial judgement, are appeals *stricto sensu*; they are of a corrective nature and are not trials *de novo*.[1181] Trial Chambers are vested with a broad discretion in determining an appropriate sentence, due to their obligation to individualise the penalties to fit the circumstances of the accused and the gravity of the crime.[1182] As a general rule, the Appeals Chamber will not revise a sentence unless the Trial Chamber has committed a "discernible error" in exercising its discretion or has failed to follow the applicable law.[1183] It is for the Appellant to demonstrate how the Trial Chamber ventured outside its discretionary framework in imposing his sentence.[1184]

As we have noted earlier, Article 25 of the ICTY Statute provides that:

1. The Appeals Chamber shall hear appeals from persons convicted by the Trial Chambers or from the Prosecutor on the following grounds:
   (a) an error on a question of law invalidating the decision; or
   (b) an error of fact which has occasioned a miscarriage of justice.

The "discernible error" test mentioned in *Celebici* and *Galic* would seem then to represent something of an extension or elaboration of the Statute. Dana (2004) also notes that it is not included in the Statute or the Rules of Procedure and Evidence. According to Dana, this concept first appears in the *Tadic* sentencing judgment, paragraph 22. But even here there is no jurisprudence cited or analysis of the term "discernible error." In the *Aleksovski* judgment, paragraph 187, the judges ruled that:

> In applying that test to the instant case the Appeals Chamber finds that there was a discernible error in the Trial Chamber's exercise of discretion in imposing sentence. That error consisted of giving insufficient weight to the gravity of the conduct of the Appellant and failing to treat his position as commander as an aggravating feature in relation to his responsibility under Article 7(1) of the Statute. The sentence imposed by the Trial Chamber was manifestly inadequate.

Here too, however, there are no rationales or explanations from case law to elucidate this concept or to ascertain how it relates to the standards of appeal expressly provided for in the ICTY Statute. As well, the errors cited – failure to properly recognize the gravity of the conduct and failure to appreciate the command authority of the accused as an aggravating factor – are interesting in that they are errors of degree, not of kind. That is, the Trial Chambers erred not in failing to consider these factors at all, but rather by failing to accord them their proper degree of importance. These were not, apparently, errors of omission or commission, but errors regarding the degree of emphasis to be placed on these sentencing determinants.

Interestingly, while this brief analysis suggests that the ICTY Appeals Chamber has elaborated upon the standards of review in appeals against sentencing beyond what is expressly provided for in its statute, such jurisprudence does not seem to have engendered significant debate. Subsequent appellate judgments have (as we have shown here) repeatedly cited paragraph 725 in the *Celebici* judgment on discernible error. The "discernible error" test seems to have generated much debate outside the tribunals. Indeed, Dana (2004, n 64) notes that an analysis of "discernible error" would make for a "worthy topic" for a law review.

We would argue that the development of this concept represents something of a modest, yet nonetheless progressive development of international law. The statutes speak of the need for judges to consider errors of law and errors of fact, principally, if not implicitly in relation to the verdicts. *Celebici* follows this by analogy when it asserts in paragraph 725 that the Appeals Chamber will substitute its judgment for a Trial Chamber's only if the law was not followed or the Trial Chamber committed an error in using its discretion. But it goes one step further when it articulates the "discernible error" test. Presumably errors of law or fact regarding appeals against sentencing must be discernible, which again leaves significant discretion in the hands of the Appeals Chamber on sentencing matters. Hence, this development of the law preserves the power of the judges to make key sentencing determinations, just as the previous discussion regarding individualized sentences.

Role of Gravity in Sentencing

The final matter that is at issue in a case paragraph and is cited at least twenty-five times is the role of gravity in sentencing. Gravity is typically listed first when the trial

chambers are specifying the characteristics of a crime that determine the severity of
the sentence to be imposed. Interestingly, it is often the Trial Chamber judgments
that have been mentioned most by scholars and judges as well, such as this phrase
from the *Celebici* Trial Chamber decision, "By far the most important consideration,
which may be regarded as the litmus test for the appropriate sentence, is the gravity
of the offence."[35] The paragraph we find cited most often, however (paragraph 182
cited thirty-six times), comes from the *Aleksovski* Appeals Chamber judgment:

> The nub of the Prosecutor's appeal is to be found in the third ground as sum-
> marised above, namely the weight to be given to the gravity of the Appellant's
> conduct. Consideration of the gravity of the conduct of the accused is normally
> the starting point for consideration of an appropriate sentence. The practice of
> the International Tribunal provides no exception. The Statute provides that in
> imposing sentence the Trial Chambers should take into account such factors as the
> gravity of the offence.[348] This has been followed by Trial Chambers. Thus, in the
> *Celebici* Judgement, the Trial Chamber said that "[t]he most important considera-
> tion, which may be regarded as the litmus test for the appropriate sentence, is the
> gravity of the offence."[349] In the *Kupreškic* Judgement, the Trial Chamber stated
> that "[t]he sentences to be imposed must reflect the inherent gravity of the criminal
> conduct of the accused. The determination of the gravity of the crime requires a
> consideration of the particular circumstances of the case, as well as the form and
> degree of the participation of the accused in the crime."[350] The Appeals Chamber
> endorses these statements.

The paragraph enshrines the primacy of the gravity of the offense as the dominant
consideration in determining punishment. Given that the gravity of the offense
is the only substantive sentencing criteria listed in the tribunals' statutes (with the
exception of the catch-all, "individual circumstances" of the accused and sentencing
practices in the home country of the accused) this jurisprudence does not appear
to break new ground. It does, however, position the judges as the ultimate deciders
of punishment and does not provide for any sentencing schedules. It preserves the
prerogatives of judges to make all such determinations regarding punishment. The
other most commonly cited paragraph comes from *Celebici* (paragraph 731, cited
twenty-six times) and largely restates these same points:

> The Trial Chamber found, in its general considerations before addressing the factors
> relevant to each individual accused, that "[b]y far the most important consideration,
> which may be regarded as the litmus test for the appropriate sentence, is the gravity
> of the offence."[1242] In the subsequent *Aleksovski* Appeal Judgement, the Appeals
> Chamber expressly endorsed this statement of the *Celebici* Trial Chamber, and
> also expressed its agreement with the following statement of the Trial Chamber in
> the *Kupreškic* proceedings:

---

[35] Celebici Case, Case No. IT-96-21-T, Trial Chamber, November 16, 1998, para 1225.

> The sentence to be imposed must reflect the inherent gravity of the criminal conduct of the accused. The determination of the gravity of the crime requires a consideration of the particular circumstances of the case, as well as the form and degree of the participation of the accused in the crime.[1243]

> The Appeals Chamber reiterates this endorsement of those statements and confirms its acceptance of the principle that the gravity of the offence is the primary consideration in imposing sentence. It is therefore necessary to consider whether the Trial Chamber in fact gave due weight to the gravity of the offences for which Mucic was convicted in the sentence it imposed.

Nonetheless, we would make two observations regarding the importance of this confirmation of the relevance of the gravity criterion. First, the statutes specify that the judges *should* take into consideration the gravity of the crimes. This certainly does not mandate such decision making, and leaves open the possibility that other broad categories of sentencing determinants might also be utilized. Second, and closely related to this point, many observers of the tribunals have bemoaned what they perceive as a fixation of the tribunals on the gravity criterion, especially insofar as it reflects the primacy given to retribution as the overall aim of punishment (Drumbl 2007a; Findlay and Henham 2005, 2010; Henham 2003, 2007; Kelsall 2010; Sloane 2007b). Henham (2003, 68) writes, " . . . retribution in international criminal justice has been more readily equated with the concept of victor's justice, vindication and western exculpation." These critics question whether punishment grounded in retribution and its accompanying emphasis on the gravity of the offense can bring a true and relevant justice to the people who have been most affected by such crimes. There seems to be an implicit assumption underlying such critiques that the primacy of retribution and gravity reflects a conscious choice by the judges, who might have given if not primacy then due regard for other considerations, such as restorative justice, expressive punishment and other penological theories. If one accepts the basic premise of this reasoning, then the tribunals' focus on gravity as a sentencing determinant does represent a conscientious decision to move sentencing jurisprudence in a particular direction.

Whether this represents a progressive development of the law given its clear grounding in the founding documents of the tribunals is debatable. Yet, one could argue that the emphasis on gravity of the crimes and the retributive element of punishment highlights the need to make such punishment severe enough so as to dissuade others from embarking on such misdeeds. In this sense, the emphasis on gravity in sentencing reflects, in part, a concern for human rights insofar as it contributes to deterrence.

We conclude from this review of these three types of sentencing issue that are among the most frequently cited paragraphs of the tribunals' jurisprudence that there has been a modest, progressive development of the law. First, all of these paragraphs regarding individualized sentencing, the standard of review for sentences and the importance of the gravity of the crime have been cited frequently. Second, they would seem to be commonly accepted and adhered to. Each of the most frequently cited paragraphs builds upon foundations established in previous decisions, quotes from them and solidifies their acceptance. There would appear to be little disagreement emanating from the tribunals regarding these rulings. Third, we also find evidence that, in varying degrees, each represents an extension or progressive development of international law from the guidance provided to the tribunals in their statutes. There is the most evidence in the case of the jurisprudence on individualized sentencing, where clearly the judges have held fast to preserving their own discretion, rather than articulating a set of clear guidelines and/or a sentencing schedule. Punishment is the prerogative of the trial chamber judges and is not to be surrendered to a set of bureaucratic formulations. There is less evidence that the standard of review for sentences and the criterion of "discernible error" represent a progressive development of the law. While the "discernible error" criterion seems to be an original contribution of the judges in sentencing jurisprudence, it does not appear to be a significant break from the criteria laid out in the statutes. And the jurisprudence on the gravity of the crime, while surely important as an articulation of a key determinant and an acknowledgement of the importance of retribution as a guiding theory of punishment, also does not break any new ground, except insofar as it plants jurisprudence firmly in one theoretical grounding rather than other penological justifications, such as restorative justice, rehabilitation, or deterrence.

Appellate Procedures

We next move on to discuss one area where we found a tremendous number of citations, but which was not part of our original set of hypotheses. There is extensive evidence that cases and paragraphs that deal with the most basic aspects of the appellate procedures are frequently and extensively cited. With regard to the ground rules of the novel appeal process it is not surprising that some of the most cited paragraphs pertain to issues about the formal requirements of the Appellant's brief. Concerns about the smooth development of proceedings and assurance of fairness in the justice delivered, have prompted appellate judges to make multiple reference to the elements invalidating the ground of appeals. Portions of some judgments related to the preliminary issues of formality have been cited on more than sixty occasions and, over time, these types of paragraphs have become increasingly more detailed. The most cited paragraph regarding formal requirements of the appellant's brief comes from the *Blaskic* Appeal Judgment. Paragraph 13, cited sixty-eight times, reads:

> The Appeals Chamber reiterates that an appeal is not a trial de novo. In making its assessment, the Appeals Chamber will in principle only take into account the following factual evidence: evidence referred to by the Trial Chamber in the body of the judgement or in a related footnote; evidence contained in the trial record and

referred to by the parties; and additional evidence admitted on appeal. In setting out its contentions on appeal, a party cannot merely repeat arguments that did not succeed at trial, unless that party can demonstrate that rejecting them occasioned such error as to warrant the intervention of the Appeals Chamber. Arguments of the party which do not have the potential to cause the impugned decision to be reversed or revised may be dismissed immediately by the Appeals Chamber and need not be considered on the merits. With regard to requirements as to form, an appealing party is expected to provide precise references to relevant transcript pages or paragraphs in the judgement being challenged. The Appeals Chamber will not give detailed consideration to submissions which are obscure, contradictory, or vague, or if they suffer from other formal and obvious insufficiencies. Thus, in principle, the Appeals Chamber will dismiss, without providing detailed reasons, those submissions which are evidently unfounded.[36]

The language from the *Blaskic* decision has been repeated numerous times in many other cases, which in turn refer to several, other appellate judgments of the ICTY and ICTR creating a complex 'network' of citations (Pelc 2014). Portions of judgments dealing with formal requirements of appeals cited more than thirty times also come from *Vasilevic, Kunarac, Kupreskic,* and *Gacumbitsi*.[37] As mentioned above, through the citations of these cases appellate judges have developed two important requirements for the admissibility of appeals. First, the precise reference to the sections of the trial chamber decision being challenged and, second, the relevance of the issue challenged to the outcome of the trial chamber decision (Book 2011). While the list of requirements has become more detailed over time, in all cases the appeals chamber has been very attentive on monitoring the compliance with the judges' established prerequisites and in promptly pointing out when briefs are lacking and grounds of appeal are dismissible (Boas et al. 2013).

Once we move from the appellants' briefs to the more specific aspects of appellate process, some of the most cited issues address the observance of a "margin of deference" to the Trial Chamber's assessment of facts. Paragraph 18 of the Appeals Chamber judgment in the case of the *Prosecutor v. Musema*, cited sixty-one times, is instructive and reads:

> The Appeals Chamber recalls that in determining whether or not a Trial Chamber's finding was reasonable, it will not lightly disturb findings of fact by a Trial Chamber. In the first place, the task of weighing and assessing evidence lies with the Trial Chamber. Furthermore, it is for the Trial Chamber to determine whether a witness

---

[36] The Prosecutor v. Tihomir Blaskic, Case No. IT-95-14-A, July 29, 2004, para 13.

[37] The Prosecutor v. Vasiljevic, Case No. IT-98-32-A, February 25, 2004, para 12, cited 62 times; The Prosecutor v. Kunarac, Case No. IT-96-23 & IT-96-23/1-A, June 12, 2002, paras 43, 47–48, cited, respectively, fifty-two, forty and fifty-one times; The Prosecutor v. Kupreskic, Case No. IT-95-16-A, October 23, 2001, paras. 30–32, 39, cited, respectively, fifty-five, forty-one, forty-six and thirty-seven times; The Prosecutor v. Gacumbitsi, Case No. ICTR-2001-64-A, July 7, 2006, para 10, cited thirty-seven times.

is credible or not. Therefore, the Appeals Chamber must give a *margin of deference* (emphasis added) to a finding of fact reached by a Trial Chamber.

The rationale behind the establishment of this rule is clearly based on the tasks and procedures followed by the trial chambers. Evidence and testimonies are heard by trial chambers' judges and they have access to a wealth of information on the facts of the case. Thus, they are advantaged in assessing the consistency and reliability of the evidence collected (Rohan 2010; Jayawardane and Divin 2014).

Furthermore, the "reasonableness" standard further strengthens the margin of deference the appeals chambers give to the trial chambers' assessment of factual findings. The principle has been defined in paragraph 64 of the *Tadic* appellate judgment, which is the most cited paragraph of any appellate judgment:

> The two parties agree that the standard to be used when determining whether the Trial Chamber's factual finding should stand is that of unreasonableness, that is, a conclusion which no reasonable person could have reached.[38]

The miscarriage of justice element, added as a further strengthening component in the possible reevaluation of the trial chambers decisions, represents another of those issues that we expect to impact considerably the development of international criminal justice procedures. Indeed, its importance is particularly shown by the amount of times judges refer to the miscarriage of justice standard defining it as "a grossly unfair outcome in judicial proceedings, as when a defendant is convicted despite a lack of evidence on an essential element of the crime."[39] Specifically, the paragraph from the *Furundzjia* Appeal judgment has been cited thirty-seven times.

With regard to the specific right of the accused to a reasoned opinion, first and foremost, we find that appellate judges have been mindful once again of the novel structure of a two tier international criminal justice system. They have recalled in several and extensively cited paragraphs of judgments that a trial chamber can, at its discretion provide explanations about standards of law or facts and that it "is not required to articulate in its judgement every step of its reasoning in reaching particular findings."[40] We quote a specific section of paragraph 23 of the *Kvocka* Appeal Judgment, which is cited eighty-five times:

> [. . .] the Trial Chamber is not under the obligation to justify its findings in relation to every submission made during the trial. The Appeals Chamber recalls that it is in the discretion of the Trial Chamber as to which legal arguments to address. With

---

[38] The Prosecutor v. Tadic, Case No. IT-94-1-A, para 64 cited ninety-seven times. Similarly see Aleksovski appeal judgment, para 63 cited eighty-five times and Furundzija appeal judgment, para 37, cited eighty-five times.

[39] The Prosecutor v. Furundzija, Case No. IT-97-17/1-A, July 21, 2000, para 37.

[40] Celebici Case, Case No. IT-96-21-A, Appeal Judgment, February 20, 2001, para 481 cited thirty-eight times.

regard to the factual findings, the Trial Chamber is required only to make findings of those facts which are essential to the determination of guilt on a particular count. It is not necessary to refer to the testimony of every witness or every piece of evidence on the trial record.[41]

We also see that given the aims of the appellate judges to protect the right of appeal, it is not surprising that some of the most cited paragraphs of appellate judgments deal with the limitations imposed on the Trial Chamber's discretion in handing down a "reasoned opinion." The *Kupreskic* Appeal Judgment, paragraph 32, cited forty-six times, establishes that:

> Th[e] discretion [of the Trial Chamber] is, however, tempered by the Trial Chamber's duty to provide a reasoned opinion, following from Article 23(2) of the Statute. In the *Furundžija* Appeal Judgement, the Appeals Chamber considered the right of an accused under Article 23 of the Statute to a reasoned opinion to be an aspect of the fair trial requirement embodied in Articles 20 and 21 of the Statute.

It comes as no surprise that appeals chambers judges have spent considerable time developing a web of citations that has created *ex novo* complex procedures and regulations shaping the role of the appellate chambers and the function of the appellate jurisdiction. Lacking precedents on which to rely and scant statutory direction, the procedural aspects of the appellate jurisdiction have represented one of the best opportunities for judicial entrepreneurialism and the development of international criminal courts' procedures. Judges have contributed to the creation of a significant body of regulations that tackle the most compelling appellate procedural matters, from the admissibility of procedural and substantive issues, to the novel relationship in international criminal justice between the appeals chambers and the trial chambers. Most importantly, judges have paid considerable attention to the complexity of the trial chamber decisions and the frequency with which they are appealed. Hence, it is not surprising that rules and regulations governing the formal requirements of the parties' briefs are of particular importance for the smooth and expeditious development of the proceedings. Vague and overly general grounds could overburden the appellate re-examination of a case, while appeals that focus on and contest the facts would tend to undermine the appellate process, which is not meant to be a *de novo* trial on the same facts, but a more focused re-analysis of possible legal and factual errors committed by the court of first tier. Yet, the initial versions of the Rules of Procedure and Evidence regulating the work of the ad hoc tribunals and the founding documents of the two institutions were extremely scant about the appropriate content of appellate briefs (Calvo-Goller 2006) and left ample discretionary power to the appeals chambers to assess whether the briefs clearly stated the grounds and challenges to the trial chambers' decisions. Of particular

---

[41] Some of the most cited paragraphs by appellant judgments on this point are the Prosecutor v. Kvocka, Case No. IT-98–30/1-A, Appeal Judgment, February 28, 2005, para 23, cited eighty-five times.

importance to the judges were the types of issues and challenges that could warrant reconsideration of the case by the appeals chamber.

The Progressive Development of the Crime of Rape

Lastly, we examine an issue that was neither one of our hypotheses nor one of the subjects of importance revealed in our quantitative analysis. The topic of rape and sexual assault, however, has generated tremendous interest in the scholarly community (Askin 1997 and 2003; Franke 2006; Gekker 2014; Goldstone 2002; Meron 1993; Schomberg and Peterson 2007). Matters involving the perpetration of the crime of rape represent one of the areas of international criminal law less developed by prior jurisprudence. Because of definitional issues with the crime and the determination of the burden of proof, it is primed for the development of international jurisprudence. However, we find that for the most part the development of the law with regard to the crime of rape has been performed by the Trial Chambers of the ad hoc tribunals rather than by the Appeals Chambers. We also find that issues pertaining to the definition of the crime, the circumstantial evidence, and the burden of proof of the crime have not triggered controversial debate among judges. Most of the decisions handed down show mostly an "incremental" character to the different facets of the international crime of rape. From the *Akayesu* case at the ICTR and the *Kunarac et al.* case at the ICTY (the first indictment to focus mostly on charges of rape), judicial decisions at the international tribunals have defined and refined the crime of rape, adding and specifying the elements of the crime, but with little significant controversy.

We find that the definition of the criminal actions identified as amounting to rape were mostly determined by the jurisprudence of the trial chambers and that appeals chambers have frequently referred to the language developed by the trial chambers of the ad hoc international tribunals while citations to earlier appellate decisions have been infrequent. The following definitions provided by the cases of *Akayesu* and *Furundzija* have been frequently mentioned by Appeals Chambers. The ICTR judges in *Akayesu* defined rape as:

> physical invasion of a sexual nature, committed on a person under circumstances which are coercive. The Tribunal considers sexual violence, which includes rape, as any act of a sexual nature which is committed on a person under circumstances which are coercive. Sexual violence is not limited to physical invasion of the human body and may include acts which do not involve penetration or even physical contact[42]

Sometime later the ICTY Trial Chamber provided a more detailed definition and a much needed description of the actus reus in the case of *Furundzija*, whose relevant paragraph we reproduce here:

[42] The Prosecutor v. Jean-Paul Akayesu, Case No. ICTR-96–4, Trial Chamber Judgement, September 2, 1998, para 688.

the following may be accepted as the objective elements of rape:

(i) the sexual penetration, however slight:
   (a) of the vagina or anus of the victim by the penis of the perpetrator or any other object used by the perpetrator; or
   (b) of the mouth of the victim by the penis of the perpetrator;
(ii) by coercion or force or threat of force against the victim or a third person.[43]

Rather than simply repeating the definition given in *Akayesu*, in the case of *Furundzija* the Trial Chamber qualified the circumstances in which rape occurred as *coercive, forceful, and threatening*, developing a more complex definition of the crime, centered on factual and circumstantial evidence.

The Appeals Chambers further developed the definition of the crime by according the proper qualification of the coercive circumstances, assessing the relative burden of proof that those conditions were present, and by qualifying the requisite mens rea specifically with regard to the accused's knowledge of the coercive circumstances. These matters were developed by the Appeals Chambers of the ICTY and ICTR in the cases of *Kunarac et al.* and *Gacumbitsi* respectively. In *Kunarac et al.* the judges established that, in cases in which women were raped while being held in military headquarters and in residences controlled by officers, the crimes in front of the bench were committed in such circumstances as to presume the lack of consent.[44] In the Appeal case of *Gacumbitsi v. The Prosecutor* the judges espoused the "circumstantial interpretation" of the elements of the crime of rape, suggesting that "non-consent [can be inferred] from background circumstances, such as an ongoing genocide campaign or the detention of the victims."[45] As per the knowledge of lack of consent by the perpetrator, the judges established that the Prosecution must show that the accused knew of the coercive circumstances that undermined the possibility of a genuine consent.

As briefly mentioned above, while the recognition of rape as an international crime committed in times of war has been welcomed as one of the most important milestones reached by the ad hoc international tribunals, the jurisprudence developed has not warranted extensive deliberation and citations by the appeals chambers. In analyzing appellate decisions of the ICTY and ICTR we found that judges have repeatedly relied on the position expressed by the trial chambers' decision and, when further elements of the crime were elaborated by appeals chambers, subsequent appellate decisions have simply reiterated the positions of earlier judgments. This does not mean that the progressive development of the law with regard to rape has not been significant and groundbreaking, but it indicates that there is a general

---

[43] The Prosecutor v. Anto Furundzija, Case No. IT-95–17/1-T, Trial Judgment, December 10, 1998, para 185. Also paras 174–186.

[44] The Prosecutor v. Kunarac et al., Case No. IT-96–23-A & IT-96–23/1-A, June 12, 2002.

[45] The Prosecutor v. Sylvestre Gacumbitsi, Case No. ICTR-2001–64-A, July 7, 2006, para 155.

and common understanding about the different components of the crime of rape that has not yielded significant debate.

We would make different observations regarding the absence of extensive appellate citations for one of the most groundbreaking advancements that the ad hoc international tribunals have made. First and foremost, as the tribunal for the former Yugoslavia was being created by the Security Council there was a growing awareness of the widespread gendered violence that was occurring during that country's bloody dissolution. As reported in the case of *Furundzija*:

> [the United Nations Security Council] resolutions [leading to the establishment of the Tribunal] condemned the systematic rape and detention of women in the former Yugoslavia and expressed determination to put an end to such crimes and to take effective measures to bring to justice the persons who are responsible for them. [...] The general question of bringing to justice the perpetrators of these crimes was, therefore, one of the reasons that the Security Council established the Tribunal.[46]

As the tribunals became operational investigations revealed that acts of "unspeakable brutality"[47] had been committed against women. A swift and firm response was needed. We would suggest that as evidence of the widespread perpetration of the crime of rape as a weapon of war was collected by investigators and submitted to judges, it became evident the need "for a rapid adjustment" (Meron 1993, 1) of the international criminal law system to address these crimes. This, in turn, may have strengthened the judicial will to provide a comprehensive and undisputed definition of the crime, which left very little room for future adjustments and debates.

Lastly, we agree with scholars (Franke 2006; Haffajee 2006; Phelps 2006) that although the advances made by the ICTY and ICTR in terms of the definition of the crime of rape in times of war are extremely important, the cases dealing with charges of rape have been few and far between. The difficulties associated with the prosecution of the crime of rape, which requires extensive testimony from witnesses who carry the brunt of extreme violence, and often the stigma and shame that a traditional society imposes on them (Haffajee 2006, 205) have slowed down considerably the prosecution of the crime of rape. The paucity of the cases and the relative consistency of the circumstances surrounding the perpetration of the crime of rape have very likely contributed to the small of number of citations generated by appellate courts.

CONCLUSION

The results of our hypothesis testing have been rich in their diversity and complexity. We found two hypotheses strongly confirmed, and one that evidenced little empirical

[46] The Prosecutor v. Anto Furundzija, Case No. IT-95-17/1-A, July 21, 2000, para 201.
[47] Ibid, footnote 275 referring to the United Nations Security Council Resolution No. 798 (1992).

support. And we also found instances where the results suggested other hypotheses might be more in order. First, we found that there are a great many citations to key rulings on command and control and sentencing. The jurisprudence of the tribunals is replete with key rulings being cited dozens of times across tribunals and across time. We would expect that the numbers will only continue to grow with future rulings of international tribunals, such as the ICC. Therefore, we assert that there is substantial evidence that judges have progressively advanced international law in these issue domains. They have clarified ambiguities in the law, as we saw numerous times in the case of command and control decisions and especially joint criminal enterprise issues. When ambiguities preserved their own discretion and judgment, however, as we saw with regard to sentencing, judges have been content to live with a lack of clarity or certainty. They have confronted definitional issues by specifying, for example, factors to be taken into consideration when determining whether superiors should be expected to know about the behavior of their subordinates.

At the same time, however, judges have set key precedents in other areas of international law where we did not expect to see such activity, while they have not created nearly the level of jurisprudence we had predicted in issues we argued were ripe for judicial entrepreneurship. The number of citations to issues involving the appellate process dwarfed all other subjects. The appeals chambers consistently cited the same rulings from earlier cases again and again to the point where such references seemed automatic or even perfunctory. The standards of appeal, the right to a reasoned decision and the importance of adhering to proper procedure were hallmarks of such rulings and demonstrate that such encompassing and fundamental issues, especially in embryonic international law, are a given. At the same time we also found that where we had expected evidence of substantial citation – the issue of bias crimes – we found none. To be sure, there have been many widely analyzed rulings in this issue domain, but few that have gained a widespread currency across tribunals. Could it be that this issue area is so new that no appeals chamber has arrived at a definition resolution on issues such as the meaning of protected groups? Or is it that the ICTR, which has heard the majority of genocide cases, has not been cited by the ICTY to the same extent ICTY decisions have been cited by the ICTR? There are several possible answers to this question that require much deeper analysis.

Because of the textual analysis performed on the cases in which bias crimes were adjudicated, we suggest that among the possible answers to this question one resonates as more likely than others. In fact, we noticed that in the adjudication of bias crimes judges have relied on legal discourses that have focused more on the international and regional instruments defining such crimes rather than citing prior judgments. In cases dealing with genocide – such as the *Krstic* and *Jelisic* cases above cited – judges have relied extensively on the definitions provided by the Convention on the Prevention and Punishment of the Crime of Genocide, as well as on the numerous reports published by UN commissions monitoring the status of human rights in Rwanda and the ex-Yugoslavia in the wake of violence. Similarly, judges have relied on multiple human rights instruments to define the crime of persecution and identify those who can be considered victims of such crimes. We might conclude that in relying on these instruments rather than on a fictitious international rule of *stare decisis* judges have sent two different messages. First, judges might have wanted to strengthen the validity of their reasoning by relying on universally recognized principles of human rights protection and in so doing shaping a consistent interpretation of these principles across cases without necessarily proceeding to a self-serving internal citation. Second, judges might have seized the opportunity to once again reinforce the focus of the international criminal justice system on victims and on the protection of innocent civilians, through the use of the international instruments created for the protection of human beings, rather than focusing on the reasoning through which punishment for other indictees had been reached.

We contend that across all of these issue domains, with the possible exception of rulings on procedural matters, international judges have demonstrated a substantial interest in advancing international law in such a way that also advances human rights. Judges have advanced the cause of human rights by ensuring that individuals would be held to account for their criminal misdeeds, regardless of their position. They have advanced human rights by ensuring that those convicted of serious crimes would be given serious penalties. They have advanced human rights in small ways that do not always appear in our analyses by expanding the types of crimes that qualify as genocide and by developing a more holistic and appropriate definition of rape. To be sure the tribunals have endeavored to protect the rights of defendants, but they have shown consistently that human rights, especially of innocent civilians, are the foremost value they seek to achieve through justice. It is to how the judges give voice to these values through the expressive language that we next turn.

We note, however, that there are limitations to our research strategy. There have been several issues that have generated significant controversy in the academic world that our analyses do not capture, because they have not tended to generate a significant number of citations. The *Celebici* Trial Chamber judgment has been well-remarked upon for its jurisprudence regarding superior liability and especially its definition of effective control. As well, there have been extended debates regarding what has been termed "successor liability" (whether superiors are responsible for actions taken by subordinates under a previous commander) which is an issue that has not been cited frequently. Thus, do we see that both in instances where jurisprudence may be regarded as fairly settled (e.g., *Celebici*), and instances where there are still ambiguities in interpretation our count of citations does not always concur with the amount of discourse in the international legal community. In general, however, we believe that the count of citations is effective at identifying what are the truly consequential rulings.

4

The Expressive Function of Judgments

INTRODUCTION

"In the all too long, sad and wretched history of man's inhumanity to man, the Pionirska street and Bikavac fires must rank high. At the close of the 20th century, a century marked by war and bloodshed on a colossal scale, these horrific events remain imprinted on the memory for the viciousness of the incendiary attack, for the obvious premeditation and calculation that defined it, for the sheer callousness, monstrosity and brutality of herding, trapping and locking the victims in the two houses, thereby rendering them helpless in the ensuing inferno and for the degree of pain and suffering inflicted on the victims as they were burnt alive."[1]

On July 20, 2009, Judge Patrick Robinson, the presiding judge in the case of the *Prosecutor v. Milan Lukic and Sredoje Lukic,* pronounced these words in front of an audience, who had listened for more than thirty minutes to a short, but vivid description of the crimes for which the accused stood trial. Through the narrative of apocalyptic imagery, the audience was taken outside the courtroom – to the street of Pionirska and the Bikavac settlement in Visegrad – where, trapped in the basement of buildings, fifty-nine Muslim women, children and elderly and sixty Muslim civilians, respectively, were burnt alive. Under the defiant eyes of the accused, who repeatedly shook their heads in disapproval of Judge Robinson's account, the judicial bench went beyond its duty of handing down a sentence; it stated a moral condemnation and proclaimed a collective indignation for crimes whose gravity may never find an appropriate punishment.

Statements like those pronounced by Judge Robinson in the *Lukic* case stand out in international justice. Paragraphs marked with words of vivid condemnation and stigmatization of criminals have emerged as a potent expression of moral indignation. One may find words such as "evil," "repugnant," "unspeakable" and others in judicial

[1] The Prosecutor v. Milan Lukic and Sredoje Lukic, Case No. IT-98–32/1-T, July 20, 2009, para 740.

statements which resonate more as a moral condemnation of the crimes rather than a legal assessment of the guilt. On judgment day, judges sitting on the bench pronounce dramatic words that are a clear and loud message of reprobation for these crimes.[2]

Some of those judicial statements have remained in the collective memory more than the actual punishment. On the day Judge Mumba delivered the judgment in the case of the *Prosecutor v. Kunarac et al.* she stated that "[. . .] the evidence shows that Muslim women and girls, mothers and daughters together, [were] *robbed of the last vestiges of human dignity*, women and girls treated like chattels, pieces of property at the arbitrary disposal of the Serb occupation forces, and more specifically, at the beck and call of the three accused"[3] (emphasis added). In directly addressing one of the accused, judged Mumba added, "You were a soldier with courage in the field, somebody whom your men undisputedly are said to have held in high esteem. By this natural authority you could easily have put an end to the women's suffering. Your active participation in this *nightmarish scheme of sexual exploitation is therefore even more repugnant*"[4] (emphasis added). The words of Judge Mumba were widely reported by the media and would seem to have resonated very close to the hearts and minds of the victims, as the world watched the trial come to an end.

In the broader international judicial context within which these tribunals operate – one set up to fulfill goals of retribution, deterrence, peace and reconciliation – these statements, stand out. They seem to go beyond the clinical and objective assessment of the crimes and the establishment of the actus reus and mens rea, adding a subjective nuance to an otherwise detached and objective legal process. Thus, we must wonder whether judges are employing a rhetorical exercise that has no practical value for the dispensation of international justice. Or, is the purpose of these statements to be found in other, more abstract and moral aims? We do not believe that these statements are void of meaning beyond their immediate impact. We consider international judges as operating in a purposive manner; we think of the words, paragraphs, and chapters of judgments as aiming at affecting a specific and worthy goal of international criminal justice. In a word we perceive these words as serving an "expressive" purpose in the law.

In this chapter we examine two fundamental questions relating to what we call "judicial expressivism" – the use of words to convey a moral judgment rather than serve a legal purpose. The first investigates the rationale behind ethical statements. The second concerns the extent to which judges address their audience with such words of moral reprobation and recognition of the human element of these crimes. More specifically, we contend that the motivation behind moral statements and

---

[2] It should be noted that these summary judgments are not the official judgments of the tribunals. As well, not all summary judgments are published by the tribunals.

[3] Summary of Judgement, Prosecutor v. Kunarac et al., Case No. IT-96–23/1, February 22, 2001, p. 2.

[4] Ibid., p. 5.

harsh rhetorical condemnation of crimes is the result of a complex series of considerations, which find their roots in the intrinsic shortcomings of international justice in addressing heinous crimes and aim at speaking to a multifaceted audience. As Sloane (2007, 43) has argued, "ICL's ability to contribute to the lofty objectives ascribed to it depends far more on enhancing its value as authoritative expression than on ill-fated efforts to identify the 'right' punishment, whatever that could mean, for often unconscionable crimes." We intend to explore the rationale behind these statements by looking specifically at how entrepreneurial international judges fill the shortcomings of retributive elements of international criminal law by using moral rhetoric which contributes to the condemnation of crimes and reinforces the "social disapproval of a particular form of behavior" (Feinberg 1970 as cited by Wringe 2006, 176).

We rely on the concept of the "expressive function of the law" elaborated by previous scholarship (Drumbl 2007b; Feinberg 1970; Sloane 2007; Sunstein 1996). In particular, we contend that judges, as judicial entrepreneurs, utilize the expressive function of the law to characterize the nature of the crime as not only forbidden by law, but morally wrong as well. We believe that it is through emotionally charged moral statements that international judges propel international criminal justice in a dimension that goes beyond the imperfect remedy of retribution and punishment. We then discuss how judges use the same rhetoric to address their audiences: victims, the defendants, prosecutors, the affected population, and the global community at large. We envision the audience as being both a passive *receptor* of judicial statements and an active *propagator* of the judges' message, reinforcing the power of international criminal justice's goals for the future generations.[5] We then use textual analysis to locate and analyze the use of expressivism in the judgments of the tribunals and discuss just when such condemnation seems most likely and what ultimate purposes it serves.

THE RATIONALE OF MORAL EXPRESSIVISM – REDEFINING THE GOALS OF INTERNATIONAL CRIMINAL JUSTICE

Over the years there has been a widespread skepticism about international criminal justice's ability to hand down punishments that can fulfill the goals established by the founding documents of the institutions (Drumbl 2007b; Henham 2003, 2007). Paradoxically the list of goals of international tribunals – retribution, deterrence, peace and reconciliations – have, in some ways, made international criminal prosecutions an inadequate answer to the past decades' atrocities. In particular, the emphasis placed on goals such as retribution and deterrence have revealed an intrinsic weakness of the international criminal justice system. Scholars (Wippman 1999;

---

[5] See Cassese (1998): "a fully reliable record is established of atrocities so that future generations can remember and be made fully cognisant of what happened" (p. 4).

Damaska 2008; Ku and Nzelibe 2006) have indicated how the deterrent effect of international criminal prosecutions is mostly lacking, as individuals who committed crimes against humanity or genocide are frequently moved by deep seated hatred. Moreover, the reasons behind the crimes which international tribunals address are moved by illogical behavior and concern individuals who often accept the risk of being punished thus defying deterrence altogether (Damaska 2008).

Even more than other goals, retribution has come under heavy criticism as an unattainable goal (Drumbl 2007b; Koskenniemi 2002; Tallgren 2002; DeGuzman 2012; Sloane 2006). On the one hand, the political elements of the process through which the institutions operate affect the harmony of the international justice system and in some ways detract from the objective dispensation of punishments. Some believe that crimes that have outraged the international community have received rather lenient sentences, and that the absence of clear guidelines of sentencing has created inconsistent punishments for similar crimes (Drumbl 2007b). On the other hand, scholars have indicated that the "physical and moral distance from the crimes and affected communities" makes international criminal law unsuccessful in "exacting retribution" as effectively as national criminal law (Sloane 2007, 50–51; deGuzman, 2012, 302, n 186). Along the same lines, in her lucid analysis of the shortcomings of retribution for the punishment of international crimes, Arendt compares the necessity of a legal response to the horrific crimes masterminded by a state apparatus, and the inadequacy of the same legal response to redress the monstrosity of crimes that can never find the right punishment (Arendt 1963, 1992).

In examining the jurisprudence of the recent international criminal tribunals, it seems that these observations have some basis. The principle of retribution, according to which punishment must reflect the gravity of the crime finds several obstacles in its implementation, chief among them the horrific brutality of the criminal behavior. It seems as if the human-made international legal system is inadequate to redress acts committed by individuals who have seemingly lost their humanity. Even when international judges have handed down harsh punishments such as life in prison, they have come across as inadequately reflecting the horrific magnitude of human suffering. Yet, the international tribunals' judgments are replete with statements recalling that the "litmus test" in the imposition of an appropriate sentence is the gravity of the offence.[6] The principle honors some of the most basic tenets of a legal system aiming for the dispensation of a fair and retributive justice.

However, there are considerable challenges in judging crimes of unbelievable violence and handing down sentences that reflect the gravity of the offense and the international reprobation for the harm inflicted on society. In practice, most

---

[6] The Prosecutor v. Tihomir Blaskic, No. ICTY IT-95-14-A, July 29, 2004, para 683. The Prosecutor v. Zlatko Aleksovski, Case No. ICTY IT-95-14/1-A, March 24, 2000, para 182. The Prosecutor v. Dario Kordic and Mario Cerkez, Case No. IT-95-14/2-A, December 17, 2004, para 1061. The Prosecutor v. Goran Jelisic, Case No. IT-95-10-A, July 5, 2001, para 94. The Prosecutor v. Dragan Nikolic, Case No. IT-94-02-A, February 4, 2005, para 18.

of the sentences meted out by the international tribunals have been considered inappropriate given the gravity of the crime[7] and have been criticized as being disproportionally lenient (Szoke-Burke 2012). What is the proper punishment for those who organized the slaughter of eight hundred thousand people in a few months, as in Rwanda? What are the penalties that can quell the pain and suffering of those who lost loved ones in the Srebrenica massacre? Each count of a crime of genocide and of a crime against humanity, if proven, is a violation not only of the law, but of the most elementary rules of human dignity. While retribution appears to be one of the most prevalent goals (Woods 2012), there is a common sentiment among practitioners and scholars alike that there is no just dessert proportional to the harm inflicted. Retribution might just be no more than an empty promise in the eyes of the victims.

As we examine the atrocities that have led to the establishment of international criminal institutions, it seems that the purely legalist purposes in the dispensation of justice are inadequate. Good legal processes and retributive consequences should be able to reflect a moral judgment of the crimes committed and a stigmatization of the individuals charged, none of which belongs to the clear pragmatic aspect of international criminal proceedings. On this point, speaking of the goals of punishing international crimes of terrorism, Drumbl (2009) debated whether deterrence, retribution, rehabilitation, and reconciliation are goals which indeed fulfill the mission of international criminal justice or whether the purpose of international "punishment [should be] something more communicative and pedagogical." Scholars (Sloane 2006; Szoke-Burke 2012) have analyzed at length the concept of "retributive expressivism."

The interpretation and usage we give of the word "expressivism" is rather different than found in prior scholarship. We would certainly concur with those who argue that retributive expressivism can be reflected in punishment *as* punishment – that is a lengthy sentence for severe crimes committed by senior figures – expresses condemnation of the crimes and the individual for orchestrating such violence (Drumbl 2007b; Sloane 2007). In such a perspective, however, the communication of the sentence largely accomplishes the expression of the condemnation. We do not know, however, what meaning individuals in the local or international context will attach to this expression of values as punishment. As such, these analyses are more focused on the underlying rationales of punishment rather than the precise nature of the message or the use of particular words and phrases to express values. We do not contend that harm-based sentences (Szoke-Burke 2012) or cumulative sentences better express the reprobation and condemnation for the crimes adjudicated. On the

---

7 As Drumbl and Gallant reported in 2002 the mean sentence handed down by the ICTY was sixteen years and the highest sentence, at the time of their writing, was forty-six years for the crime of genocide in the *Krstic* case. We note that since then judges have handed down life in prison punishments. See the Prosecutor v. Popovic et al., Case No. IT-05–88, June 10, 2010; the Prosecutor v. Lukic and Lukic, Case No. IT-98–32/1, July 20, 2009.

contrary, we suggest that international judges build a "memorial of words," which speak loudly of the magnitude of the crimes, of the extent of the suffering, and of the reprobation for these crimes. Where retribution fails to reflect the atrocities committed and where a precise term of incarceration does not speak to the pain and suffering of individuals, then authoritative and moral words may better communicate the horrific magnitude of the events probed. Hence, rather than assessing how the more macro-level, institutional interests in expressivism are realized through punishment more generally (Sloane 2007) or the selection of cases (DeGuzman 2012), we focus on the micro-level. We analyze the language in judgments used to express norms and values. Ours is a focus on the practice of expressivism rather than its theoretical role.

We believe that international judges are fully aware of the difficult task they face in handing down a forty-year sentence for the killing of three thousand individuals, for example. We think that judges are sensitive to the criticisms about non-retributive sentences and to the lack of support by local communities affected by the crimes. It is because of these shortcomings that we contend judges articulate moral opinions and give an additional impetus to the retributive aspect of punishment. In a sense international judges act as entrepreneurs by reinforcing the sentencing with moral statements, by creating a moral standard against which crimes are punished, and by indicating that what criminals are judged for is not only prohibited but it is altogether wrong (Tallgren 2002). As judicial entrepreneurs who are not content to employ legalese to confront crime, they strike out beyond these roles and speak as humans, not just judges.

Lastly, as judges who hear evidence and as individuals who must listen to numerous witnesses retelling many horrific, personal stories, we must believe that they are affected as humans by these narratives. The acts which judges probe violate the core of human dignity and provoke horror and disgust. As cogently stated by the presiding judge of the Eichmann trial "while on the bench a judge does not cease to be flesh and blood, possessed of emotions and impulses. However he is required by law to subdue these emotions and impulses, for otherwise a judge will never be fit to consider a criminal charge which arouses feelings of revulsion, such as treason, murder or any other grave crime."[8] We hypothesize that while in their judicial robes judges must maintain such decorum, but that in their judgments they will as seemingly demanded by the horrific nature of the crimes, express a more human condemnation of this violence.

We believe that judges seek to leave a lasting memory of the horrors they adjudicate to develop a message that speaks clearly, forcefully and morally of their recognition of the human cost of these tragedies. We believe they seek to move beyond punishment and acknowledge the pain of victims and local communities

---

[8] The Trial of Adolf Eichmann, Session 6, April 17, 1961. The transcripts can be found at: http://www.nizkor.org/hweb/people/e/eichmann-adolf/transcripts/Sessions/.

and communicate this suffering to the larger international community. In a certain way, moral condemnation does what retribution and punishment alone cannot do; it shrinks the "physical and moral distance" (Sloane 2007) between the victims and the communities shattered by the events and the legal proceedings adjudicating the crimes. It creates empathy among individuals and it sends a clear message to a multifaceted audience, through the creation of a "historical narrative," the objective and public account of the crimes, which stigmatizes violence and criminals in a deeper and more meaningful way than any punishment can (Drumbl 2007b, 1182).

THE AUDIENCE

As suggested in the introductory paragraph to this section, we submit that, while expressing moral condemnation for the crimes committed reinforces retribution and punishment, the messages articulated by international judgments aim at addressing audiences beyond those who are party to the case. Scholars (Szoke-Burke 2012; DeGuzman 2012; Damaska 2008) have indicated that generally speaking any legal system expresses the values for which a society stands and uses punishment to send a message of condemnation to a large audience.[9] The same scholars have also suggested that taking into consideration an audience is of utmost importance to build the legitimacy of international criminal justice. International courts and tribunals are as strong as the support they receive from audiences that can reinforce the values that international criminal law represents. deGuzman (2012) argues that the adjudication of cases in support of global norms and values of a "constitutive community"[10] is of particular importance for the legitimacy of the ICC. While deterrence and retribution remain major objectives, the inadequate amount of resources at the disposal of the ICC, for example, which force the court to select only a handful of cases among the many violations of international law, make the attainable goal of expressing global norms and values even more important than for the other international tribunals.

We contend that it is not only through punishment that judges acknowledge the importance of the audience, but through the articulation of moral statements of condemnation. We envision the audience as one that comprises the victims, the local community affected by the crimes, the defendants, and the international community. We believe that judges address with their to words these audiences because it satisfies the need to send a message to those whose lives have been violated by international crimes, signal the importance of the human rights and humanity

---

9 See Amann (2002) writing that "The intended audience of such exhortations is not just the wrongdoer of most concern to deterrence and retributive theorists. It is also the Everyone of most interest to expressive theorists: the law-abider and the lawmaker, the activist and the private citizen, and even the potential victim, today and tomorrow" (p. 124).

10 deGuzman (2012) speaks of an "appropriate community of interests" as the intended target of the justice being meted out by international tribunals (p. 278).

of the victims, and can increase the resonance and perhaps even the legitimacy of international justice. We suggest that each and every audience to which international judges send their message is relevant. Victims, local communities, practitioners and international policy makers see the operation of the international justice system as important for specific reasons typical of the interests of their own organization or community.

We do not argue that all moral statements of condemnation are meant for the entire audience, but we believe that whenever judges go beyond their duty to deliver a punishment and express disgust, disdain, and horror for the crimes probed, they are speaking to some of these audiences for a specific reason. We envision the messages articulated by the judges as moving through a complex network of actors and interests. Judicial statements can satisfy a specific actor's interest that may increase the support and trust provided by that group and foster the increased legitimacy of the institutions working for the implementation of international criminal law. We examine the relevance, interest and support each actor comprising the audience carries and we describe a network of communication between judges and the relevant audience which ultimately explains why judges use moral rhetoric in their judgments. Each judgment becomes more than the conclusive act of a lengthy proceeding; it becomes a memorial of the crimes and a permanent archive of the horrors committed and suffered by individuals.[11]

Victims

Among the actors comprising the relevant audience to which judges speak through their judgments, victims are perhaps the most important. In the long and troubled history of international criminal justice the role and relevance of victims in the dispensation of justice has been controversial. Only the international criminal justice system post-Nuremberg has seen an increasing shift of attention toward the victims of the crimes being adjudicated. While prior to the establishment of the ICTY and ICTR the focus of the Nuremberg trials was on the role of the perpetrator, international judges and prosecutors at the ad hoc institutions created in the 1990s advocated for more "victim oriented" (Moffett 2014) legal proceedings in which individuals who had suffered the brunt of war and long-lasting psychological scars, would participate in the proceedings and see their suffering acknowledged by the international community. In this sense, the trials held at the ad hoc tribunals have become the opportunity for victims to tell their stories and set a historical account of their truth and suffering.[12] The ICC statute and its Rules of Procedure and Evidence provide even more "victim oriented" provisions through the institutionalization of

---

[11] See Amann (2002) writing that "Condemnation, the process of compiling a record of evil and expressing repulsion, received as much attention as punishment" (p. 121).

[12] Stover, Eric (2005). *The Witnesses. War Crimes and the Promise of Justice in The Hague*, University of Pennsylvania Press: Philadelphia, p. 110.

victims' participation and reparation (Moffett 2015). Yet the founding documents of the international tribunals do not speak of acknowledging the emotional needs of the victims or providing a remedy for the disruption of their lives (Moffett 2014). In the legalist framework within which international criminal law operates, victims are supposed to be satisfied by the punishment handed down to those found guilty of crimes.

However, the situation has changed considerably in the past decades. Over time the perception of what victims need from an international criminal justice system has changed. The lengthy and strenuous account of the events through which victims suffered redefines the scope of international criminal justice. International judges do not rely only on documentary evidence; they stand in the same courtroom with those who have come forward to tell their story. They listen to the horrors suffered, they see the trauma caused by the crimes on the faces of the witnesses, and hear the desperation over the loss of loved ones. We suggest that judges know that punishment and the consequences for the guilty do not match that pain witnessed in the courtroom. Thus, rather than relying solely on the punitive consequences assigned by the law, we suggest that judges seek to realize a moral condemnation of criminal actions to better communicate to the victims.

We believe that judges acknowledge the pain and suffering of the victims in two different ways. Judgments and especially trial chambers' judgments are replete with witnesses' statements recalling the events for which the accused stood trial. For example, in the case of the *Prosecutor v. Radislav Krstic* the trial chamber included in the judgment numerous statements of Witness DD recalling how her son had been snatched away from her and begging the judicial bench to ask Krstic whether he knew of her son's whereabouts. Most of these witness statements are used to support legal conclusions and demonstrate the liability of the accused. Hence, their purpose and importance is understood mostly on legal grounds. At the same time, however, the inclusion of these statements also gives voice to victims and may make judgments resonate with witnesses and other victims by giving such international prominence to their words and suffering.

Additionally, through the words of victims and judges' acknowledgment of their experiences, the judges reinforce and validate the suffering of victims and witnesses. They add to the dry accounting of events a vivid description of the images and of the deep fear and desperation of victims. They build upon these words in order to amplify a message, which is often one reflecting moral values. For example, the judges described the account of Witness DD in the *Krstic* case as the most emblematic depiction of the campaign of terror during the Srebrenica genocide and a clear example of the "ultimate suffering" of the population.

In this particular case, the testimony of Witness DD represented one of the most crucial moments in the acknowledgment of the victims' suffering and in the validation that Bosnian Muslims had been the subjects of a genocidal campaign. Through the words of Witness DD the judges spoke of "a patriarchal society, such as the one in which the Bosnian Muslims of Srebrenica lived [in which] the elimination of virtually all the men [...] made it almost impossible for the Bosnian Muslim women who survived the take-over of Srebrenica to successfully re-establish their lives"[13] and to return home. Through the quoting of Witness DD's words about details of the events, such as the repetition of her son's last words, judges provided something more than the factual historical record, they vividly marked in the memory of all the words of a boy without a name and the suffering of a mother.

In the few cases so far adjudicated at the ICC, while judges have not shown the same kind of moral rhetoric as those sitting at the ICTY, they have nonetheless devoted extensive space in their judgments to victims' and experts' testimony, while at the same time showing some "empathy" toward those testifying in front of the bench (Hayes 2015, 834). In several passages in the *Lubanga Dyilo* judgment, the Chamber describes in detail the testimonies of victims, particularly focusing on the living conditions of children enlisted as soldiers or body guards of commanders. Lengthy paragraphs describe the trauma and punishments suffered by children and the consequent apprehension to come forward as witnesses.[14] In one instance judges detailed very closely the testimony of a witness who worked in the child protection program of the United Nations Organization Mission in the Democratic Republic of the Congo who recalled:

> meeting two particular little boys. [...] They were eleven and thirteen years old respectively, and had been frightened by the military. [The witness] thought they were very afraid because they did not know where they were being taken or what was to become of them, and when she began asking them questions one of them broke down in tears. [...] Given they were so upset, [the witness] merely took down the names of their parents and their ages before referring them. [The witness] *recalled holding the hand of the younger child when crossing the street. Her evidence was that "[h]e was so small* [emphasis added]."[15]

Once again, as in the case of Krstic and Witness DD, the reported details of this testimony seemingly aim at giving an identity to a child whose name is unknown and whose suffering can only be recounted by those who met him. Judges have included such statements and justified their presence even as some have questioned the accuracy of many witnesses, particularly at the SCSL and ICTR (Combs 2013). At the same time ICC judges have justified the inconsistencies in the victims' oral testimonies as a consequence of the fear instilled in them by the perpetrators of crimes and as the result of the painful and shameful memories they had to relive during court proceedings. In particular, judges have directly acknowledged the pain

---

[13] The Prosecutor v. Radislav Krstic, Case No. IT-98-33-T, August 2, 2001, para 91.

[14] See Situation in the Democratic Republic of the Congo in the Case of The Prosecutor v. Thomas Lubanga Dyilo, Case No. ICC-01/04-01/06, March 14, 2012, paras 883-896.

[15] See Situation in the Democratic Republic of the Congo in the Case of The Prosecutor v. Thomas Lubanga Dyilo, Case No. ICC-01/04-01/06, March 14, 2012, para 653.

suffered by victims and the consequent confusion on recounting the events in court. On one occasion, recalling the inconsistent testimony of a victim of rape in the *Katanga* judgment, the bench stated:

> The Chamber thus considers that although P-132's testimony about the events is at times inconsistent due to, *and this must be repeated* [emphasis added], her difficulty in reviving such painful memories, it can be relied on to establish that the three persons who attacked her in Bogoro intentionally committed the crime of rape.[16]

In addressing the victims' suffering and making sure that their judgments speak to those most affected by the crimes perpetrated, the SCSL went even further than the ICC and ICTY. In all adjudicated cases the judges did not spare details of the crimes that were perpetrated and of the suffering the victims must have gone through as a consequence of the atrocities committed during the ten years lengthy civil war. In judgments the benches went through the gruesome facts of the crimes with a vivid depiction of the particulars. In the Civil Defense Forces case against Moinina Fofana and Allieu Kondewa, the SCSL judges indicated that

> Many of the victims of these crimes were young children and women, and therefore belong to a particular vulnerable sector of society. For instance, we note our findings of the hacking to death by the CDF/Kamajors of a boy named Sule at a checkpoint in the Tongo area, the murder of a 12 year old boy in Talama, the murder of an unidentified woman who was alleged to have cooked for the rebels in Bo, and the atrocious murder of the two women in Koribundo [. . .][17]

In almost all cases adjudicated by the SCSL, judges proceeded very methodically in listing the number of victims, when possible, as in the above example, gave the names of the victims, and spared no details of the brutality with which crimes were perpetrated. Although sometimes shorter in length than judgments handed down by the other tribunals, the SCSL judgments are replete with words such as "brutal," "heinous" and "sanctity of human life."[18] In all cases the SCSL judges indicated as the crimes were directed against the civilian population and in particular against the most vulnerable elements, namely women and children. Most certainly the acknowledgment of the victims' pain is central to the SCSL judgments.

We believe that giving space to victims' statements, showing empathy for the conditions suffered and the consequent trauma, and reinforcing the testimony with words of condemnation are instruments judges use to make the message of international justice more understandable to the victims. More than any punishment,

---

[16] See Situation in the Democratic Republic of the Congo in the Case of The Prosecutor v. Germain Katanga, No. ICC-01/04-01/07, March 7, 2014, para 992.

[17] Judgment of the Sentencing of Monina Fofana and Allieu Kondewa, Case No. SCSL-04-14-T, October 9, 2007, para 48.

[18] Prosecutor v. Issa Hassan Sesay, Morris Kallon, and Augustine Gbao, Case No. SCSL-04-15-T, April 8, 2009, para 52.

statements of condemnation by the judges and the use of moral language stand out as universal reminders of the horrors committed during war. These judgments stand out because they have collected the memories and provide a permanent record of those whose names or existence might be easily forgotten – the children, the women, and men who became the object of international crimes.

The moral condemnation of the crimes and the stigmatization of those who have perpetrated the horrors of war can empower the victims and bridge the distance often felt with the international justice system. We contend that the empathy shown by judges toward those who come forward to testify about their experiences during war heightens the legitimacy of the tribunals in the eyes of the individuals and fosters support for international prosecutions. It creates a basis for the justification of the exercise of the authority by international judges and their emphasis on the human rights of victims, who through words of compassion demonstrate their ability to capture the human experience beyond the legal definition of the crimes.

Local Communities

On a broader scale, we contend that expressing moral reprobation for these international crimes addresses some of the needs of the local communities as well. Often judges refer to the crimes committed as having a "devastating impact on the community"[19] or "catastrophic" consequence[20] for the societies affected by human rights violations and persecutions. We think of the local community as comprising two different elements. First, there is the local community in general whose social functioning is disrupted by human rights atrocities. Scholars have indicated that the damage caused to the social structure of communities affected by wars is particularly widespread and touches upon the different strata of a society through the "loss of loved ones, jobs, political institutions and arrangements, and social networks" (Fletcher 2004, 1023). Thus, human rights violations, genocide, and crimes against humanity are not only violations of international criminal law, they represent the fall of a society's values and the disappearance of social order. International prosecutions and punishment are meant to rebuild social order and trust in the rule of law.

There is also that part of the local community who supported the crimes; the bystanders who stood passively by as crimes were committed; those who might have facilitated, even in minor ways, the commission of crimes; the public and private supporters of campaigns of violence; and those who are eventually released after serving their sentences. The stigmatization of the crimes as a form of collective responsibility and as a disruption of societal order, although contrary to the principle of individual accountability, sends a clear message that crimes of this magnitude cannot be perpetrated without the support of the collective. As cogently stated by

---

[19] The Prosecutor v. Popovic et al., Case No. IT-05-88, June 10, 2010, para 866.
[20] The Prosecutor v. Radislav Krstic, Case No. IT-98-33-T, August 2, 2001, para 90.

Gustafson (1998, 68–69) "a Hitler – like a Stalin, a Karadzic, a Tudjman, a Mao – is only as strong as the power of mass obedience and support" and that the collective carries the moral burden as well as the brunt of the crimes committed. The messages of moral reprobation and condemnation pronounced by international judges are meant to restore the strength of law and shape a culture of *collective* moral indignation against irrational hatred and ethnic violence.

In nearly all cases of mass atrocity we find that after the crimes have been committed a denial industry arises and elected officials, self-appointed historians, journalists and others begin claiming that no such crimes ever took place. Whether it is the Holocaust, the Armenian genocide, the crimes of the Bosnian war or the Rwandan genocide, one finds these individuals arguing that whatever crimes occurred were random and involved a small number of victims. They scoff at the notion that crimes were planned and targeted thousands if not more victims. Because so much emphasis has been placed on the role of the tribunals as objective truth tellers, their role in countering these denials is critically important.

However, in this task the international criminal justice system faces challenges. Despite the incredible attention given by the international community to the crimes occurring in countries like the former Yugoslavia and Rwanda, the distance between international prosecutions and the needs of a local society to go back to normality have been growing over the years. Whether because of inadequate outreach programs or because of a lack of understanding of local realities (to say nothing of the individualized nature of criminal trials), international justice focuses more on the individuals, whether victim or perpetrator, than on the society against which crimes have been perpetrated or within which crimes were masterminded. By trying to reduce the perception of a collective guilt for the crimes committed, the international criminal justice system has neglected to determine the effects that prosecutions might have on societal peace and the fact that individuals are members of a larger society within which the memory of crimes is reinforced and reiterated. The distance becomes greater when international punishments for the crimes committed are too lenient compared to the corresponding national criminal punishments. While the focus on individual liability, especially political and military leaders, for violations of international law is legally appropriate and justifiable, the lack of attention accorded the role of societies in creating criminally permissive environments may well undermine the deterrence and peace-enhancing elements of international justice (Drumbl 2007b).

We believe that international judges can contribute to reconciling victims, perpetrators, and societies by expressing outrage for violations of principles of humanity that go beyond the legal and political rationale conflicting parties may use to justify their actions, by allowing the collective to see the horror of the acts detached from the legal and political consequences of adjudication. The most important aspect of the moral condemnation delivered by judges in their final judgment is the ability to remind us that, beyond a courtroom, a criminal legal definition, and a punishment, there are memories to pass on to future generations so as to avoid the repetition of the horrors. In this regard what is most important is that the moral condemnation becomes part of a collective memory of the people that can stop society's aberrations and reinforce the protection of individuals. As stated by Schabas (1997):

> for the victims, and for the public in general, the thirst for justice may be better satisfied by *society's condemnation* of anti-social behavior than by the actual punishment of the offenders. What is desired is a judgment, *a declaration by society*, and the identification and stigmatization of the perpetrator. This alone is often sufficient redress. What is actually done to the offender as a result of conviction may be far less important. (emphasis added)

Prosecutors and the Global Community of Courts

In handing down their sentences and lengthy judgments, international judges express moral norms that address a larger, global, judicial community, which has become particularly relevant during the past two decades. While the legacy of the Nuremberg and Tokyo tribunals had remained dormant for some fifty years, the work of the ad hoc tribunals in the 1990s has fostered the creation of numerous other international and hybrid courts, which have taken most of their legal and procedural frameworks from the ICTR and ICTY. In a short period of time, the ad hoc tribunals have become more than "legal precedents" – they have become bearers of global moral norms that are intended to change the perception of the crimes adjudicated and reframe the role that international criminal justice plays in adjudicating crimes. Specifically, we argue that merely describing international law violations and adjudicating cases is insufficient when sitting in judgment of horrific crimes. The law alone has limited power to constrain behavior or express moral judgments. We view judges as operating within a complex network of the international judicial communities and communicating with them about the importance of defining breaches of international humanitarian law as "violations of principles of humanity [. . .] and breaches of norms of morality" (Kelsen 1943) against which international law alone may just be deficient or powerless.

The task upon which international judges embark in addressing the international community, which works for the implementation of international criminal justice, is somewhat easier than sending the same message to victims and local communities. At the international level, international criminal law is already viewed as a "vehicle of global justice" (DeGuzman 2012, 280) and of moral obligation toward those victimized by human rights violations and as a vessel of global, moral values. Making moral judgments is an important aspect of the establishment of international global order, which is widely expected by the "global community." International judges see their work as expressing not only principles of illegality, but reflecting a specific order of societal values and, more precisely, of what an international order "esteems and what it abhors" (Amann 2002, 118).

We see this global community as one that comprises prosecutors and international judges operating in different international courts. We believe that judges intend to address prosecutors with their moral statements to heighten the human context of crimes and underlie the importance of prosecutorial independence from political and financial constraints. In an international justice framework in which international prosecutors enjoy a certain amount of prosecutorial discretion, judges have often found themselves disagreeing about charges not being included in the indictments and individuals not being charged. It is known that, challenged by limited resources, facing strict deadlines set up by the Security Council, and striving to establish legitimacy in the early years of the ad hoc tribunals, prosecutors rushed to charge war criminals with counts that could be easily proven and secure certain convictions. Despite ICTY Prosecutor Richard Goldstone's aspiration to see the highest ranking officials standing trial, the prosecuting team had to start rapidly and charge lower ranking officials, with readily proven counts based on the gathering of evidence while the conflict was still ongoing. In the midst of pursuing a rapid international justice some of the more difficult charges to prove, such as rape, were not as thoroughly investigated and the time invested in pursuing high ranking officials was limited. Judicial ethical statements send a message that the principles through which cases shall be investigated and judged should not be dictated by political considerations. It indicates that the interest of justice resides in the moral obligation to prosecute human rights violations by looking at the principles at the core of the protections established by the international community – namely human dignity and morality.

We also see international judges as interacting in a global dialogue with other judges operating within the international criminal justice system. We believe that through moral reprobation judges try to create a community of practitioners expressing the values of the international community in general. We suggest that one goal in utilizing the expressive capacity of the law is to bridge the divide between the purely legal goals established for the tribunals and the values and morals for which the international justice system stands.

There are many reasons that justify the use of rhetorical moral condemnation by the judges. As mentioned above, chief among them is the need to fill the shortcomings of international criminal justice in the face of crimes of a horrific magnitude, as well as the need to close the gap between a geographically and morally distant courtroom and the affected communities. We believe that criticisms depicting international justice as "too normative and abstract, and lacking context and historical background" (Banjeglav 2013, 35) are at the core of "judicial expressivism." Through moral condemnation judges enter a public sphere – one in which we find the victims, the local and international communities – and show that the international criminal justice system is anchored in moral values and fully aware of the need of responding to the violence of the past with something more than verdicts. With their words, judges direct their audiences to think about the events adjudicated as a historical account of the suffering, in which victims are given back the humanity taken from them through the crimes.

We also believe that on judgment day, while sitting on the bench and pronouncing words of reprobation in front of the indictees, prosecutors, defense lawyers, victims, and the community at large, judges send a stronger and more permanent message than they could ever send with any punishment. They stigmatize individuals and their roles; deprive crimes of any political and legal justification, and write, in the pages of the judgments, the names, the stories, and the pain of common people so that these are not forgotten. We believe that judges use moral condemnation to deprive humanity of the chance of condoning itself for what happened and justifying inertia in the wanton destruction of the most basic rules of humanity.

DATA COLLECTION AND METHODS

Having argued that judges will utilize judgments for expressive purposes we next turn to assessing the validity of this general hypothesis. While others have made such arguments (e.g., Sloane 2007), there has been no attempt to determine the extent to which judges engage in this conduct with which we are familiar. We are embarking into unexplored terrain. Rather than adopting one particular methodology to determine when, where or how judgments might be used for expressive purposes, we sought evidence of such opinion writing through numerous strategies. We utilized textual analysis programs, word and phrase searches, and other types of mechanisms by which to ascertain whether we could find language in judgments, both trial and appellate, that a reasonable observer could argue represented expressive language.

As a first step in this process we sought to define exactly what is meant by this term "expressivism" or more precisely, "expressive language." In a general sense all language is expressive since it attempts to communicate or express ideas whether simple and direct, or complex and deeply meaningful. Judgments at the tribunals convey a great deal of information from reviews of procedural matters, descriptions of evidence, analysis of witness statements, theories of liability to assessments of these matters in totality to reach conclusions. The judgments also review the arguments put forward by the prosecution and the defense in order to evaluate their plausibility. Thus, on one level a great deal – quite likely the vast majority – of language in judgments is present because of instrumental purposes. More precisely, judgments are filled with language designed to take the reader through the evidence and arguments in order to reach a verdict, determine a sentence or decide whether to uphold a particular ground of appeal. A great deal of this language is descriptive/analytical, while the rest is opinion and reflects the judges' assessment of the accuracy of the evidence or evaluation of the legal doctrines at issue. These are the primary purposes of the judgment – they are legal documents with a judicial purpose. Thus, we should not attach any particular expressive purpose to language that is designed to serve this fundamental aim. Instead, we argue that expressive language is "extra" language that is not a necessary element of the need for the judges to reach legal conclusions. Thus, because expressivist statements are designed to convey broader moral reasoning, exhortations or condemnations they are, in effect dicta, or:

> A statement of opinion or belief considered authoritative because of the dignity of the person making it. The term is generally used to describe a court's discussion of points or questions not raised by the record or its suggestion of rules not applicable in the case at bar. Judicial dictum is an opinion by a court on a question that is not essential to its decision even though it may be directly involved.[21]

Expressivist statements, however, are more than just additional, non-binding language that does not directly pertain to the fundamental purposes of a judgment.

Expressivist statements are also expressions of morality, and thus serve a much broader purpose than dicta, which typically pertain to legal matters. They are, in a sense, meta, macro or universalist statements designed to convey a moral opinion regarding the issues and actions that are being litigated. While they express a moral or ethical evaluation, they are not designed to reach any kind of legal conclusion regarding the defendant's culpability or the legality of the actions at issue. Rather, they represent a moral judgment, evaluation or interpretation of the action itself – the massacre of thousands of individuals or the brutal violence perpetrated upon one individual – that we, the larger international community, should condemn regardless of who committed the violence and the liability of any one individual for such violence. They are, in effect, an attempt by the judges to find a universal ground of morality upon which the whole of the international community can appreciate and understand the actions of the defendant.

Implicit in this conceptualization of expressive language is intentionality. Judges deliberately include such language in their opinions to provide a moral judgment. These are not passing references or perfunctory descriptions of heinous behavior. Nor are we seeking to infer larger meanings and messages from ordinary or legally germane language. Given that the vast majority of the language of judgments is intended to reach legal conclusions, the inclusion of statements that are not so designed represents, we believe, a perceived need to step outside the legal purposes of judgments and acknowledge that the behavior of which the defendants are accused is of an exceptional nature. Such actions should not be treated as typical. We contend that judges, as moved by their own individual consciences and morality feel compelled to set aside their role as adjudicators and adopt a larger role of judges as moral arbiters to recognize exceptional violence for what it is, condemn it or place it in a larger moral universe. Perhaps they may even find instances of good behavior they wish to highlight.

---

[21] As from the Cornell University Law School Legal Information Institute found at https://www.law.cornell.edu/wex/dicta.

In sum, we contend that expressivist statements are those that (1) do not serve a specific legal purpose; (2) represent a moral statement regarding the actions being litigated; and (3) are intentionally included in opinions by judges when they feel compelled to write as human observers rather than legal adjudicators. Utilizing this definition we sought to find instances of expressivist language in both trial chamber judgments and appellate judgments at all four tribunals.

The first strategy we adopted to search the judgments for evidence of such language focused on the second element of the definition. That is, we sought to find examples of certain words or terms of moral condemnation or reasoning in the judgments by using various search strategies and computer-based textual analyses of opinions. This strategy, however, proved to be ineffective. In order to utilize search engines to find such language we developed dictionaries of various moral or judgmental words and phrases to determine the frequency with which they were utilized. These words or phrases were ones involving emotional or moral opinions of the defendant's actions. This resulted in numerous issues and complications with many false positive and false negative findings. Many of the words and terms we used were already part of the legal terminology of international law, such as cruel, outrage, heinous, and many other words that are part of the legal lexicon and even appear in the statutes of the tribunals. Thus, we could not conclude the usage of such words fit our definition because their employment served a legal purpose. We were also concerned that while we might build a rather impressively sized set of terms that would be largely inclusive of words used to morally condemn or adjectives used to describe violence, we could not develop a listing that was as inclusive as possible. We were concerned that some terms might be left out, or that the judges might use less evocative language to reach exceptional conclusions.

Therefore, we elected instead to focus on the third element of the definition and search for evidence of the trial chamber and appellate judges communicating their views, evaluations and opinions as human observers. In effect, we sought language that would clearly indicate the judges "owned" these statements. This necessitated a very different search strategy in which we looked for all examples of the trial chambers and the appellate chambers intentionally conveying their opinions. Put simply, we searched for every single instance in which the words "the trial chamber," "the chambers" or the "appeals chamber" appeared as the subject of a sentence, as in "the Trial Chamber finds . . . ," or "the appeals chamber observes . . . ".[22] This strategy resulted in thousands of such "hits." For example, we found many instances of phrases such as "the trial chamber finds that evidence provided by Witness A . . . .," or "the chambers is of the view that the doctrine of joint criminal enterprise . . . " or "the appeals chamber rejects the arguments put forward by the defense . . . ". This represented the first step in the process. As every usage of such language was found

---

[22] The word "we" often appears in judgments, but we found that, in general, the judges more consistently relied on speaking of themselves in the third person.

we then read the text thereafter to determine what the judges were seeking to convey by speaking in the first person plural. The vast majority of the time the purpose was to reach a legal conclusion or to note the procedural aspects of the case and thus did not represent, in our judgment, the use of expressivist language. We relied on our own interpretation of the language coming after the use of these first person pronouncements.

By reading the text that appeared after every instance in which the words, "the trial chamber," "the chambers" or "the appeals chamber" occurred we had to rely on our own interpretation of the text, and thus our particular subjective interpretation of the words. This leaves open the possibility that we too might make false positive and false negative assessments of the occurrence of expressivist language. To guard against the occurrence of such errors we have taken the following steps. First, to reassure the reader that we have kept the potential for the occurrence of false positive errors (claiming we have found an instance of the use of expressivist language when in fact there was no such usage of language by the judges) to a minimum we have included in the appendix every occurrence where we believe we found expressivist language. The reader may judge for herself whether the passages we list are actually instances of expressivist language or if the judges were seeking to convey a different meaning. Reducing the likelihood of false negative findings in which we overlook the use of truly expressivist language is significantly more difficult to address. There may well be occasions in which our interpretation of the language differs from another reader's.

Because there is what we would consider to be an unacceptably significant probability that our readings of the judges' words were not always the correct one, if such near perfect accuracy is even possible, we chose to utilize a more conservative method of analysis. Rather than attempting to utilize any of the empirical and quantitative methods we have employed in other chapters to predict the occurrence of the expressive use of language, we elected instead to use a more qualitative approach and provide the reader with examples and textual analyses of the use of such language. Hence, our aim is to discuss the purpose and prevalence of expressivist language as a (hopefully) first step in the development of a theory of the use of expressivist language.[23] We would not claim that our list is exhaustive of all uses of expressive language for the moral import of some judgments and some writing might not have signaled to us that the judges were engaged in such behavior. We do believe,

---

[23] We note at the outset that our methodology does not capture all of the likely uses of expressive language and that we do not examine the summary judgments that are announced directly from the bench (but would make an excellent subject of further analysis). Some number of such uses occur in passages that are not preceded by our key words, such as "The trial chambers said . . . ," but we cannot be certain how many. There are tens of thousands of pages of these judgments that makes reading all of them to identify such uses a lengthy and difficult operation. Thus, we must be content for now with knowing that we have one particular sample of such uses and put these data to effective use.

however, that we have found ample evidence that judges do use judgments for expressive purposes.

We have chosen what we believe is a representative and illustrative number of examples of expressivist language to assess what we perceive to be the purposes behind the use of such language. These and other instances of expressive language we identified through our search strategy are found in the Appendix. In our examination of the uses of expressive language we noticed several trends in what we perceived to be the reasoning behind the words and the purposes for which the words were communicated. We do not suggest that the inductively derived taxonomy we develop is final or complete or that there could not be other categories used to describe the language. Nonetheless, we believe our taxonomy captures the most basic purposes of messages being conveyed through the tribunals' judgments. These uses of expressive language, we contend, are evidence of the judges acting as entrepreneurial decision makers who find reason to go beyond the basic purposes of judgments to reach moral and universal conclusions that speak to the wider audiences we described earlier.

Before we begin, however, we must make note of one trend in the data that both authors observed independently of one another. We found that a substantial majority of the instances of expressive language came mostly from the ICTY, and also the SCSL. In part this is because the ICTY is the oldest tribunal and has issued by far the most judgments, especially in comparison to the SCSL and the ICC. We believe that given the number of judgments issued and the length of these judgments as measured in the number of words, that, roughly, the ICTY and the SCSL contributed what we perceived to be their "fair share" of expressive language. In our search of all the trial and appellate judgments, we found almost no instances of the ICTR or the ICC using expressive language. In the case of the ICC this is not entirely surprising given the paucity of judgments thus far (four individuals have had their cases adjudicated at the time of writing). What was unexpected and quite surprising to us was that neither author found instances in which we could plausibly argue that the ICTR trial chambers or appellate judges used expressive language. We suspected that given the brutality, efficiency and enormity of the Rwandan genocide that there would be ample opportunity for the judges to step outside their role as adjudicators and speak to the need for moral condemnation of such violence. But while we found many instances, using our particular search strategy in which ICTR judges detailed such violence, they do so to convey the facts. Indeed, we found that considerable attention was devoted to describing witness testimony and attempting to reconcile differences among the testimonies of individuals and between an individual's written statement and verbal testimony. Perhaps too because most of those charged by the ICTR played a critical role in the deaths of some eight hundred thousand individuals singling out some individuals or some conduct for special condemnation did not seem nearly so urgent or compelling. The level of violence and brutality in Rwanda was the norm while in Yugoslavia there were more cases of individuals being charged for "lesser crimes." By contrast, the violence in Sierra Leone was also consistently horrific across a number of years and yet the SCSL judges did use expressive language in a number of instances to condemn such violence. Ultimately, we are truly puzzled by the absence of expressive language from the ICTR.

After having read through the ICTR judgments ourselves we employed research assistants to thoroughly read and review all language of judgments in a select sample of six cases (e.g., *Akayesu*, *Kambanda*, *Bagosora*) where we thought there would be ample opportunity for judges to use expressive language. We thought of these as "easy" test cases for our expectations regarding the prevalence of expressive language given the high profile nature of these cases, which we might expect to reach a large audience. And while our research assistants did find some instances of what might be expressive uses of language in ICTR judgments, even in these cases we found that the ICTR judgments did not quite reach that threshold as the legal purposes of the language seemed to dominate. For example, in the Appellate decision in the *Bagosora* leadership case, the judges opined:

> 729. In light of the foregoing, the Appeals Chamber need not address the parties' remaining contentions. The Appeals Chamber underscores that the desecration of Prime Minister Uwilingiyimana's corpse constituted a profound assault on human dignity meriting unreserved condemnation under international law.[1680] Such crimes strike at the core of national and human identity. However, the Appeals Chamber finds, Judge Pocar dissenting, that Bagosora was not charged on this basis, and thus cannot be held legally responsible for this act.[24]

While the language *might* be viewed as expressing moral condemnation, we are also struck by the fact that the defendant was not charged with this crime. Thus, whatever moral ambitions might have emanated from such language are quickly and brusquely undermined by noting the defendant's lack of liability. We looked very closely at the *Kambanda* decisions. Given that he was prime minister during the genocide and had confessed his crimes, we might have expected this case to be primed for the use of expressive language. Instead, we find uses of language such as, "the crimes for which Jean Kambanda is responsible carry an intrinsic gravity, and their widespread, atrocious and systematic character is particularly shocking to the human conscience."[25] There is nothing wrong with such sentiments, but the words do not seem to do justice to the crimes.

As mentioned earlier, we are less puzzled by the absence of such expressive language at the ICC. Judges have shown little preoccupation with the explicit moral condemnation of the crimes committed. There are no statements which go beyond the legalist determination of guilt, similar to those handed down by the ICTY or the SCSL, which could be *directly* attributed to the ICC judges. The extensive use of victims' statements and experts' testimony has provided a painstaking account of the

[24] Theoneste Bagosora and Anatole Nsengiyumva v. The Prosecutor, ICTR-98–41-A, December 14, 2011, para 729.
[25] The Prosecutor v. Jean Kambanda, ICTR 97–23-S, September 4, 1998, para 61.

events charged in the cases against Thomas Lubanga Dyilo and Germain Katanga, for example. However, short of the victims' voices and experts' accounts, judges have been very methodical in reporting the events, using very few remarks showing moral outrage over the facts of the cases. On this, some have noted how the opening paragraphs of the *Lubanga Dyilo* judgment – which gives a brief but detailed history of the case – are in stark contrast with Moreno-Ocampo's explanation for charging only "offenses related to child soldiers," which called for a "moral duty" to adjudicate crimes that "jeopardize humankind" (Amann 2013, 418–419). We believe that the absence of expressive statements such as those present in the ICTY and SCSL judgments might be attributable to three different factors. On the one hand, the court has only so far adjudicated a handful of cases and thus the number of possible judicial statements on which we can rely is limited. Additionally, we believe that the relatively unfettered judicial discretion with which the judges of the ICTY operated is absent at the ICC. Statutory regulations and stricter Rules of Procedures and Evidence give the ICC judges an extensive legalese vocabulary on which to rely. Lastly, we must remember that, when the ICTY brought to light the crimes perpetrated during the war in the ex-Yugoslavia the international community was shocked by the images of men, children and women being deported and confined in camps. Those images reignited the memory of the horrors of the Holocaust and very likely triggered a greater moral outrage by the judges adjudicating the cases.

In our reading of the occurrences of expressive language we have chosen to categorize these instances into five separate groupings. First, there are those occasions in which the judges used expressive language to call attention to the magnitude and scale of the crimes. Second, there are those instances where the judges utilized expressive language to condemn the heinousness or brutality of the violence. Third, there were instances where the judges sought to use the words of the victims and the accused to convey a moral message. Fourth, there were instances where the judges sought to affix a moral or personal responsibility on the accused rather than a legal liability. Fifth, there were occasions when the judges issued universalist, moral condemnations of the violence as well as used non-legalistic language to describe the violence, such as the use of the word "tragedy." Because these are subjective interpretations, and because many uses of expressive language do not always neatly fall into one category, we chose not to count their occurrence, but to highlight instead the most noteworthy examples.

THE USE OF EXPRESSIVE LANGUAGE

The Magnitude and Scale of the Crimes

The enormity of the atrocities committed in the former Yugoslavia, Rwanda, Sierra Leone and the Congo (most notably for the ICC) was chief among the reasons the United Nations and the international community sought to punish the guilty.

The Rwandan genocide was likely the most efficient genocide in history – eight hundred thousand humans were slaughtered in one hundred days. The wars of the former Yugoslavia dragged on throughout the 1990s leaving millions of victims and refugees in their wake. The civil wars in Sierra Leone and the Congo also took place over many years and created massive loss and disruption of life. The scale of these crimes was so enormous that the guilty could not be ignored and left to destroy their societies further. The international community was forced to take notice, and so too have judges felt compelled to recognize in their opinions that they were addressing no "ordinary" violations of international law, but ones whose size demanded an "extraordinary" response.

We find several instances, especially in the case of the ICTY, of judges pausing in their adjudicatory roles to recognize such massive human suffering. Their motivation may stem from a desire to recognize such crimes as historical fact and deliver the verdict of history, especially so that little doubt might exist in the future that such crimes did occur. Judges may wish to recognize the suffering of the victims and acknowledge the enormity of the events they experienced. They may seek to deliver a message to the world about the seriousness of the crimes committed and the number of lives lost. Whatever their more specific motivations, judges have engaged in what we argue are expressive uses of language to address the magnitude of the crimes committed. The passage below from the judgment of the Trial Chamber in the case of Momcilo Krajisnik, former member of the Bosnian Serb collective presidency, is instructive. Krajisnik was found responsible for the political campaign and national efforts to establish a Bosnian Serb state through ethnic cleansing and other widespread war crimes and crimes against humanity in Bosnia-Herzegovina during the first half of the 1990s. The Trial Chamber wrote:

> There is no need to retell here the countless stories of brutality, violence, and depravation that were brought to the Chamber's attention. But hidden amidst the cold statistics on the number of people killed and forced away from their homes, lies a multitude of individual stories of suffering and ordeal – psychological violence, mutilation, outrages upon personal dignity, rape, suffering for loved ones, despair, death. A sentence, however harsh, will never be able to rectify the wrongs, and will be able to soothe only to a limited extent the suffering of the victims, their feelings of deprivation, anguish, and hopelessness.[26]

Here we see the judges not only alluding, in very human terms, to the suffering of victims, but also asserting that punishments for such crimes can never do justice to this suffering. They recognize that the evidence on the violence of war is not just a collection of statistics, but a compendium of many stories of personal loss.

There is similar if even more grandiloquent use of expressive language in the ICTY's first judgment regarding the genocide at Srebrenica in the *Krstic* case. The

[26] The Prosecutor v. Momcilo Krajisnik, Case No. IT-00–39-T, September 27, 2006, para 1146.

Trial Chamber in this case appeared to be fully aware of the historical import of the crime and their first judgment upon it. We quote from a rather lengthy passage to convey the full depth of the emotion apparent in the judgment which appears almost immediately in the second paragraph of the judgment:

> The events of the nine days from July 10–19 1995 in Srebrenica defy description in their horror and their implications for humankind's capacity to revert to acts of brutality under the stresses of conflict. In little over one week, thousands of lives were extinguished, irreparably rent or simply wiped from the pages of history. The Trial Chamber leaves it to historians and social psychologist to plumb the depths of this episode of the Balkan conflict and to probe for deep-seated causes. The task at hand is a more modest one: to find, from the evidence presented during the trial, what happened during that period of about nine days and, ultimately, whether the defendant in this case, General Krstic, was criminally responsible, under the tenets of international law, for his participation in them. The Trial Chamber cannot permit itself the indulgence of expressing how it feels about what happened in Srebrenica, or even how individuals as well as national and international groups not the subject of this case contributed to the tragedy. This defendant, like all others, deserves individualised consideration and can be convicted only if the evidence presented in court shows, beyond a reasonable doubt, that he is guilty of acts that constitute crimes covered by the Statute of the Tribunal ("Statute"). Thus, the Trial Chamber concentrates on setting forth, in detail, the facts surrounding this compacted nine days of hell and avoids expressing rhetorical indignation that these events should ever have occurred at all. In the end, no words of comment can lay bare the saga of Srebrenica more graphically than a plain narrative of the events themselves, or expose more poignantly the waste of war and ethnic hatreds and the long road that must still be travelled to ease their bitter legacy.[27]

The expressive language in this passage conveys several ideas. First, and oddly enough the judges use expressive language to, in a sense, deny that they are in fact doing precisely that. They note in non-legal language the depths of the tragedy, and argue they must leave it to others to understand just why such events like Srebrenica occur. The judges protest that they cannot allow themselves "the indulgence" of expressing their feelings, yet they have just done that. While rightfully noting that their verdict must be fair and dispassionate, they also recognize the human dimension of their job as they attest to the immensity of the tragedy. And like the passage from the *Krajisnik* opinion, they also claim that words, like statistics, cannot do justice to the suffering of the victims. Thus, the passage neatly captures both a human awareness of the events at issue while recognizing that their principal function is not to pontificate on the meaning of what happened at Srebrenica, but to sit in judgment of one man's role.

We find similar language used in the *Galic* Trial Chamber judgment, which was also quoted, verbatim, in General Galic's appeals decision. General Galic was found

---

[27] The Prosecutor v. Radislav Krstic, Case No. IT-98–33-T, August 2, 2001, para 2 as found at http://www .icty.org/x/cases/krstic/tjug/en/krs-tjo10802e.pdf.

guilty of liability for war crimes and crimes against humanity during the siege of Sarajevo in which many civilians were deliberately targeted by Bosnian Serb snipers and artillery that ringed the city throughout the three-year war:

> The gravity of the offences committed by General Galic is established by their scale, pattern and virtually continuous repetition, almost daily, over many months. Inhabitants of Sarajevo – men, women, children and elderly persons – were terrorized and hundreds of civilians were killed and thousands wounded during daily activities such as attending funerals, tending vegetable plots, fetching water, shopping, going to hospital, commuting within the city, or while at home. The Majority of the Trial Chamber also takes into consideration the physical and psychological suffering inflicted on the victims. Sarajevo was not a city where occasional random acts of violence against civilians occurred or where living conditions were simply hard. This was an anguishing environment in which, at a minimum hundreds of men, women, children, and elderly people were killed, and thousands were wounded and more generally terrorized.[28]

The *Galic* language is less expressive perhaps than some of the other opinions cited here, but it is also noteworthy for being reiterated verbatim by the Appeals Chamber. The Appeals Chamber, however, used these words in part to demonstrate that the sentence handed down by the Trial Chamber was manifestly inadequate given the scale of the violence as the Chamber itself had described. In effect, the Appeals Chamber used the Trial Chamber's very words to demonstrate the inadequacy of the punishment.

The *Kupreskic* Trial Chamber judgment parallels much of the structure and content of many of these passages in detailing the magnitude of the crimes committed. This case involved the destruction wrought in the Bosnian Muslim village of Ahmici that was carried out by Bosnian Croat forces during the brief war that erupted between these two communities in the midst of the larger war against the Bosnian Serbs. Here the judges write:

> The massacre carried out in the village of Ahmici on 16 April 1993 comprises an individual yet appalling episode of that widespread pattern of persecutory violence. The tragedy which unfolded that day carried all the hallmarks of an ancient tragedy. For one thing, it possessed unity of time, space and action. The killing, wounding and burning took place in the same area, within a few hours and was carried out by a relatively small groups of members of the Bosnian Croatian military forces: the HVO and the special units of the Croatian Military Police, the so-called Jokers. Over the course of the several months taken up by these trial proceedings, we have seen before us, through the narration of the victims and the survivors, the unfolding of a great tragedy. And just as in the ancient tragedies where the misdeeds are never shown but are only recounted by the actors, numerous witnesses have told the Trial

[28] The Prosecutor v. Stanislav Galic, Case No. IT-98-29-T 5, December 5, 2003, para 764 as found at http://www.icty.org/x/cases/galic/tjug/en/gal-tj031205e.pdf.

Chamber of the human tragedies which befell so many of the ordinary inhabitants of that small village.[29]

The judges call the events that took place in the village of Ahmici by elements of the Bosnian Croat forces against the town's Muslim population a "tragedy." In fact, the judges use the word "tragedy" five times within this single paragraph. They note how the events, which took place by one set of military forces against a small town in a quite brief period of time, resemble so many others tragedies of the past. They recognize the enormity of what happens through the many narratives shared by the witnesses and others. Indeed, it appears as though the judges are writing of the events at Ahmici as though they were a Greek tragedy. This harkening back to other events and to a universal appreciation for what a tragedy entails shows the judges speaking in universal terms to place this tragedy in a broader human context.

Heinousness and Brutality

We found numerous instances of the judges using their opinions to call attention to the exceptional brutality of certain crimes or the zeal with which the defendant(s) carried out their atrocities. Often such language is used in determining the sentences meted out to the guilty, particularly in the discussion of aggravating factors. On other occasions the judges conclude their description of a particularly horrific incident to reflect upon its savagery and condemn the violence. In the passage below from the first Trial Chamber judgment in the *Celebici* prison camp case in which Bosnian Muslims were found guilty of war crimes and crimes against humanity perpetrated on Bosnian Serbs, the judges were focused on determining whether rape could be considered a form of torture. Hence, while reaching a legal conclusion, the judges sought to also demonstrate they recognized the trauma of the crime as well:

> The Trial Chamber considers the rape of any person to be a despicable act which strikes at the very core of human dignity and physical integrity. The condemnation and punishment of rape becomes all the more urgent where it is committed by, or at the instigation of, a public official, or with the consent or acquiescence of such an official. Rape causes severe pain and suffering, both physical and psychological. The psychological suffering of persons upon whom rape is inflicted may be exacerbated by social and cultural conditions and can be particularly acute and long lasting. Furthermore, it is difficult to envisage circumstances in which rape, by, or at the instigation of a public official, or with the consent or acquiescence of an official, could be considered as occurring for a purpose that does not, in some way, involve punishment, coercion, discrimination or intimidation. In the view of this Trial Chamber this is inherent in situations of armed conflict.[30]

---

[29] The Prosecutor v. Zoran Kupreskic et al., Case No. IT-95–16-T, January 14, 2000, para 754, as found at http://www.icty.org/x/cases/kupreskic/tjug/en/kup-tj000114e.pdf.

[30] The Prosecutor v. Zejnil Delalic et al., Case No. IT-96–21-T, November 16, 1998, para 495 as found at http://www.icty.org/x/cases/mucic/tjug/en/981116_judg_en.pdf.

In one concise paragraph, the Trial Chamber recognizes the inhumanity and trauma of rape as well as the enduring pain and shame it causes. The judges recognize that rape is widespread and endemic during armed conflict. They argue that when rape is committed by public offices, it is not just a sexual assault, but an act of coercion and intimidation. It is this latter finding that is used to anchor the judges' reasoning that rape is also a form of torture for those acts involve the infliction of pain by public officials to acquire information or further a policy.

One finds several fairly emotional passages from the case of *Lukic and Lukic* at the ICTY as the judges grappled with the horrors inflicted by these Bosnian Serb members of a paramilitary force in Visegard, Bosnia-Herzegovina. While there were several acts for which the two were convicted, the incidents in which the Lukic cousins herded men, women, children and the elderly into homes and then set them ablaze led the judges to issue especially pointed condemnations:

> The serious gravity of these multiple murders and savage beatings must be recognized individually, even as the Trial Chamber considers the particular gravity of the monstrous mass killings that Milan Lukić committed in the Pionirska street fire and the Bikavac fire. The Trial Chamber reiterates that the Pionirska street fire and the Bikavac fires exemplify the worst acts of inhumanity that one person may inflict upon others. The Trial Chamber recalls its observations that these horrific events remain imprinted on the memory for the viciousness of the incendiary attack, for the sheer callousness and cruelty of herding, trapping, and locking the victims in the two houses, thereby rendering them helpless in the ensuing inferno, and for the degree of pain and suffering inflicted on the victims as they were burned alive.[31]

This chapter began with a passage from the same trial chamber judgment, in which the judges recognized that the defendants had committed acts that, even in the roster of horrors of the former Yugoslavia, stood out for their exceptional ruthlessness and cruelty. Indeed, even in the passages in the judgment that merely seek to describe these events, the words possess a particular vividness that evokes revulsion and horror. Perhaps because these acts were so personal and discreet, as opposed to many of the more "orderly" atrocities carried out with bureaucratic efficiency, they seem to demand a moral response.

Judgments from the Special Court for Sierra Leone contain many references to the brutal atrocities that characterized that civil war as found in this judgment in the case of Moinina Fofana and Allieu Kondewa who were responsible for numerous crimes committed against innocent civilians:

> The Chamber considers these crimes to have had a significant physical and psychological impact on the victims of such crimes, on the relatives of the victims, and on those in the broader community. The testimony of witnesses heard by the Chamber

---

[31] The Prosecutor v. Milan Lukic and Sredoje Lukic, Case No. IT-98–32/1, July 20, 2009, para 1061. As found at http://www.icty.org/x/cases/milan_lukic_sredoje_lukic/tjug/en/090720_j.pdf.

during the trial, and appended to the Prosecution brief in Annex D, indicates the impact of such events such as amputations and the loss of family members has had on the lives of victims and witnesses. As appropriately described and summarized by our sister Trial Chamber II, "victims who had their limbs hacked off not only endured extreme pain and suffering, if they survived, but lost their mobility and capacity to earn a living or even to undertake simple daily tasks. They have been rendered dependent on others for the rest of their lives." In particular, the Chamber notes the lasting effect on these crimes on victims such as TF2–015, who was the only survivor of an attack on 65 civilians who were hacked to death by machete or shot, and who was himself hacked with a machete and rolled into a swamp on top of the dead bodies in the belief that he was dead."[32]

In the above passage the Trial Chamber sought to communicate the consequences of the savagery organized and perpetrated by the accused. And while the judges are more descriptive than moralistic in their choice of certain words, in some sense vividly conveying the events and recognizing their awful consequences on the victims speaks loudly enough.

When describing the heinousness of the crimes committed, judges also often seek to place these events in their social context to illustrate the full scope and depth of the consequences of these actions, especially to audiences that may not be aware of these crimes or downplay their significance. We quote from the sentencing judgment for the leaders of the Revolutionary United Front in a case of exceptional cruelty. In this case the judges condemned the behavior of three of the most senior leaders of this rebel group that had been involved in the Sierra Leone civil war for many years. They wrote:

> We therefore recall our finding that the brutal manner in which women and girls were debased and molested, in the naked view of their protectors, the fathers, husbands and brothers deliberately destroyed the existing family nucleus, and flagrantly undermined the cultural values and relationships which held the societies together. 216 The Chamber observes that the shame and fear experienced by victims of sexual violence, alienated and tore apart communities, creating vacuums where bonds and relations were initially established.[33] P13

The judges recognize that the violence and the shame associated with rape and sexual slavery implicate whole families and villages which witnessed these atrocities. Indeed, victims' family members were often forced to watch these crimes to further add to their stigma and destroy communities.

---

[32] The Prosecutor v. Moinina Fofana and Allieu Kondewa, Case No. SCSL-04–14-T, Sentencing Judgment, October 9, 2007, para 49.

[33] The Prosecutor v. Issa Hassan Sesay, Morris Kallon and Augustine Gbao, Case No. SCSL-04–15-T, April 8, 2009, para 134.

The sentencing judgment in the case of Charles Taylor, the Liberian president who was the mastermind behind the violence of RUF and others, serves to encapsulate the shocking brutality of the crimes committed in Sierra Leone. Taylor had funded and manipulated rebels inside Sierra Leone that helped fuel the fighting and numerous atrocities. Here the judges wrote:

> In determining an appropriate sentence for the Accused, the Trial Chamber has taken into account the tremendous suffering caused by the commission of the crimes for which the Accused is convicted of planning and aiding and abetting, and the impact of these crimes on the victims, physically, emotionally and psychologically. The Trial Chamber recalls the tremendous loss of life – innocent civilians burned to death in their homes, or brutally killed by maiming and torture. The amputation of limbs was a hallmark of terror and cruelty visited upon innocent civilians. For those who survived these crimes, the long-term impact on their lives is devastating – amputees without arms who now have to live on charity because they can no longer work; young girls who have been publicly stigmatized and will never recover from the trauma of rape and sexual slavery to which they were subjected, in some cases resulting in pregnancy and additional stigma from the children born thereof; child soldiers, boys and girls who are suffering from public stigma, highlighted by the identifying marks carved on their bodies, and enduring the after-effects of years of brutality, often irreparable alienation from their family and community, all as a consequence of the crimes for which Mr. Taylor stands convicted of aiding and abetting and planning. The Defense aptly described "the pain of lost limbs, the agony not only of rape in its commonly understood sense, but also the rape of childhood, the rape of innocence, possibly the rape of hope." The Trial Chamber witnessed many survivors weeping as they testified, a decade after the end of the conflict. Their suffering will be life-long.[34]

The Taylor judgment was perhaps the most visible and noteworthy of the SCSL's decisions. Charles Taylor was the most prominent of all the defendants, and had been particularly notorious for the violence he perpetrated not just in his home country of Liberia, but also in neighboring countries by his funding of other rebel groups. His conviction was, in many respects, the culmination of the SCSL's work and represented a final condemnation of the horrors of the Sierra Leone civil war.

The Words of the Victims and the Accused

Judges can also use expressive language by communicating through the voice of another. While there are occasions in which judges quote from witness testimony or statements made by the accused, these words are often used in a more instrumental fashion when establishing the existence of a chain of events or the liability of the

[34] The Prosecutor v. Charles Taylor, Case No. SCSL-03–01-T, May 30, 2012, para 71. As found at http://www.rscsl.org/Documents/Decisions/Taylor/1285/SCSL-03-01-T-1285.pdf.

accused. On other occasions judges will use the words of witnesses or the accused to make a larger, concluding point or to give a more personal voice to convey a particularly poignant story or a compelling admission. Such use of language allows the judges to communicate emotions or ideas that may not always be appropriate in a strictly legal sense, but which provide a human context in the midst of an otherwise dry recitation of events. Such words may also express what judges are feeling, but do not wish to usurp the voice of the victims.

Below we provide a lengthy quotation from the sentencing judgment of Milan Babic at the ICTY. Babic was the leader of the self-declared Serbian Autonomous Region (SAO) Krajina, and then president of the Republic of Serbian Krajina (RSK) in north-eastern Croatia. Babic pled guilty to a variety of crimes that were characterized as "persecution" because of the efforts by the Croatian Serbs to ethnically cleanse their "republic" of Croats and others through forcible expulsion, violence and the destruction of property. Babic pled guilty and was sentenced to thirteen years in prison. What attracted the attention of the Trial Chamber judges who determined his sentence, was his extensive recognition of the crimes committed under his leadership. The judgment quotes from his statement:

> I come before this Tribunal with a deep sense of shame and remorse. I have allowed myself to take part in the worst kind of persecution of people simply because they were Croats and not Serbs. Innocent people were persecuted; innocent people were evicted forcibly from their houses; and innocent people were killed. Even when I learned what had happened, I kept silent. Even worse, I continued in my office, and I became personally responsible for the inhumane treatment of innocent people.138

He continued:

> These crimes and my participation therein can never be justified. I'm speechless when I have to express the depth of my remorse for what I have done and for the effect that my sins have had on the others. I can only hope that by expressing the truth, by admitting to my guilt, and expressing the remorse can serve as an example to those who still mistakenly believe that such inhuman acts can ever be justified. Only truth can give the opportunity for the Serbian people to relieve itself of its collective burden of guilt. Only an admission of guilt on my part makes it possible for me to take responsibility for all the wrongs that I have done.[35]

Scholars have called attention to the role envisioned for international tribunals in advancing peace and reconciliation (Clark 2015; Meernik 2005, 2011). It is rare, however, to find a defendant recognizing that his actions were not only wrong and created great harm, but expressing the depth of remorse as Babic does. By according Babic's confession such prominence the Trial Chamber judges help advance several goals. First, such admissions of guilt help to counteract the denial that exists among

---

[35] *The Prosecutor v. Milan Babic*, Case No. IT-03–72-S, June 29, 2004, para 83. As found at http://www.icty.org/x/cases/babic/tjug/en/bab-sj040629e.pdf.

some groups in the former Yugoslavia that such crimes were even committed. Second, confessions may also encourage others to come forward and admit their guilt. And third, if the larger truths of the wars of the former Yugoslavia can be communicated to those in the region, perhaps their recognition of the wrongdoing will help prevent future atrocities. This, at least, is what an international justice idealist might argue. And while the lasting impact of one confession may not tip the scales significantly toward peace and reconciliation, the judges may believe that publicizing acts of contrition will bolster the weight of justice on those scales.

In the *Celebici* trial judgment, in which Bosnian Muslims stood accused of crimes committed against Serbs, the judges chose to conclude a powerful statement describing a defendant's sexual assault with some very simple words from the mouth of one witness:

> Hazim Delic is guilty of torture by way of the deplorable rapes of two women detainees in the Celebici prison-camp. He subjected Grozdana Cecez not only to the inherent suffering involved in rape, but exacerbated her humiliation and degradation by raping her in the presence of his colleagues. The effects of this crime are readily apparent from the testimony of the victim when she said " . . . he trampled on my pride and I will never be able to be the woman that I was."[36]

The words are very simple and direct when it is often difficult, one would imagine especially so for male judges, to convey the pain and suffering of sexual assault. They also convey the deeper and personal impact of rape on victims in a manner where clinical or legal terms may fall so far short as to be insulting. This passage from the *Krstic* judgment describing the toll taken on the survivors by the genocide is also powerful in its emotional simplicity:

> This heartbreak and anguish is no better reflected than in the words of Witness DD whose young son was torn away from her in Potocari:
>
> > . . . I keep dreaming about him. I dream of him bringing flowers and saying, "Mother, I've come" I hug him and say, "Where have you been, my son?" and he says, "I've been in Vlasenica all this time."[37]

A video of the witness making this statement is one of the most powerful and moving of the testimonies of all witnesses. One of the authors has shown this video clip numerous times in classes and can attest to the emotional impact of these words on student audiences.

We quote from a series of witness statements that the *Tolimir* Trial Chamber included in its judgment to describe the horrors of the genocide at Srebrenica. Zdravko Tolimir was a high-ranking Bosnian Serb general who was sentenced to life

---

[36] The Prosecutor v. Zejnil Delalic et al., Case No. IT-96–21-T, November 16, 1998, para 1262, as found at http://www.icty.org/x/cases/mucic/tjug/en/981116_judg_en.pdf.

[37] The Prosecutor v. Radislav Krstic, Case No. IT-98–33-T, August 2, 2001, para 93, as found at http://www.icty.org/x/cases/krstic/tjug/en/krs-tj010802e.pdf.

imprisonment for his role in that massacre that left approximately eight thousand Bosnian Muslim men dead:

> The accounts of survivors of these events who escaped their imminent death and lived to provide their testimony is harrowing. The Chamber feels compelled to highlight some of these accounts, and considers that they are illustrative of the experience of the thousands who were not so fortunate. PW-004, a sole survivor of killings that took place at the Jadar river in Bratunac on 13 July 1995, recalled how shortly before being shot at by Bosnian Serb Forces, he and the other men "waited for our lives to end there, and we expected – there was half a minute of silence, and just then the images of my children appeared in my mind, and I thought I was done for."3150 Shot in the hip, PW-004 threw himself into the river in an attempt to escape, continuing to be shot at by Bosnian Serb Forces still standing at the banks of the river.3151 PW-006, a survivor of the between 600 and 1000 Bosnian Muslim men who were killed at the Kravica Warehouse by Bosnian Serb Forces on 13 July 1995, described being shot, pretending to be dead, and climbing over dead bodies to escape through a window of the warehouse from where he fell into a cornfield.3152 A soldier approached him and shot him in the right shoulder, asking him whether he wanted another one; PW-006 pretended to be dead.3153 He remained in this spot throughout the night, and heard the sound of excavators.3154 He heard soldiers shooting individuals who were not yet dead. 3155 He crawled to a nearby river, where he saw two men shot in the head.3156 He ultimately found his way to Zepa which at the time had not yet fallen, and was evacuated.3157

> The Chamber recalls here the testimony of a witness to the executions in Orahovac on 14 July that he observed a child of about five or six years old standing up from the pile of bodies which he described as "a pile of flesh in bits,"3158 and calling out for his father "Baba, where are you?" The child was in shock, covered in blood stains and bits of others' bowel and tissue. He was taken to a hospital and Zvornik, treated for his injuries and survived.

> On 16 July 1995 PW-016 and PW-073 were directed to a meadow at Branjevo Military Farm in Zvornik, where they saw the bodies of those shot before them; they were lined up, shot at, and heard the summary executions of individuals who had not died after the first burst of gunfire.3160 PW-016 and PW-073 pretended to be dead to avoid being shot.3161 They subsequently managed to escape the killing fields, wandered around aimlessly for the next few days looking for food and water, and ultimately gave themselves up to the same forces they had escaped from, in the hope of survival.3162 PW-016 and PW-073 were then taken to Batkovic camp where they stayed until their release in December 1995.[38]

The words and stories of the victims describe, at a very personal level, the experiences of those individuals who survived the Srebrenica massacre in a way statistics and

[38] The Prosecutor v. Zdravko Tolimir, Case No. IT-05–88/2-T, December 12, 2012, para 755. As found at http://www.icty.org/x/cases/tolimir/tjug/en/121212.pdf.

numbers cannot. The use of expressive language to convey these narratives helps humanize legalistic judgments so that they speak more forcefully to the audience beyond the international legal community, especially the victims of these crimes.

A Greater Responsibility

Those who are responsible for planning and ordering the commission of international crimes are liable not only as architects of these crimes, but also as the moral authors of this violence. They are found guilty on the basis of their legal responsibility, but their moral failings as leaders, one can argue, represent a deeper form of culpability. As leaders they are responsible for ensuring the safety and well-being of their people. By failing to provide such security for the victims, and instead exploiting their position for nefarious ends, such leaders have violated the basic compact between citizens and their government. The decision to abdicate moral responsibility as leaders to all their people to commit acts of unspeakable violence represents a form of responsibility that the statutes of the tribunals do not, and cannot really, address. More than legal determinations are necessary to call attention to this moral failure of leadership.

Furthermore, the crimes adjudicated at the international tribunals are distinguished not only by the role played by the leaders who are tried, but the many who carried out their violent plans and generally not subject to international justice, and only occasionally national justice. As such, the leaders not only do violence to the victims, they also criminalize and victimize the direct and indirect perpetrators. As we saw in the case of Drazen Erdemovic, who appeared to have suffered psychological harm as a result of his involvement in the Srebrenica massacres, as well as those others who have confessed their crimes, there are likely enduring, negative consequences and trauma that results from participation in these crimes. Thus, by implicating these individuals in the commission of criminal actions, leaders bear another form of responsibility and have attracted additional condemnation by the judges for their failures as leaders who should have been looking after the best interests of those in their command.

We found several instances in which judgments moved beyond asserting the defendant's legal liability to describe in more personal terms the moral responsibility of the accused for organizing such crimes and involving so many others in their commission. This passage from the *Krstic* Trial Chamber is illustrative:

> The Trial Chamber's overall assessment is that General Krstic is a professional soldier who willingly participated in the forcible transfer of all women, children and elderly from Srebrenica, but would not likely, on his own, have embarked on a genocidal venture; however, he allowed himself, as he assumed command responsibility for the Drina Corps, to be drawn into the heinous scheme and to sanction the use of Corps assets to assist with the genocide. After he had assumed command of the Drina Corps, on 13 July 1995, he could have tried to halt the

use of Drina Corps resources in the implementation of the genocide. His own commander, General Mladic, was calling the shots and personally supervising the killings. General Krstic's participation in the genocide consisted primarily of allowing Drina Corps assets to be used in connection with the executions from 14 July onwards and assisting with the provision of men to be deployed to participate in executions that occurred on 16 July 1995. General Krstic remained largely passive in the face of his knowledge of what was going on; he is guilty, but his guilt is palpably less than others who devised and supervised the executions all through that week and who remain at large. When pressured, he assisted the effort in deploying some men for the task, but on his own he would not likely have initiated such a plan. Afterwards, as word of the executions filtered in, he kept silent and even expressed sentiments lionising the Bosnian Serb campaign in Srebrenica. After the signing of the Dayton Accords, he co-operated with the implementers of the accord and continued with his professional career although he insisted that his fruitless effort to unseat one of his officers, whom he believed to have directly participated in the killings, meant he would not be trusted or treated as a devoted loyalist by the Bosnian Serb authorities thereafter. His story is one of a respected professional soldier who could not balk his superiors' insane desire to forever rid the Srebrenica area of Muslim civilians, and who, finally, participated in the unlawful realisation of this hideous design.[39]

The judges' description of Krstic's responsibility seems directed specifically at those who are not the ringleaders of genocidal crimes, but those who are the necessary cogs in the political and military machinery that carry out such complex crimes. While each individual may deny his involvement or argue his role was insignificant, the judges assert that such self-serving rationales cannot disguise the truth. They also call attention to the need for individuals, who might even recognize the criminality of their superiors' plans, to take action to stop such crimes. While sometimes such exhortations to do the right thing may seem unrealistic in nations where the concepts of right and wrong have become upended and the formerly illegal becomes the new normal, the judges argue that individual agency still exists. Individuals can still decide to exit such murderous regimes.

Then there are those individuals, more often accused of crimes of a lesser magnitude than General Krstic, who deny their responsibility and argue that their actions were insignificant or that others did worse. The next paragraph, from one of the ICTY's very first judgments in the case of Dusko Tadic, is instructive. Tadic, of course, committed various abuses of human rights, although he was never in a position of leadership:

In his final statement, Dusko Tadic offered a list of persons whom he suggested were more responsible than he for the horrific events that transpired. At trial, he testified

---

[39] The Prosecutor v. Radislav Krstic, Case No. IT-98–33-T, August 2, 2001, para 724. As found at http://www.icty.org/x/cases/krstic/tjug/en/krs-tj010802e.pdf.

that "I do not think that anybody is guilty." TP 6137 (Tuesday, 29 October 1996). Likewise, in closing submissions at trial, his counsel at that time quoted from a letter from the then President of the United States, Abraham Lincoln, in the period of the Civil War in the United States in the mid-nineteenth century, in which he stated: "Each man feels an impulse to kill his neighbour, lest he be first killed by him." *Abraham Lincoln: Speeches and Writings 1859–1865* (1989), p 523. However, what was not pointed out by that counsel was that the Executive Order which President Lincoln issued in response to that conflict, the Instructions for the Government of Armies of the United States in the Field, better known as the Lieber Code, has been recognised as one of the foundations of the Law of The Hague, setting limits on the conduct of armed conflicts. *See* Frits Kalshoven, *Constraints on the Waging of War* (2 ed., 1991), pp 11, 12, 13. Thus, this quote from President Lincoln should not be construed as excusing criminal conduct even when committed during a time of armed conflict. The International Tribunal was established to adjudge individual guilt or innocence, and it discharges that responsibility without recognising as justifications the exigencies some say are inherent in the nature of armed conflict.[40]

In addition to asserting Tadic's guilt and the necessity of punishment, the judges also seek to correct Tadic's misreading of history and international jurisprudence. To deny one's culpability and misuse the very laws that have developed in response to war crimes would seem to be doubly problematic for the judges and call forth a forceful response.

Speaking to a Larger Audience

Our last category of expressivism is the use of language that deliberately seeks to reach beyond the parties to a case and the tribunals' stakeholders to speak to the world now and the world of the future. Sometimes these passages are quite brief, but powerful, as the quote below from the judgment against Drazen Erdemovic. Erdemovic pled guilty to taking part in the Srebrenica massacre against his will and subsequently proved to be one of the most helpful "insider" witnesses at the ICTY:

> With regard to a crime against humanity, the Trial Chamber considers that the life of the accused and that of the victim are not fully equivalent. As opposed to ordinary law, the violation here is no longer directed at the physical welfare of the victim alone but at humanity as a whole.[41]

Similar language is found in the Trial Chamber's first sentencing judgment against Dusko Tadic:

---

[40] The Prosecutor v. Dusko Tadic, Case No. IT-94-1-T, July 14, 1997, para 71. As found at http://www .icty.org/x/cases/tadic/tjug/en/tad-sj970714e.pdf.

[41] The Prosecutor v. Drazen Erdemovic, Case No. IT-96-22-T, November 29, 1996, para 19. As found at http://www.icty.org/x/cases/erdemovic/tjug/en/erd-tsj961129e.pdf.

Thus, the Trial Chamber does not accept that Dusko Tadic's actions were anything but criminal, constituting offences against individuals, and indeed, against all mankind. To condone Dusko Tadic's actions is to give effect to a base view of morality and invite anarchy.[42]

In the SCSL's sentencing judgment against those defendants involved in the Congress for Democratic Change trial, the judges spoke of the universal rejection of the defendants' crimes no matter what local sentiment might be. The defendants had been found guilty of numerous crimes involving rape, amputations and other violations of human rights:

> What should be one of the paramount considerations in the sentencing of an accused person convicted of crimes against humanity and war crimes is the revulsion of mankind, represented by the international community, to the crime and not the tolerance by a local community of the crime; or lack of public revulsion in relation to the crimes of such community; or local sentiments about the persons who have been found guilty of the crimes.[43]

And lastly we observe the words of the SCSL in sentencing the defendants in this case, Moinina Fofana and Allieu Kondewa:

> We again observe, however, that the crimes for which the accused tried and convicted remain very serious crimes, and both Fofana and Kondewa will bear the stigma of conviction after we have pronounced their sentences. The Chamber hopes that this Judgment will send a message to future pro-democracy armed forces or militia groups that notwithstanding the justness of propriety of their cause, they must observe the laws of war in pursuing or defending legitimate causes, and that they must not recruit or use children as agents of instruments of war. It will, in addition, remind them of their obligation to protect civilians who are unarmed and not participating in hostilities, and whose aspiration is only to protection, regardless of their perceived affiliation.[44]

The judges speak to other, would-be war criminals around the world, most especially those who believe they are trying to advance democracy. Whatever one may believe about the righteousness of one's cause, the temptations to commit acts of unspeakable violence are always there. As we have argued previously, we believe judges are very conscious of their legacy not just in international criminal jurisprudence, but in the verdict of history. Some judges seize opportunities to move beyond the formal

---

[42] The Prosecutor v. Dusko Tadic, Case No. IT-94-1-T, July 14, 1997, para 72. As found at http://www.icty.org/x/cases/tadic/tjug/en/tad-sj970714e.pdf.

[43] The Prosecutor v. Moinina Fofana and Allieu Kondewa, Case No. SCSL-04-14-A, May 28, 2008, para 564. As found at http://www.rscsl.org/CDF_Appeals_Chamber_Decisions.html.

[44] The Prosecutor v. Moinina Fofana and Allieu Kondewa, Case No. SCSL-04-14-T, Sentencing Judgment, October 9, 2007, para 96. As found at http://www.rscsl.org/Documents/Decisions/CDF/796/SCSL-04-14-T-796.pdf.

requirements of their opinions to adjudicate legal matters and speak to history. This, ultimately, is the essence of the use of expressive language.

DISCUSSION AND CONCLUSIONS

As we have examined the passages from the tribunals' judgments that met our definition of expressive language we have seen that such words can serve multiple purposes and address multiple audiences. Judges have employed expressive language to recognize the enormity of the damages wrought on entire societies, and they have been utilized to condemn the horrific abuses of the few. The judges use such language to speak to the whole of humanity and place the suffering of the victims into a historical context that recognizes their tragedy as a personal loss and as an exemplar of loss alongside other tragedies throughout history. Judges also speak through the words of witnesses when their descriptions cannot resonate with the same forceful and simple clarity of the victim's own words. And they even employ the words of the accused, when those are offered in a spirit of genuine remorse and desire for reconciliation. And when the legal analysis of a defendant's liability cannot capture their human and moral responsibility for their crimes, they speak of a deeper personal ownership that defendants must bear.

Undoubtedly there are different perspectives or interpretations of this expressive language that would call attention to other judicial motivations, and thus we do not claim this categorization to be complete or perfect. We recognize that the uses of expressive language will not include all such instances. Our project was not to develop an exhaustive list of such instances, but rather as large a representative sample of expressive language as we could identify. We do believe that it can serve as a productive approach for analyzing what we have argued is the "entrepreneurial" decision making judges engage in that moves beyond the technical dimensions of reaching verdicts and meting out punishment.

As we have stressed, judges act within the bounds of their statutes and rules governing procedure and evidence, but they are not "mere" bureaucrats who deliver judgments with machine-like precision. They understand both their role in the larger scope of the international judicial community and international relations. Such an understanding of these broader roles, we contend, can produce a need to speak to the larger communities that make up their audience. We believe that some judges may use the power of their judgments and their stature as prominent, international jurists to call attention to the human element in these tragedies through the use of expressive language as well as the development of jurisprudence that might help to avert such crimes in the future.

Indeed, judges cannot help but recognize their institutions were created to deal with unique and horrible events that cannot always be interpreted through a legal lens. They understand that irrespective of the necessity of assessing evidence in a dispassionate and objective manner, there is the cumulative suffering of many individuals that has created the need for international justice. To lose sight of the human element, we would argue, risks turning international judicial proceedings into simply ledgers of the evidence for and against the accused. Should these tribunals approach the adjudication of these crimes in the same manner as a judge might reach a decision on the legality of a business tax break, they might well undermine the impact of their justice. That is why we believe judges will, on occasion, seek to bring this human element back into the judicial accounting.

While there are still many unanswered questions about the causes and nature of judicial expressivism, one that is particularly puzzling and critical to understand is, why we don't find more instances of such language? We are quite puzzled by the lack of instances of expressive language from the ICTR, especially given the scale and brutality of their Rwandan genocide. Was it that nearly all the accused were charged with horrible crimes that somehow lessened the need to condemn these actions in any one case in more human terms? Were there too many other challenges of operating a tribunal under difficult circumstances in Arusha that reduced the likelihood of expressivism? What role is played by the individual judge in the use of expressive language? Indeed, are there some judges, regardless of the setting, who because of some personal or professional characteristics are more likely to use this language? For example, we are struck by the fact that many of the uses of expressive language at the ICTY come from the *Krstic* and *Lukic and Lukic* judgments. Was it the crimes or the judges that motivated expressive language? We would urge a rigorous and systematic analysis of these judgments, perhaps using textual analysis software, to better understand their origin.

We are aware that the operations of the ICTR have been fraught with logistical complications, which might have left very little space to judges to engage in judicial expressivism. Discussing the moral and physical evidence of the ICTR from Rwanda, Clark (2013) mentions how the tribunal has seemed particularly detached by the everyday stories of those still living in Rwanda. He quotes the words of one of the judges, who, asked if he had ever been in Rwanda to see the effects of justice on local communities, replied:

> I have never been to Rwanda and I have no desire to visit. Going there and seeing the effect we are having would only make my work more difficult. How can I do my job – judging these cases fairly – with pictures in my mind of what is going on there. This task is already complicated enough.[45]

We also believe that there might be two additional reasons as to why the ICTR judges have not used expressive language in their judgments as much as at the ICTY. First, we agree with Clark (2013) that similarly to the ICC, the ICTR has been branded as the product of neo-colonial policies, a solution to a conflict imposed from external actors to further control Africa. On this point, we also believe that many of

---

[45] Clark (2013), p. 155 and n. 4, p. 165 "Interview with an ICTR judge in Arusha, 7 February 2003."

the crimes adjudicated were being identified as caused by old European colonial policies, imposing ethnic divisions and fomenting ethnic hatred, therefore probably limiting the willingness of judges to pronounce a moral *j'accuse* of societal collapse. Second and sadly, we also suggest that the ICTR has received far less attention than the ICTY; judges might have been aware that their words resonated much more loudly among practitioners and the global community at large if pronounced in The Hague rather than in Arusha.

However, these are suppositions based on our knowledge of the work of these tribunals. We would strongly encourage more research into the use of expressive language in the judgments of international tribunals. While the judicial record of these institutions in holding fair and effective trials of the most dangerous war criminals is surely their most important institutional and political legacy, their historical legacy may well rest upon their ability to speak to those affected by these crimes and the greater international community today and into the future. To send a message of historical and educational importance, the words of any speaker must resonate with her audience. The words must be heard or read, understood and make sense. The words must be words that the audience can appreciate. Legal language must be employed in the interest of fairness and to speak to the more immediate audiences in a case. But other words and messages must be employed to reach the rest of the world. This, we believe, is the ultimate purpose of expressive language and why judges sometimes act as entrepreneurs in seeking to reach this audience.

In this sense, they are judicial entrepreneurs with a moral as well as a legal mission to use the vehicle of their judgments to speak to human values that transcend legal necessities. We saw in the previous chapter that judges progressively develop the law because of a variety of interests related to their concern for human rights and their legacy. In this chapter we see something very similar. Judges use the vehicle of their judgments here as well and because of their concern for human rights and their legacy. Thus, the means and the motives remain the same across both acts of judicial entrepreneurship. The difference here is that judges engage in moral observation and criticism instead of legal interpretation and evaluation. They are servants of the law and humankind with attendant needs to reach both to advance protection of human rights and to ensure international justice has both a legal and a moral legacy.

5

Punishing the Guilty

INTRODUCTION

The international community created international criminal tribunals to bring justice, peace and reconciliation to some of the most intractable conflicts in the world. Where once international inaction might have allowed massive human rights atrocities and blatant violations of humanitarian law to go unchecked and war criminals to go unpunished, the impunity of the past has now been steadily eroded by the accomplishments of the present international justice system. The international community has invested billions of dollars in the operations of these criminal tribunals to ensure that those who committed crimes will be tried and punished. Despite the notable successes of the tribunals in delivering justice, however, there has been substantial debate in particular over their sentences for some scholars see them as inconsistent and inadequately justified (Clark 2007; D'Ascoli 2011; De Roca and Rassi 2008; Harmon and Gaynor 2007).

Once guilt has been proven, the judges have tremendous discretionary power regarding punishment. There is little in the way of detailed guidance on what theories of punishment should inform sentencing and which specific sentencing determinants should be assessed. For example, we count approximately 34,322 words in the latest version of the ICTY Rules of Procedure and Evidence. Yet of those 34,322 words, only 289 – eight-tenths of 1 percent – are devoted to sentencing. More to the point, the judges themselves recognize their tremendous power over punishment. The ICTR opined in the *Kayishema and Ruzindana* judgment that, "This chamber also finds that it possesses unfettered discretion to go beyond the circumstances stated in the Statute and Rules to ensure justice in the matters of sentencing."[1] As well, in the Hadzihasanovic decision the judges wrote:

---

[1] The Prosecutor v. Clément Kayishema and Obed Ruzindana, Case No. ICTR-95–1-T, Trial Chamber, May 21, 1999, para 4.

While the Statute and Rules provide the Trial Chambers general guidelines for determining sentences by requiring that they take into account aggravating and mitigating factors, the material and personal circumstances of the Accused, the gravity of the offence, and the general practice regarding prison sentences in the former Yugoslavia, they do not exhaustively define the points of fact and law which the Trial Chambers may consider when determining sentences. Chambers therefore have broad discretionary power in determining such matters.[2]

That judges have considerable discretionary power to determine what is a just and fair punishment is in little doubt (Henham 2007). We discussed in Chapter Three how the judges progressively developed international law on issues such as sentencing. Thus, our goal here is not so much to review how the law has developed, but to analyze how the law has been applied on matters of sentencing.

The focus of this chapter is to analyze the punishments handed down by the international criminal tribunals to assess the degree to which the broad objectives of the tribunals – to right the scales of justice through retribution, promote deterrence and advance peace are reflected in the punishments they hand down. Furthermore, we seek to identify and gauge the importance of specific sentencing determinants derived from these broad objectives that judges utilize in locating a proper punishment for those who are convicted. Our goal is to demonstrate that the judges have developed consistent practice on sentencing by remaining faithful to the broad goals established by their founding documents, and using a consistent set of factors to determine punishment. Hence, in contrast to the arguments of many that the judges have been highly inconsistent in their sentencing behavior (Clark 2007; D'Ascoli 2011; De Roca and Rassi 2008; Harmon and Gaynor 2007), we demonstrate that there is a great deal of consistency in judicial decision making regarding sentences.

We shift our focus somewhat away from the judicial entrepreneurial conception of decision making to argue that in the practice of sentencing, as distinct from jurisprudence on sentencing that we addressed in Chapter Three, judges possess ample discretion to exercise their judgment on such matters as best they see fit. Therefore, we do not seek to demonstrate that judges engage in substantial entrepreneurial decision making in meting out punishment, but rather that judges mostly possess the requisite power they need to sentence according to their best judgment. Where we argued in Chapters Three and Four that judges engage in entrepreneurial decision making to advance human rights and ensure the legacy of the tribunals, here we argue that the protection of human rights and judicial legacy can be advanced mostly within the scope of the judges' authority. We conclude that what unites the progressive development of the law, the use of expressive language and the

[2] The Prosecutor v. Enver Hadzihasanovic and Amir Kubura, Case No. IT-01-47-T, Trial Chamber, March 15, 2006, para 2068.

punishment of the guilty is the expansion and consolidation of judicial power to advance justice, human rights and the legacy of the tribunals.

The chapter proceeds as follows. In the first section, we review the guidance on sentencing provided to the tribunals and discuss how judges have interpreted their authority. In the second part of the chapter we examine what the judges have written about the importance of the three purposes of the international tribunals and the role they play in punishment. We analyze in turn, the role and importance played by (1) retribution, (2) deterrence and (3) peace and reconciliation in the rationales articulated in the written opinions. In part three we develop a model of sentencing decisions by judges premised on those factors that the judges have relied on and that pertain to the three goals. We conclude with a discussion of the evolution of sentencing and punishment since the creation of the ICTY and how we might expect ICC judges to sentence the convicted in the future.

THE RATIONALE OF PUNISHMENT

Background

Before proceeding we must outline the relevant language in the statutes of the tribunals pertaining to judgments and penalties. The language in the ICTY and ICTR Statutes and Rules of Procedure and Evidence are largely identical so we reproduce here just the germane language from the ICTY. In Article 23, the ICTY Statute provides that:

1. The Trial Chambers shall pronounce judgements and impose sentences and penalties on persons convicted of serious violations of international humanitarian law.
2. The judgement shall be rendered by a majority of the judges of the Trial Chamber, and shall be delivered by the Trial Chamber in public. It shall be accompanied by a reasoned opinion in writing, to which separate or dissenting opinions may be appended.

While Article 24 contains the following:

1. The penalty imposed by the Trial Chamber shall be limited to imprisonment. In determining the terms of imprisonment, the Trial Chambers shall have recourse to the general practice regarding prison sentences in the courts of the former Yugoslavia.
2. In imposing the sentences, the Trial Chambers should take into account such factors as the gravity of the offence and the individual circumstances of the convicted person.

3. In addition to imprisonment, the Trial Chambers may order the return of any property and proceeds acquired by criminal conduct, including by means of duress, to their rightful owners.[3]

The ICTY's Rules of Procedure and Evidence state that:

(A) A convicted person may be sentenced to imprisonment for a term up to and including the remainder of the convicted person's life. (Amended 12 Nov 1997)
(B) In determining the sentence, the Trial Chamber shall take into account the factors mentioned in Article 24, paragraph 2, of the Statute, as well as such factors as:
   (i) any aggravating circumstances;
   (ii) any mitigating circumstances including the substantial cooperation with the Prosecutor by the convicted person before or after conviction;
   (iii) the general practice regarding prison sentences in the courts of the former Yugoslavia;
   (iv) the extent to which any penalty imposed by a court of any State on the convicted person for the same act has already been served, as referred to in Article 10, paragraph 3, of the Statute.[4]

Article 19 of the Statute of the Special Court for Sierra Leone states that:

1. The Trial Chamber shall impose upon a convicted person, other than a juvenile offender, imprisonment for a specified number of years. In determining the terms of imprisonment, the Trial Chamber shall, as appropriate, have recourse to the practice regarding prison sentences in the International Criminal Tribunal for Rwanda and the national courts of Sierra Leone.
2. In imposing the sentences, the Trial Chamber should take into account such factors as the gravity of the offence and the individual circumstances of the convicted person.
3. In addition to imprisonment, the Trial Chamber may order the forfeiture of the property, proceeds and any assets acquired unlawfully or by criminal conduct, and their return to their rightful owner or to the State of Sierra Leone.[5]

Its Rules of Procedure and Evidence indicate in Rule 101 that:

(A) A person convicted by the Special Court, other than a juvenile offender, may be sentenced to imprisonment for a specific number of years.

3 ICTY Statute, Articles 23–24, as found at http://www.icty.org/x/file/Legal%20Library/Statute/statute_sept09_en.pdf.
4 Rules of Procedure and Evidence of the ICTY as found at http://www.icty.org/x/file/Legal%20Library/Rules_procedure_evidence/IT032Rev49_en.pdf.
5 Statute of the Special Court for Sierra Leone as found at http://www.sc-sl.org/LinkClick.aspx?fileticket=uClndiMJeEw%3d&tabid=176.

(B) In determining the sentence, the Trial Chamber shall take into account the factors mentioned in Article 19 (2) of the Statute, as well as such factors as:

  (i) Any aggravating circumstances;
  (ii) Any mitigating circumstances including the substantial cooperation with the Prosecutor by the convicted person before or after conviction;
  (iii) The extent to which any penalty imposed by a court of any State on the convicted person for the same act has already been served, as referred to in Article 9 (3) of the Statute.

(C) The Trial Chamber shall indicate whether multiple sentences shall be served consecutively or concurrently.

(D) Any period during which the convicted person was detained in custody pending his transfer to the Special Court or pending trial or appeal, shall be taken into consideration on sentencing.[6]

The key provisions on sentencing from the ICC from the Rome Statute, Articles 77 and 78, provide that:

Article 77(1). Subject to article 110, the Court may impose one of the following penalties on a person convicted of a crime referred to in article 5 of this Statute:

(a) Imprisonment for a specified number of years, which may not exceed a maximum of 30 years; or
(b) A term of life imprisonment when justified by the extreme gravity of the crime and the individual circumstances of the convicted person.

Article 78(1). In determining the sentence, the Court shall, in accordance with the Rules of Procedure and Evidence, take into account such factors as the gravity of the crime and the individual circumstances of the convicted person.

Article 78(3). When a person has been convicted of more than one crime, the Court shall pronounce a sentence for each crime and a joint sentence specifying the total period of imprisonment. This period shall be no less than the highest individual sentence pronounced and shall not exceed 30 years imprisonment or a sentence of life imprisonment in conformity with article 77, paragraph 1(b).[7]

The ICC Rules of Procedure and Evidence provide further guidance, and some in particular that provides more detail than found in such rules for the ad hoc tribunals. Judges are instructed to give consideration to:

... the extent of the damage caused, in particular the harm caused to the victims and their families, the nature of the unlawful behaviour and the means employed to execute the crime; the degree of participation of the convicted person; the degree

---

[6] Rules of Procedure and Evidence of the SCSL as found at http://www.sc-sl.org/LinkClick.aspx?fileticket=Psp%2bFho%2bwSI%3d&tabid=176.

[7] Rome Statute of the International Criminal Court as found at https://www.icc-cpi.int/NR/rdonlyres/ADD16852-AEE9-4757-ABE7-9CDC7CF02886/283503/RomeStatutEng1.pdf.

of intent; the circumstances of manner, time and location; and the age, education, social and economic condition of the convicted person.

As well the types of mitigating and aggravating circumstances the judges are to evaluate are described and listed to include such factors as efforts to compensate the victims and diminished mental capacity (mitigating factors), as well as abuse of power, heinousness of the actions and the defenseless nature of the victims (aggravating factors). While these lists of circumstances are not exhaustive they provide considerably more guidance than that found in the equivalent documents at the ad hoc tribunals.[8]

While the statutes and rules of procedure and evidence of the tribunals provide insight into the broad parameters of sentencing, in practice the judges have displayed considerable discretion in utilizing this guidance to a greater or lesser degree, as their statutes themselves allow. Much has been written about international sentencing that has sought to determine on what basis or theory of punishment judges ground their sentences (Clark 2007; D'Ascoli 2011; De Roca and Rassi 2008; Harmon and Gaynor 2007; Hola, Smeulers and Bijleveld 2009, 2011a 2011b, 2012; King and Greening 2007; Meernik 2003, 2011; Meernik and King 2003, 2011; Meernik, King and Dancy 2005). What specific factors determine the severity of sentences? Are these sentences consistent within and even across tribunals? Is there something akin to a sentencing regime emerging from the work of the tribunals?

Adhering to Their Framers' Intentions

The goals set out for the tribunals in these documents – most especially to redress violations of international crimes, deter their future occurrence, promote peace and advance reconciliation do provide broad guidance in judicial decision making regarding sentencing. While in other aspects of the law judicial discretion was more circumscribed, here the dearth of language has given the judges as much freedom as they need and more to arrive at sentencing decisions. Judges may well believe that the development of a theory of punishment would subject them to a legal straitjacket. Reliance on a single vehicle for determining punishment might limit the types of evidence, circumstances and other, even non legal case characteristics the judges might find useful in allocating punishment. This, in turn, could lead to actual problems with significant sentencing disparities and appeals for sentencing revision on the basis of neglect of individual circumstances. Furthermore, the judges have evinced considerable reluctance in being bound to any particular frameworks, such as the sentencing practices of the states over which they exercise jurisdiction. They are especially zealous of guarding their responsibility for consideration of individual

---

[8] Rules of Procedure and Evidence of the International Criminal Court, Chapter 7, Rule 145 as found at https://www.icc-cpi.int/iccdocs/PIDS/legal-texts/RulesProcedureEvidenceEng.pdf.

circumstances and their prerogative to prioritize sentencing determinants as they see fit. As the ICTR opined in the *Kayishema and Ruzindana* judgment, "This Chambers also finds that it possesses unfettered discretion to go beyond the circumstances stated in Statute and Rules to ensure justice in matters of sentencing."[9] Thus, by grounding punishment in the goals set forth in their founding documents (e.g., justice, deterrence), and especially the need to consider the individual circumstances of the accused, judges retain tremendous latitude. There is little need to go beyond their founding documents as they provide all the freedom judges could wish for in this regard. In effect, the founding documents allow judges to become fairly entrepreneurial within very wide bounds.

A Reluctance to Make Law on Punishment

More importantly, judges no doubt understand that the development of a "theory" of punishment or the articulation of the values and policy preferences undergirding a sentencing tariff is rightly the province of politicians and legislators. As Ashworth (2010, 76) has written, "It is one thing to agree that judges should be left with discretion . . . it is quite another to suggest that judges should be free to choose what rationale of sentencing to adopt in particular cases or types of cases." To be sure judges in general play a role in the development of punishment rationales and sentencing guidelines, but as charged to do so by legislatures and in cooperation with others involved in the criminal justice enterprise, such as attorneys, victim rights groups and the public. Even though sentencing frameworks, such as those set forth in the US Federal Sentencing Guidelines, often provide judges with discretion in imposing penalties, this discretion is granted within a legislatively authorized process.

More fundamentally, punishment rationales and sentencing guidelines have their roots in societal views of crime and punishment that then form the basis of public policy. For example, Tonry (2001, 4) notes:

> . . . prevailing beliefs vary greatly among policymakers about the causes of crime and the capacity of criminal justice policy changes to affect crime rates. In the United States and more recently in England and some Australian states, many policymakers believe that crime is primarily the result of bad or irresponsible people, not criminogenic conditions and inadequate socialization, and that harsher and more restrictive punishments will reduce crime rates through deterrent and incapacitative processes.

Such assumptions and values regarding crime and punishment are reflected both in the policies governments adopt to address crime, and in the individuals who are socialized and trained in the criminal justice system of a particular society.

---

[9] Prosecutor vs. Clement Kayishema and Obed Ruzindana. ICTR-95–1 T, May 21, 1999, para 4.

Thus, we find important differences across states not only within the western world, but between the western world and other legal cultures, such as those based on Islamic or Confucianist principles. As Tonry (2001, 7) also argues, "National differences in imprisonment rates and patterns result not from differences in crime but from differences in policy." Hence, judges are apt to arrive at the international tribunals with a significant diversity of experience regarding criminal sentencing that may have also worked against the development of more regimented sentencing criteria.

We contend that despite their substantial discretionary power, judges largely confine their punishments to align with the guidance in their statutes and rules of procedure and evidence – principally the gravity of the crime, the culpability of the accused and the individual circumstances of the accused. They stay within the parameters established by the international community (e.g., UN Security Council, Assembly of States Parties) and generally do not seek to go beyond the bounds of what is politically permissible.[10] Thus, even though scholars and advocates have called for judges to develop more coherent rationales for sentencing and more clearly articulate the relative weight accorded to various sentencing determinants, the judges have persistently refused to set down such a theory or set of assumptions that would guide them.

In order to begin exploring their sentencing decisions we look first to the importance of the overall goals of the several tribunals and the manner in which the judges have given voice to these objectives in their punishment strategies. We demonstrate how the judges have premised their decisions on these goals – retribution, deterrence and peace and reconciliation – and subsequently show through our statistical analysis that judges have derived consistent sentencing determinants from these goals that also provide them with considerable flexibility.[11]

THE GOALS OF PUNISHMENT

Retribution

At its most fundamental and human purpose, punishment is about retribution. Society's official sanction of the guilty seeks to provide just desserts to those who

---

[10] It is not clear what sort of alternative punishment scheme the judges might have developed that went beyond the dictates of their statutes given the broad latitude they possess. Perhaps they might have sought to emphasize a restorative justice framework or sought greater involvement in rehabilitation. With little guidance or experience in devising alternative methods of punishment, however, it is difficult to imagine how such systems might have been developed.

[11] While we do discuss the expressive function of punishment in communicating the international community's condemnation of these crimes, the expressive goal is served principally by the punishment itself and whatever language is used to demonstrate judicial stigmatization of international crimes. Expressivism does not directly inform punishments in specific cases.

have ruptured the equilibrium of the community and to right the scales of justice. Thus, when the judges as well as the international legal community speak of justice, they are alluding to an official reckoning that concludes with a punishment that fits the crime. Retribution is at once both legally straightforward and morally dense. While we must concede that given the scale and ferocity of international crimes no punishment can ever be considered commensurate with the damage done, there is assumed to be something of a rough, linear relationship between the magnitude of the crimes and the severity of the punishment. The greater the severity of the crimes, the longer the sentence is likely to be. It is the moral calculation underlying this equation in which we find scholars and jurists alike striving to articulate just how proportionate punishment is just and appropriate and is not simply a modern-day version of "eye for an eye" punishment as revenge.

Indeed, one finds two currents of thought coursing through the judgments handed down by the tribunals. On the one hand, judges stress that punishment must fit the crime and make numerous references to the importance of the gravity of the human rights abuses on which individuals are convicted. On the other hand, the judges are at pains to stress that despite the emphasis on the gravity of the crimes and the acknowledgement of the central importance of the concept of retribution, their punishments are not merely a latter day version of vengeance. We elaborate on this observation and the central place of retribution in judges' sentencing behavior first by assessing the weight placed on this goal in their own words. Subsequently, we analyze the degree to which the retribution goal finds effect in the severity of the sentences judges hand down.

In their very first judgment, the trial chamber of the ICTY that sentenced Drazen Erdemovic acknowledged that they were given almost no guidance to arrive at appropriate sentences. It is worth quoting at length for the judges describe the very beginning of their efforts to grapple with deriving a just punishment given the objectives the UN Security Council bequeathed them. They wrote:

> Neither the Statute nor the Report of the Secretary-General nor the Rules elaborates on the objectives sought by imposing such a sentence. Accordingly, in order to identify them, the focus must be on the International Tribunal's very object and purpose, as perceived by the Member States of the Security Council of the United Nations and by the International Tribunal itself. The International Tribunal's objectives as seen by the Security Council – i.e. general prevention (or deterrence), reprobation, retribution (or "just deserts"), as well as collective reconciliation – fit into the Security Council's broader aim of maintaining peace and security in the former Yugoslavia. These purposes and functions of the International Tribunal as set out by the Security Council may provide guidance in determining the punishment for a crime against humanity.[12]

---

[12] The Prosecutor v. Drazen Erdemovic, Case No. IT-96-22-T, Trial Chamber, November 29, 1996, para 58.

The judges look to the very goals of the ICTY to determine what its objectives ought to be in that most fundamental of international justice outcomes – punishment of the guilty.[13]

Subsequently, judges began to argue that the single most important sentencing objective is retribution. One of the most elegant descriptions of its role in sentencing comes from the *Todorovic* decision where the judges declared:

> The principle of retribution, if it is to be applied at all in the context of sentencing, must be understood as reflecting a fair and balanced approach to the exaction of punishment for wrongdoing. This means that the penalty imposed must be proportionate to the wrongdoing; in other words, they hold to the principle that the punishment be made to fit the crime.[14]

In *Kupreskic* the Trial Chamber stated that:

> The Trial Chamber is of the view that, in general, retribution and deterrence are the main purposes to be considered when imposing sentences in cases before the International Tribunal. As regards the former, despite the primitive ring that is sometimes associated with retribution, punishment for having violated international humanitarian law is, in light of the serious nature of the crimes committed, a relevant and important consideration.[15]

Despite their continual reliance on retribution as a justification for punishment, the judges are always at pains to declare that this concept is not simply a modern-day version of revenge. Indeed, one finds enough rationalizations for reliance on retribution to begin to wonder if the judges doth protest too much. The *Celebici* Trial Chamber refers negatively to the "primitive theory of revenge."[16] In an oft-quoted passage from the *Alexovski* Appellate judgment, the judges declare that "An equally important factor is retribution. *This is not to be understood as fulfilling a desire for revenge but as duly expressing the outrage of the international community at these crimes*" (emphasis added).[17] While the reminders that justice is more than old fashioned retribution can, at times, seem awkward, it does appear that the judges are striving to both condemn monstrous crimes while at the same time maintain their legal impartiality in judging the individual.

[13] Interestingly, while judges reference what will eventually become the two most frequently cited objectives of punishment – retribution and deterrence – they also argue that the expressive function of their ruling is critical to the Tribunal's existence. "On the basis of this, the International Tribunal sees public reprobation and stigmatisation by the international community, which would thereby express its indignation over heinous crimes and denounce the perpetrators, as one of the essential functions of a prison sentence for a crime against humanity". The Prosecutor v. Drazen Erdemovic, Case No. IT-96-22-T, Trial Chamber, November 29, 1996, para 65.
[14] The Prosecutor v. Stevan Todorovic, Case No. IT-95-9/1-S, July 31, 2011, para 29.
[15] The Prosecutor v. Kupreskic et al., Case No. IT-95-16-T, January 14, 2000, para 848.
[16] Prosecutor v. Zejnil Delalic et al., Case No.: IT-96-21-T, Trial Chamber, November 16, 1998, para 1225.
[17] The Prosecutor v. Zlatko Alexovski, Case No. IT-95-14/1-A, March 24, 2000, para 185.

Perhaps the most eloquent articulation of the meaning of retribution as well as its larger role in the expressive capacity of the law comes from the *Mrda* Trial Chamber decision. In it the judges write:

> As a form of retribution, punishment expresses the society's condemnation of the criminal act and of the person who committed it and should be proportional to the seriousness of the crimes. The Tribunal's punishment thus conveys the indignation of humanity for the serious violations of international humanitarian law for which an accused was found guilty. In its retributive aspect, punishment may reduce the anger and sense of injustice caused by the commission of the crimes among victims and in their wider community.[18]

Here the judges are able to at once convey the importance of retribution as not just punishment that is proportionate to the crime, but is also reflective of the will and values of the international community whose laws have been violated. Thus, in nearly every opinion we find the judges declaring that retribution, with its modern and polished veneer, is at the heart of the sentences they hand down. We also see that the judges also call attention to the expressive function of punishment to publicize the condemnation of violations of international law, which it is hoped will communicate the international community's intolerance of these crimes as well as the stigmatization of those found guilty.

Yet, despite its widespread acceptance among the international tribunals, we find a great deal of scholarly debate regarding whether this punishment rationale can ever be scrubbed clean of its ancient roots and whether such a reliance on a primitive concept can help people seeking to repair the violence done to their communities. Many scholars and advocates question whether the emphasis on retribution in punishment for violations of international law does more harm than good. Henham (2003, 68) writes, "... retribution in international criminal justice has been more readily equated with the concept of victor's justice, vindication and western exculpation." They question the most basic assumptions and theories underpinning sentencing and suggest that more attention be accorded to restorative justice with its emphasis on local needs. Many advocate a more inclusive method of punishment that takes greater notice of victim rights and societal interests (Drumbl 2007a; Findlay and Henham 2005, 2010; Henham 2003, 2007; Kelsall 2010; Sloane 2007b). Retribution, with its emphasis on punishment and incarceration and the expression of moral outrage, may provide an effective legal rationale, but does it serve the needs of those most directly affected by international crimes? How important of a consideration should this problem be if the international community views itself equally as an aggrieved party and as the one responsible for delivering justice? Thus, although there is widespread acceptance of retribution within the halls of the tribunals, the reliance on this concept as the underlying rationale for the tribunals' work has

---

[18] The Prosecutor v. Darko Mrda, Case No. IT-02–59-S, March 31, 2004, para 14.

left many wondering how effective international justice can be at the grassroots level.

Having argued that retribution is the key objective of punishment, judges have sought to operationalize this concept in order to pass down the appropriate sentence. One finds nearly universal acceptance of the notion that the gravity of the offense is key. The *Celebici* Trial Chamber decision has been cited many times in this regard: "By far the most important consideration, which may be regarded as the litmus test for the appropriate sentence, is the gravity of the offence."[19] This notion was later elaborated upon by the *Kupreskic* Trial Chamber in another passage one finds cited almost reflexively in subsequent decisions: "The sentences to be imposed must reflect the inherent gravity of the criminal conduct of the accused. The determination of the gravity of the crime requires a consideration of the particular circumstances of the case, as well as the form and degree of the participation of the accused in the crime."[20]

The gravity of the crime, while certainly denoting its seriousness, is a catchall concept that can reference every aspect of the law violation from the number of victims, the severity of the human rights abuse, the damage caused materially, socially and psychologically to the heinousness exhibited by the accused in the course of committing human rights abuses. Given the many elements and effects of international crimes, the sheer impossibility of measuring all such damage, to say nothing of ranking such serious matters by their impact, it is nearly impossible for judges to arrive at some sort of common metric for assessing gravity. Instead, the judges make reference to the importance of considering the individual circumstances of the case and the individual charged in determining just how severe the crimes were. For example, in *Mrksic*, the judges find that, "In assessing the gravity of the offence the Chamber may consider the nature of the crimes, the scale and brutality of the crime, the role of the accused and the overall impact of the crimes upon the victims and their families."[21] Judges have also argued that while it is important to sentence similar crimes in a roughly analogous fashion, they have not provided any fixed criteria upon which such determinations might be made. Therefore, rather than assuming that it is impossible to measure the gravity of the crime, we choose not to accept the word of the judges that each case is unique and that the peculiar circumstances govern punishment. Instead, we seek to identify influential sentencing determinants that consistently reflect the gravity of the crime. Interestingly, despite the protestations of the judges that they do not employ common criteria across cases, we find evidence of striking and predictable patterns in the impact of sentencing determinants, as we show later.

---

[19] Prosecutor v. Zejnil Delalic et al., Case No. IT-96–21-T, Trial Chamber, November 16, 1998, para 1225.
[20] The Prosecutor v. Kupreskic et al., Case No. IT-95–16-T, January 14, 2000, para 852.
[21] The Prosecutor v. Mile Mrksic, Miroslav Radic, and Veselin Sljivancanin, Case No. IT-95–13/1-T, September 27, 2007, para 684.

Deterrence

Deterrence has been the second most frequently mentioned goal judges advance with their punishments. In the *Erdemovic* decision, the judges wrote that "In the light of this review of international and national precedents relating to crimes against humanity (or crimes of the same nature), the Trial Chamber deems most important the concepts of deterrence and retribution."[22] There is specific deterrence, which refers to preventing the convicted individual from committing further international crimes or human rights abuses, and general deterrence, which pertains to the aspirational goal of dissuading other, potential war criminals from carrying out violations of international law. With regard to specific deterrence, it is generally accepted that the likelihood any of those arrested by the international tribunals will commit future criminal acts is quite remote. The criminal acts for which they are being held to account arise in unique, historical circumstances that are unlikely to be repeated in their particular society. Therefore, general deterrence has assumed greater prominence in the jurisprudence of the tribunals.

In the *Kambanda* decision the ICTR established that:

the penalties imposed on accused persons found guilty by the Tribunal must be directed, on the one hand, at retribution of the said accused, who must see their crimes punished, and over and above that, on other hand, at deterrence, namely dissuading for good those who will attempt in future to perpetrate such atrocities by showing them that the international community was not ready to tolerate the serious violations of international humanitarian law and human rights.[23]

Subsequently, in the *Celebici* Trial Chamber decision, the judges went so far as to declare that:

Deterrence is probably the most important factor in the assessment of appropriate sentences for violations of international humanitarian law (emphasis added). Apart from the fact that the accused should be sufficiently deterred by appropriate sentence from ever contemplating taking part in such crimes again, persons in similar situations in the future should similarly be deterred from resorting to such crimes. Deterrence of high level officials, both military and civilian, in the context of the former Yugoslavia, by appropriate sentences of imprisonment, is a useful measure to return the area to peace. Although long prison sentences are not the ideal, there may be situations which will necessitate sentencing an accused to long terms of imprisonment to ensure continued stability in the area. Punishment of high-ranking political officials and military officers will demonstrate that such officers cannot flout the designs and injunctions of the international community with impunity.[24]

---

[22] The Prosecutor v. Drazen Erdemovic, Case No. IT-96–22-T, October 7, 1997, para 64.
[23] The Prosecutor v. Jean Kambanda, Case No. ICTR 97–23-S, September 4, 1998, para 28. See also the Prosecutor v. Omar Serushago, Case No. ICTR 98–39-S, February 5, 1999, para 20.
[24] Celebici Case, Case No. IT-96–21-T, Trial Chamber, November 16, 1998, para 1234.

Similarly, the *Kupreskic* Trial Chamber wrote in lofty terms of the importance of deterrence when it declared:

> As to the latter, the purpose is to deter the specific accused as well as others, which means not only the citizens of Bosnia and Herzegovina but persons worldwide from committing crimes in similar circumstances against international humanitarian law. The Trial Chamber is further of the view that another relevant sentencing purpose is to show the people of not only the former Yugoslavia, but of the world in general, that there is no impunity for these types of crimes. This should be done in order to strengthen the resolve of all involved not to allow crimes against international humanitarian law to be committed as well as to create trust in and respect for the developing system of international criminal justice.[25]

As well, the ICTR has argued that:

> This Chamber must impose sentences on convicted persons for retribution, 1 deterrence, 2 rehabilitation, 3 and to protect society. 4 As to deterrence, this Chamber seeks to dissuade for good those who will be tempted in the future to perpetrate such atrocities by showing them that the international community is no longer willing to tolerate serious violations of international humanitarian law and human rights.[26]

And that:

> With the sentence, an attempt is made to deter, that is, to discourage people from committing similar crimes. The main result sought is to discourage people from committing a second offence (special deterrence) since the penalty should also result in discouraging other people from carrying out their criminal plans (general deterrence). With respect to general deterrence, a sentence would contribute to strengthening the legal system which criminalizes the conduct charged and to assuring society that its criminal system is effective.[27]

Clearly the judges are intent on communicating a message to the world in general and would-be war criminals in particular about the international community's new-found intolerance for violations of its laws. This message has remained consistent throughout the jurisprudence of the tribunals. Subsequently, however, the Trial Chambers have been much more circumspect in the degree to which they stress the role of deterrence in determining sentence, lest they be accused by the defendants of not giving such sufficient regard to the individual circumstances of the case. The Kunarac Trial Chamber took notice of this problem of excessive emphasis on deterrence when it wrote:

> As to general deterrence, in line with the view of the Appeals Chamber, it is not to be accorded undue prominence in the assessment of an overall sentence to

[25] The Prosecutor v. Kupreskic et al., Case No. IT-95–16-T, January 14, 2000, para 848.
[26] The Prosecutor v. Clément Kayishema and Obed Ruzindana, Case No. ICTR-95–1-T, May 21, 1999, para 2.
[27] The Prosecutor v. Vincent Rutaganira, Case No. ICTR 95–1C-T, para. 110.

be imposed. The reason is that a sentence should in principle be imposed on an offender for his culpable conduct – it may be unfair to impose a sentence on an offender greater than is appropriate to that conduct solely in the belief that it will deter others.[28]

As scholars of international relations have long known, ascertaining whether the actions or words of one actor dissuaded another actor from carrying out the action in question is extremely challenging to prove in the absence of statements acknowledging such influence from the second actor. However, it may well be the case that while the justice of the international tribunals is not a sufficient condition to deter the commission of human rights atrocities, it is a necessary condition to erode the norm of impunity that has, in the past, given war criminals confidence that their actions would most likely go unpunished. Still, a nagging question remains – just how do the judges give effect to the importance of deterrence in their punishments and what sentencing determinants would allow the judges to factor the importance of deterrence into their decisions?

We also note that judges do not refer to the additional goal of stopping individuals from further escalating their criminal campaign while the conditions favoring those actions are still present – in effect, incapacitation. The goals of punishment, and in particular deterrence, are intended as ex-post remedies. We do not separate deterrence from incapacitation as our analysis is based on judicial statements and statutory documents that do not mention incapacitation as a different goal of punishment. However, as much as it is clear that international judges refer to deterrence as one of the main goals of international criminal law, it is also true that especially for indictments and proceedings occurring while wars are still ongoing, tribunals have prevented criminals from perpetrating additional crimes by arresting them or removing their political and social support through the negative stigmatization of their actions.[29]

In our view specific deterrence and incapacitation are at the same time similar and different concepts. The prevention or incapacitation of criminal activities by the same perpetrator because of his consequent political isolation, possible rehabilitation following his time in jail, or because the convicted individual will spend the rest of his life in prison, does not differ from specific deterrence – as far as both are defined as the individual's inability or unwillingness to violate the law again. We also suggest that international criminal proceedings might have concomitant deterrent and incapacitative effects through an expressive function of indictments and punishments as far as they express the moral reprobation of the international community,

---

[28] The Prosecutor v. Dragoljub Kunarac, Radomir Kovac and Zoran Vukovic, Trial Chamber, Case No. IT-96-23-T& IT-96-23/1-T, February 22, 2001, para 840, citing the Appeals Chamber in the *Tadic* case, paras 41–50.

[29] See Greenwalt (2014) speaking of the effect that the ICTY proceedings against Milosevic had on the Serbian political campaign.

thus eroding the political support of leaders standing trials. Luban (2010, 576) indicates that "trials are expressive acts broadcasting the news that mass atrocities are, in fact, heinous crimes and not merely politics by other means." We note in addition that the expressive component of sentencing and public international trials might have a greater general deterrent and, what we call, "general incapacitative" effect.

We note that in many of the discussions of deterrence it is clear that the judges are looking to speak to both the world at large and those powerful individuals who are the most critical figures in the organization and initiation of violations of international law. While a notable number of lower-ranking individuals have passed through the halls of the ICTY and ICTR, especially in their formative years, it is clear that their emphasis, as well as that of the SCSL and the ICC is on trying the most senior leaders. The tribunals' punishments are designed to speak to their role in organizing and ordering violations of international law and to warn others not to follow in their example. Thus, we should expect to find that the sentences handed down to these senior officials will take cognizance of the need to deter similarly situated individuals in other countries. We return to this prediction later when we outline our model of sentencing determinants.

Peace and Reconciliation

The tribunals are also intended to contribute to peace and reconciliation in those states over which they exercise jurisdiction. Where once violence reigned supreme and neighbor fought neighbor, through the provision of international justice – in particular the prosecution of individuals held responsible – these societies are to be encouraged to live in peace once more. The United Nations, which has promoted the ad hoc tribunals, has for many years put the promotion of peace and reconciliation through justice to the forefront of its agenda. On November 20, 2006, the UN General Assembly (GA) adopted Resolution A/RES/61/17 proclaiming 2009 the International Year of Reconciliation while recognizing "that truth and justice are indispensable elements for the attainment of reconciliation and lasting peace."[30] More recently, on April 10, 2013, during the UN General Assembly debate on the Role of International Criminal Justice in Reconciliation, the President of the UN General Assembly, Vuk Jeremic, former Serbian Foreign Minister, made a powerful and passionate statement about the role of justice in promoting reconciliation in war torn societies. Addressing the General Assembly at the opening of the debate Jeremic stated:

> I strongly believe that efforts to achieve justice and reconciliation should reinforce each other, and be bound together in what they aim to accomplish to put an end to enmity, thus breaking for good the vicious cycle of hatred. Reconciliation

[30] As found at http://daccess-dds-ny.un.org/doc/UNDOC/GEN/No6/495/45/PDF/No649545.pdf? OpenElement.

necessitates each side to accept its share of responsibility. Divorced from this context, international criminal justice can easily be perceived as an instrument of revendication, or be portrayed as complicit with attempts to assign communal blame. Such outcomes would harm efforts to strengthen the rule of law, for no legal tradition recognizes the guilt or innocence of an entire nation. Reconciliation will come about when all the parties to a conflict are ready to speak the truth to each other. Honoring all the victims is at the heart of this endeavor. That is why it is so critically important to ensure atrocities are neither denied, nor bizarrely celebrated as national triumphs. Reconciliation is in its essence about the future, about making sure we do not allow yesterday's tragedies to circumscribe our ability to reach out to each other, and work together for a better, more inclusive tomorrow.[31]

While peace, measured as the absence of violence, lends itself to mostly straightforward definition, reconciliation remains an ambiguous term with both minimalist and maximalist conceptualizations. According to Staub (2006, 868), "Reconciliation may be defined as mutual acceptance by groups of each other." Others, like Gibson (2004, 13), have taken a more holistic view of reconciliation in the context of the South African Truth and Reconciliation Commission:

> Perhaps "reconciliation" is not such a difficult and complicated concept after all. When people talk about reconciliation, they often mean nothing more than people of different races getting along better with each other – that is, a diminution of racial animosities. This may mean that people come to interact with each other more (the breakdown of barriers across races), communicate more, in turn leading to greater understanding and perhaps acceptance, resulting in the appreciation and exaltation of the value of racial diversity.

Others have argued that reconciliation is not so much a final destination as it is the journey itself in rebuilding society (Lederach 1999). Clark (2014) makes the useful distinction between "thin" and "thick" definitions of reconciliation. The former she characterizes "... as a process wherein relationships are improved to the extent that it is necessary for society to function normally" (Clark 2014, 41). Thick definitions of reconciliation emphasize greater expectations regarding the level of rebuilding of social relations and mutual acceptance among formerly warring groups. Reconciliation encompasses the health and resilience of relationships among individuals, across ethnic, religious and other types of groups. It also occurs at the societal level where, at a minimum, conflict is prevented (negative peace) and when relationships across groups socially, economically, and politically thrive and produce the fundamental conditions of peace and security (positive peace). And reconciliation encompasses everything in between among individuals, groups, and nations.

Advancing peace and reconciliation is perhaps one of the most nebulous goals over which the tribunals are intended to exercise some degree of influence. Just

[31] As found at http://www.un.org/en/ga/president/67/statements/statements/April/icj10042013.shtml.

how these legal institutions are supposed to influence personal, social and political decisions in the affected countries is never actually described. Nonetheless, one could imagine several routes by which peace and reconciliation might be indirectly facilitated through the work of the tribunal. First, by assigning blame to individuals rather than entire societies for violations of international law the tribunals are thought to lessen the need for revenge (Akhavan 2001). Second, through their truth-telling and accounting of history, the tribunals can provide a powerful counter-narrative that can challenge the lies and propaganda spread by hardline nationalist politicians. The expressive function of punishment in communicating the international community's condemnation of the crimes comes into play here as well. This, in turn, can also lessen the perceived need for revenge and create political space for those who seek to bridge ethnic divides. Third, through their outreach efforts, although not formally a part of the adjudicatory process, the tribunals can bring together people of formerly warring groups to learn more about the crimes committed in their societies, the allocation of blame and the benefits of coexistence. We do not claim ourselves that such relationships actually exist. Rather, we postulate that if the tribunals were to advance reconciliation as they are charged to do, these would seem to be the most likely avenues of influence.

While one finds far fewer references to peace and reconciliation than either retribution or deterrence in judicial opinions on sentencing, we still find eloquent declarations testifying to the importance of the tribunals' work in advancing this lofty goal. In the *Erdemovic* judgment, the judges opine that:

> The International Tribunal, in addition to its mandate to investigate, prosecute and punish serious violations of international humanitarian law, has a duty, through its judicial functions, to contribute to the settlement of the wider issues of account-ability, reconciliation and establishing the truth behind the evils perpetrated in the former Yugoslavia. Discovering the truth is a cornerstone of the rule of law and a fundamental step on the way to reconciliation: for it is the truth that cleanses the ethnic and religious hatreds and begins the healing process.[32]

In *Furundzija*, the judges stated simply that, "It is the mandate and the duty of the International Tribunal, in contributing to reconciliation, to deter such crimes and to combat impunity."[33] In the sentencing judgment for Biljana Plavsic, the judges stated, "The Trial Chamber accepts that acknowledgement and full disclosure of serious crimes are very important when establishing the truth in relation to such crimes. This, together with acceptance of responsibility for the committed wrongs, will promote reconciliation."[34] Similarly, the ICTR has found that, "Reconciliation amongst Rwandans, toward which the processes of the Tribunal should contribute,

---

[32] The Prosecutor v. Drazen Erdemovic, Case No. IT-96–22-T*bis*, March 5, 1998, para 21.
[33] The Prosecutor v. Anto Furundzija, Case No.: IT-95–17/1-T, December 10, 1998, para 28.
[34] The Prosecutor v. Biljana Plavsic, Case No. IT-00–39&40/1-S, February 27, 2003, para 80.

must also weigh heavily in the Chamber's mind when passing sentence.[35] It too has noted that guilty pleas in particular can contribute to reconciliation: "...the plea will assist in the administration of justice as well as in the process of national reconciliation in Rwanda."[36] ICTR judges have declared, "[the] Chamber will also take into account reconciliation among Rwandans towards which, pursuant to the same resolution, the Tribunal is mandated to contribute."[37] Despite the ICTR's intentions to give meaning to reconciliation through sentencing, beyond references to the role of guilty pleas in this process, it has not demonstrated how this goal is to be achieved through punishment. The SCSL has also recognized the importance of peace, as when it recognized that defendants in the CDC case had helped contribute to the peace process in Sierra Leone and that this should factor into a mitigation of their sentence.[38]

The references to peace and reconciliation are, in some sense, like similar references to those secondary sentencing determinants to which the judges must pay some respect, but which they find it difficult to address. We argue below that if the judges are to give effect to peace and reconciliation in their sentencing judgments, we are most likely to find it in their emphasis on the power of guilty pleas and expressions of remorse to help heal divided communities. While the expressive function of punishment is relevant in communicating the immorality of the atrocities of the past in contrast to the hope for reconciliation, such expressions do not typically inform the determination of specific punishments. Having described the importance attached by the judges to these three punishment rationales, we next turn to the articulation of our sentencing model. We seek to achieve three objectives. First, our analysis aims to analyze how judges give effect to these concepts, and which sentencing determinants are most powerful in predicting punishment. Second, we will show how, despite the arguments of many scholars and practitioners, the judges have been quite consistent in their sentences. Third, we demonstrate that this consistency occurs despite the fact the tribunals have argued that some of the very determinants of this consistency are not relevant in their sentences.

A MODEL OF SENTENCING

Based upon the emphasis in the tribunals' founding documents on retribution and deterrence, as well as the guidance provided in their Rules of Procedure and Evidence concerning the central role of the gravity of the crimes and the individual circumstances of the accused, we derive a parsimonious model of judicial decision making regarding sentencing. Accordingly, we begin by further developing our

---

[35] The Prosecutor v. Jean de Dieu Kamuhanda, Case No. ICTR-95–54A, January 22, 2004, para 754.

[36] The Prosecutor v. Juvenal Rugambarara, Case No. ICTR-00–59-T, November 16, 2007, para 31.

[37] The Prosecutor v. Sylvestre Gacumbitsi, Case No. ICTR-2001–64, June 17, 2004, para 336.

[38] The Prosecutor v. Moinina Fofana and Allieu Kondewa, Case No.: SCSL-04–14-A, May 28, 2008, para 67.

hypothesis that judges will give substantial weight to the gravity of the crime as measured by the broad category of offense committed. We contend that the gravity of the offense is best captured by the general type of crime which the individual is accused of committing – that is genocide, crimes against humanity and war crimes – the number of charges on which the individual was convicted, and aggravating circumstances. We note that while in some instances the judges have provided punishments for each particular charge on which an individual is found guilty, the vast majority of the sentences are pronounced as one, global punishment encapsulating the sum total of the individual's conduct. This tendency hampers our ability to distinguish whether particular crimes attract a greater or lesser punishment than others (Hola, Smeulers and Bijleveld 2011).

Gravity of the Crime

Genocide and Crimes against Humanity

All of the tribunals have consistently held that the most important function served through the punishment of the guilty is retribution. Furthermore, and most importantly for our purposes here, retribution is crucially dependent upon the exaction of a punishment that is proportionate to the crime committed. The principle of proportionality links the gravity of the crimes committed to the harshness of the punishment. Few would quarrel with the logic of this position (its moral appropriateness is another matter), but the judges have not devised any methodology or scale with which to connect the severity of the crime with the severity of the punishment. They have listed many different factors that measure gravity, as described above in the *Mrksic* decision, including, "nature of the crimes, the scale and brutality of the crime, the role of the accused and the overall impact of the crimes upon the victims and their families."[39] While the tribunals have carefully considered these factors and others to measure the gravity of the crimes, they are not fixed and easily measurable sentencing determinants that easily lend themselves to reproducibility from one trial chamber to the next, to say nothing of scholarly research. Therefore, we take the position that judges have utilized instead a rough, rank ordering of the general category of crimes to determine their severity. We hypothesize that genocide will be punished most severely, crimes against humanity, the next most severely and war crimes will be punished the least harshly.

We are cognizant of the judges' continual insistence that they do not engage in such practices. The *Krstic* judgment is worth citing at length because the judges both recognize that while it may seem appropriate to treat crimes of genocide with more severe sentences, they must nonetheless look to the underlying criminal actions to determine punishment:

---

[39] The Prosecutor v. Mile Mrksic, Miroslav Radic, and Veselin Sljivancanin, Case No. IT-95-13/1-T, September 27, 2007, para 684.

Assessing the seriousness of the crimes is not a mere matter of comparing and ranking the crimes in the abstract. It has been argued that crimes against humanity and war crimes are equally serious and that "there is in law no distinction between the seriousness of a crime against humanity and that of a war crime [...]". No Chamber has yet ruled on the ranking of crimes in a case where an individual has been found guilty of genocide. It can also be argued, however, that genocide is the most serious crime because of its requirement of the intent to destroy, in whole or in part, a national, ethnic, racial or religious group, as such. In this sense, even though the criminal acts themselves involved in a genocide may not vary from those in a crime against humanity or a crime against the laws and customs of war, the convicted person is, because of his specific intent, deemed to be more blameworthy. However, this does not rule out the Trial Chamber's duty to decide on the appropriate punishment according to the facts of each case. Genocide embodies a horrendous concept, indeed, but a close look at the myriad of situations that can come within its boundaries cautions against prescribing a monolithic punishment for one and all genocides or similarly for one and all crimes against humanity or war crimes.[476] A murder, whether qualified as a crime against humanity, a war crime or an act of genocide, may be a graver offence than imposing serious bodily or mental harm upon an individual. In this regard, the Trial Chamber ascribes to the approach taken by the Appeals Chamber that "[t]he level [of penalty] in any particular case [be] fixed by reference to the circumstances of the case.

The *Tadic* appeal against sentencing from 2000 has long been considered to be the definitive ruling in this regard:

> After full consideration, the Appeals Chamber takes the view that there is in law no distinction between the seriousness of a crime against humanity and that of a war crime. The Appeals Chamber finds no basis for such a distinction in the Statute or the Rules of the International Tribunal construed in accordance with customary international law; the authorized penalties are also the same, the level in any particular case being fixed by reference to the circumstances of the case.[40]

Nonetheless, there is also a substantial amount of scholarly work that has demonstrated that notwithstanding the judges' arguments to the contrary, the tribunals have consistently punished those convicted of genocide with longer prison terms than those convicted of other crimes, and that they have punished those convicted of crimes against humanity with longer sentences than those convicted of war crimes (Hola, Smeulers and Bijleveld 2009, 2011a, 2011b; King and Meernik 2011; Meernik 2011). Genocide is often characterized as the "crime of crimes" and is notable for not only the horrific scope of the crime, but the *dolus specialis* of the perpetrator. The "special intent" consideration also weighs into the treatment of crimes against humanity as more severe than war crimes. This intent is required for all crimes against humanity charged at the ICTR and for the oft-charged crime of persecution

---

[40] The Prosecutor v. Dusko Tadic, Case No.: IT-94-1-A and IT-94-1-A*bis*, January 26, 2000, para 69.

at the ICTY (see also Danner 2001). Thus, given the scope and special intent of genocide, as well as the typically large-scale nature of crimes against humanity, we contend that these crimes, regardless of the underlying offense, will be punished more severely. Accordingly, we hypothesize that:

Hypothesis 1: *Individuals convicted of genocide will be given longer sentences.*

Hypothesis 2: *Individuals convicted of crimes against humanity will be given longer sentences.*

Number of Guilty Counts

We also consider that the quantity of the crimes committed will matter greatly in the determination of punishment. Those convicted on more numerous charges should, *ceteris paribus*, expect to receive a lengthier prison term in recognition of the greater scale of the suffering their actions caused. The Special Court for Sierra Leone held in the Charles Taylor trial sentencing judgment that "The Trial Chamber recognizes the universally accepted principle that a person who has been convicted of many crimes should generally receive a higher sentence than a person convicted of only one of those crimes."[41] This argument has also been borne out in the work of many scholars (Hola, Smeulers and Bijleveld 2009; King and Meernik 2011; Meernik 2011). Therefore, we hypothesize that:

Hypothesis 3: *The greater the number of charges on which an individual is convicted, the greater the length of the sentence.*

Aggravating Circumstances

Judges are specifically charged with considering the individual circumstances of each case, especially including any factors that might tend to demonstrate a level of violence and cruelty that extend beyond those factors necessary to establish guilt. Aggravating factors must be proven beyond a reasonable doubt and cannot themselves be requirements for proving the category of offense or the underlying crime. While space does not permit an enumeration of the full number of factors that the judges have identified as influential in assessing the particular circumstances of the individual, we do know that the sheer number of aggravating factors that the judges specify as influential are critical in determining sentence length. Meernik (2011) finds that for each aggravating circumstance cited by the judges, punishment tends to increase sentences by 16 months on average, all other things being equal (see also Hola, Smeulers and Bijleveld 2009). Therefore, we hypothesize that:

Hypothesis 4: *The greater the number of aggravating circumstances cited by the judges as influential in their decisions, the greater the sentence.*

---

[41] The Prosecutor v. Charles Ghankay Taylor, Case No. SCLS-03-01-T, May 30, 2012, para 8.

Deterrence

Power

One of the central purposes of the international tribunals has been to deter potential war criminals and others who might commit large-scale violations of human rights. Deterrence, as such, is an effort by one actor to change the decision calculus and goals of another. Judges understand, however, that it is the collective effort by the international community, as embodied in the work of the tribunals and the apprehension of those indicted for international crimes that is the bedrock upon which the foundation of deterrence rests. To wit, in *Furundija*, the judges write, "It is the infallibility of punishment, rather than the severity of the sanction, which is the tool for retribution, stigmatisation and deterrence.[42] Sentences are but one, albeit critical component of deterrence. The trial chambers of the respective tribunals have strongly emphasized, however, that those individuals whom they seek to deter are the senior political and military officials who have the capacity to order violations of international law. Hence, when such senior officials are brought before the tribunal it is critical that the extent of their responsibility for such crimes be reflected in the severity of their punishment. According to the Appeals Chamber for the *Musema* case at the ICTR:

> This Appeals Chamber agrees with the jurisprudence of ICTY that the most senior members of a command structure, that is, the leaders and planners of a particular conflict, should bear heavier criminal responsibility than those lower down the scale, such as the foot soldiers carrying out the orders.[43]

There is also substantial research that comports with this observation and finds that the greater the level of the individual's responsibility in a political, military or civilian chain of command, the greater is the length of the imposed prison sentence (Hola, Smeulers and Bijleveld 2009; King and Meernik 2011; Meernik 2011). Therefore, we hypothesize that:

Hypothesis 5: *The greater the level of responsibility exercised by the guilty party, the greater the severity of the sentence.*

Peace and Reconciliation

Judges have often found that not only do plea bargain arrangements expedite the business of the international tribunals, they can also be a powerful tool to aid in the reconciliation process in the affected states. These arrangements whereby an individual agrees to plead guilty to a reduced quantity or quality of charges in

---

[42] The Prosecutor v. Anto Furundija, Case No. IT-95-17/1-T, December 10, 1998, para 290.
[43] The Prosecutor v. Alfred Musema, Appeals judgment, Case No. ICTR-96-13-A, November 16, 2001, para 383.

exchange for a recommendation by the Office of the Prosecutor to the trial chamber that the individual be given a lesser penalty within a specified range have been especially popular at the ICTY. Plea bargains are governed by Rule 62ter at the ICTY and Rule 62bis at the ICTR:

(A) The Prosecutor and the defence may agree that, upon the accused entering a plea of guilty to the indictment or to one or more counts of the indictment, the Prosecutor shall do one or more of the following before the Trial Chamber:
  (i) apply to amend the indictment accordingly;
  (ii) submit that a specific sentence or sentencing range is appropriate;
  (iii) not oppose a request by the accused for a particular sentence or sentencing range.
(B) The Trial Chamber shall not be bound by any agreement specified in paragraph (A).
(C) If a plea agreement has been reached by the parties, the Trial Chamber shall require the disclosure of the agreement in open session or, on a showing of good cause, in closed session, at the time the accused pleads guilty in accordance with Rule 62 (vi), or requests to change his or her plea to guilty.[44]

Twenty such agreements have been reached at the ICTY. At the ICTR there have been nine such agreements, while there have been none at the SCSL. The judges have consistently argued along the lines of the reasoning proffered by the *Deronjic* Trial Chamber:

> Truth and justice should also foster a sense of reconciliation between different ethnic groups within the countries and between the new States on the territory of the former Yugoslavia. A guilty plea indicates that an accused is admitting the veracity of the charges contained in an indictment. This also means that the accused acknowledges responsibility for his actions. Undoubtedly this tends to further a process of reconciliation. A guilty plea protects victims from having to relive their experiences and re-open old wounds.[45]

The guilty plea is thought to provide some measure of closure to the victims as well as advance a powerful counter-narrative to those who espouse ethnic hatred or revisionist histories that downplay the extent of and responsibility for the crimes committed in the Balkans, Rwanda and Sierra Leone. As Ewald (2010, 383) argues:

> Taking plea agreements and truth-telling and co-operation with the prosecution as a substantial restorative contribution, the 'discount' in sentencing for those cases can be justified not primarily with the argument of supporting the investigative process but by substantial contribution to post-conflict peace-making.

---

[44] International Criminal Tribunal for the Former Yugoslavia, Rules of Procedure and Evidence. Revision 49, May 22, 2013. Rule 62*ter* as found at http://www.icty.org/x/file/Legal%20Library/Rules_procedure_evidence/IT032Rev49_en.pdf.
[45] The Prosecutor v. Miroslav Deronjic, Case No. IT-02-61-S, March 30, 2004, paras 133-134.

Previous research has demonstrated, however, that simply pleading guilty is not sufficient to attract a lighter sentence. Rather, individuals must also be cited by the judges for cooperation with the OTP and demonstration of remorse for their actions (Meernik 2011). Typically these three characteristics tend to operate in tandem as the price the tribunals demand for reductions of sentences. Individuals who merely plead guilty for the instrumental purpose of receiving a lighter sentence have not been viewed nearly as favorably by the judges. Hence:

> **Hypothesis 6:** *Individuals who plead guilty, cooperate with the OTP and exhibit remorse will receive lighter sentences.*

Surrender

Another method by which the judges seek to facilitate reconciliation and peaceful relations among formerly warring parties is by encouraging individuals to surrender. A surprisingly large number of individuals at the tribunals, and especially the ICTY, have surrendered themselves for a variety of reasons. Many individuals do not wish to lead the life of a fugitive; many seem to believe surrender is more honorable than flight; and others may surrender because they have been induced to do so by their own government. Such actions serve the purposes of the tribunal by encouraging others to come forward and by demonstrating the legitimacy of international justice. These benefits serve to advance the goals of peace building and should be relevant in sentencing.

> **Hypothesis 7:** *Individuals who surrender to a tribunal will receive lighter sentences.*

DATA AND ANALYSIS

We created a data set containing the verdicts, punishments and other relevant factors from all trials completed at the ICTY, ICTR and SCSL. All of the information is available from the publicly accessible websites of the tribunals.[46] We analyze the sentences given to all those individuals convicted on at least one count. Those individuals who are acquitted at the trial chamber are not included in this analysis. We employ our model to explain sentencing outcomes at the trial chamber level and so do not include any revisions of verdicts or sentences provided by the Appeals Chambers. We must also account for the issuance of life sentences, which are qualitatively distinct. While the ICTY has issued relatively few such penalties (5) and the SCSL has issued none, the ICTR has issued many such sentences (twenty-eight or nearly 40 percent of its sentences). To preserve the greater information present in measuring the actual number of months for which individuals are sentenced,

---

[46] In particular, we rely heavily on the information provided by the ICTY in its case files and summary sheets, found at http://www.icty.org/sid/10095. ICTR data are found primarily at its completed cases website and it detainee status website at http://www.unictr.org/en/cases. SCSL information is found at the Residual Special Court of Sierra Leone website at http://www.rscsl.org/index.html.

we have chosen to measure life sentences as equivalent to the longest prison sentence in the data – 52 years, or 624 months. We note that the ICTY and SCSL have addressed in some manner all the indictments they have delivered and that there are no accused currently at large (one SCSL suspect is rumored to be alive). The ICTR has completed all of its trial level work with regard to ninety-three indictees. Nine individuals are still at large (three top level officials fugitives will be tried by the International Residual Mechanism for Criminal Tribunals when apprehended, while the responsibility for capturing and trying the remaining six low-level fugitives remains within the Rwandan jurisdiction). Four additional cases have been transferred and are currently ongoing in front of local jurisdictions.

The variables that we employ in this analysis include first the general type(s) of charges on which the individual is convicted or pleads guilty – genocide and crimes against humanity. Any individual found guilty on at least one count of genocide charge is coded "1" and "0" otherwise. We do the same for a crimes against humanity variable. Third, we include a variable that measures the number of charges on which an individual is convicted of or pleads guilty to. Fourth, we include a measure of the number of aggravating factors cited as influential in trial chamber opinions.[47] Fifth, we utilize a measure of the individual's level of power. For this measure we use three categories of level of individual responsibility for those charged with violations of international law. Low-level war criminals, principally ordinary soldiers and prison camp guards are coded "1"; mid-level officials, such as prison camp commanders, military officers below the rank of colonel, and political figures below cabinet level status are coded "2"; and high-level officials including military officials at or above the rank of colonel and political officials of cabinet level status or higher are coded "3." Sixth, we measure the guilty plea variable as present when the individual is cited by the judges in their decision for (a) pleading guilty; (b) cooperating with the OTP and (c) showing remorse for his or her actions. Finally, for the surrender variable we coded as "1" all those individuals who are listed in the relevant tribunal documents as having surrendered to the respective tribunals. We also include a dummy variable (coded "1" if present and "0," otherwise) for the ICTR to determine if that tribunal tends to punish individuals more severely because of the scale of the crimes committed in Rwanda with the ICTY and SCSL as the reference categories.

To analyze the data we employ the statistical software program Stata Version 13.0. We use a standard regression model that considers the impact of each of the variables when holding all others constant. Table 5.1 provides the number of individuals who were convicted of at least one count ("guilty") and those who were acquitted of all counts ("acquitted") at all four tribunals.[48] Few individuals are acquitted of all

---

[47] More information about these data can be found at http://www.psci.unt.edu/'meernik/International%20Criminal%20Tribunals%20Website.htm.

[48] We do not include the outcomes of original trials where the appeals chamber ordered a retrial. We include the verdicts of the retrial instead.

TABLE 5.1. *Verdicts at the International Tribunals*

Verdict	ICTR	ICTY	SCSL	ICC	Total
Acquitted	8	15	0	1	24
	34.7	62.5	0	4.1	100
	11.1	13.6	0	25.0	12.3
Guilty	64	95	9	3	171
	37.8	55.8	5.33	1.75	100
	88.8	86.3	100	75.0	87.6
Total	72	110	9	3	195
	37.5	56.4	4.69	2.0	100
	100	100	100	100	100

TABLE 5.2. *Summary Measures on Sentencing at the Trial Chambers of the Ad Hoc Tribunals*

Statistic	Tribunal			
	ICTY	ICTR	SCSL	Total
Mean	203*	261*	434	232*
Median	204*	360*	540	234*
Mode	240	Life	600	Life

Numbers in months / * – not including life sentences

charges at the trial level – approximately 12 percent across all four tribunals with the most occurring at the ICTY and the least (none) at the SCSL. As well, we find that three individuals were acquitted on appeal at the ICTR and seven were acquitted on appeal at the ICTY at the time of writing (results not shown). We find in Table 5.2 that the mean (excluding life sentences) sentence for the three ad hoc tribunals is 232 months in prison, while the median sentence is 234 months. The most frequently occurring sentence is life in prison. For the ICTY the mean sentence is 203 months; the median is 204 months and modal sentence is 240 months. For the ICTR the respective numbers are 261 months; 360 months and life. For the SCSL the mean sentence is 434 months; the median sentence is 540 months in prison and the modal category is 600 months in prison. There are too few data points on the ICC to make reliable estimates.

We next examine our model explaining sentence length. One of the most critical demonstrations of the power of a model is the R^2, goodness of fit indicator that tells us the degree of variation in the dependent variable that is explained by the model.[49] We see in Table 5.3 that our model explains 62 percent of the variation

[49] For example, an R^2 of 1 or 100 percent would indicate that every sentence has been perfectly predicted, while an R^2 of .5 (50 percent) indicates that 50 percent of the variation across all sentences has been explained.

TABLE 5.3. *Regression Estimates of Trial Chamber Sentences at the Tribunals*

Variable	Coefficient	Standard Error	T Statistic	P Value
Genocide	228.694	38.674	5.910	0.000
Crimes Against Humanity	111.154	27.260	4.080	0.000
Number Guilty Counts	8.308	1.907	4.360	0.000
Aggravating Factors	24.273	6.527	3.720	0.000
Power	53.932	12.718	4.240	0.000
Plea/Cooperate/Remorse	12.806	34.357	0.370	0.710
Surrender	− 42.866	23.666	− 1.810	0.072
Mitigating Factors	− 22.820	5.007	− 4.560	0.000
ICTR	− 39.684	39.323	− 1.010	0.314
Constant	− 5.141	41.427	− 0.120	0.901

$N = 170$
$R^2 = 62$

in sentencing across all four tribunals. This degree of statistical accuracy is quite good, but more importantly it demonstrates that sentencing at the tribunals is quite consistent across a wide variety of cases. One of the chief criticisms of the tribunals from many legal practitioners and academics has been that sentencing practices are inconsistent or erratic. Some defendants get off quite lightly, while others have been subject to the most severe punishment, namely life in prison. The *Celebici* Appeals Chamber opined that:

> Public confidence in the integrity of the administration of criminal justice (whether international or domestic) is a matter of abiding importance to the survival of the institutions which are responsible for that administration. One of the fundamental elements in any rational and fair system of criminal justice is consistency in punishment. This is an important reflection of the notion of equal justice.[50]

Despite this endorsement, however, we find many questioning the tribunals' sentencing practices (e.g., Bagaric and Morss 2006; Harmon and Gaynor 2007; Henham 2003, 2007). Scholars, advocates and practitioners have criticized the tribunals for perfunctory rationales of sentencing (e.g., Drumbl 2007a; Harmon and Gaynor 2007; Sloane 2007a) and insufficient attention to punishment during trials (Harmon and Gaynor 2007). "Regrettably, the ad hoc tribunals have consistently failed to define such sentencing aims, or explored their meaning in the international trial context. Nor have they intimated exactly how particular sentencing purposes might be linked to guidance in determining punishment" (Henham 2003, 69). Drumbl (2007a, 11) writes that "the sentencing practice of international institutions remains confusing, disparate, inconsistent and erratic; it gives rise to distributive inequities." Olusanya

[50] The Prosecutor v. Zejnil Delalic, Zdravko Mucic, Hazim Delic and Esad Landzo, Case No. IT-96–21-A, Appeal Judgment, February 20, 2001, para 756.

(2005, 139) is even more dramatic in his criticism of the ICTY when he writes that its sentencing practice is, "akin to a lottery system because penalties are picked randomly rather than methodically." We would disagree with such assessments as the evidence presented here demonstrates that it is possible to predict sentences fairly well with a parsimonious model. We also find that almost all the hypotheses are supported by the estimates, which further demonstrates that punishment is driven by a few, critical determinants.

We see in Table 5.3 that the coefficients for the variables measuring convictions for genocide and crimes against humanity are both statistically significant.[51] All other things being equal, when an individual is convicted of at least one charge of genocide at the trial chamber level, we can expect to see the sentence increased by 228 months. Additionally, individuals convicted of at least one crime against humanity can expect to receive an additional 111 months in prison, *ceteris paribus*. Not only is it striking that these factors exercise such a powerful influence, these findings run contrary to repeated statements over the years by the judges that no one general category of criminal offense attracts a greater punishment than another. What matters, the judges have claimed, are the underlying offenses – murder, rape, torture, and so forth. In the *Rajic* decision, the ICTY held, "the case-law of the Tribunal has consistently held that 'there is in law no distinction between the seriousness of a crime against humanity and that of a war crime'. The gravity of the crimes should be assessed in view of the particular circumstances of each case."[52] Indeed, despite their protestations the judges may well be immune from acting on the belief that genocide in particular is the "crime of crimes." The crime of genocide entails not only the effort to destroy in whole or in part an entire category of people, which is horrific in itself, but is also characterized by its special intent, by which few other crimes are defined. The intent, the goal and the scale of genocide would seem to dwarf almost all other crimes. As Sloane (2007a, 724) writes, "But if gravity means culpability in a sense other or more than a consequentialist one, then the *dolus specialis* of genocide – to destroy in whole or in part, a national, ethnic, racial or religious group, as such – matters a great deal for purposes of assessing gravity as it bears on sentencing for the 'crime of crimes.'"

Yet, as Hola, Smeulers and Bijleveld (2011, 423) astutely observe:

The question remains, however, whether the heavier sentences for genocide or crimes against humanity are related solely to the fact that cases were characterized as genocide or crimes against humanity and this characterization in itself attracts a heavier sentence (related to gravity in abstracto) or whether these cases are sentenced harsher because they are indeed the very worst cases with the greatest number of death and harm caused (related to gravity in concreto).

[51] This means that the likelihood of observing the relationship between an independent variable, such as a genocide conviction, and the dependent variable of sentencing, is statistically quite unlikely.
[52] The Prosecutor v. Ivica Rajic, a.k.a. Viktor Andric, Case No. IT-95–12-S, May 8, 2006, para 83.

TABLE 5.4. *Levels of Responsibility in Civilian, Political or Military Chain of Command for Those Convicted by the Ad Hoc Tribunals*

Power	ICTY		ICTR		SCSL		ICC		Total	
Low Level	27	28%	16	25%	0		0	0	43	25%
Mid Level	32	34%	25	40%	2	22%	0	0	59	35%
High Level	36	38%	22	35%	7	78%	3	100%	68	40%

(Tribunal spans ICTY, ICTR, SCSL, ICC)

Our results cannot speak to the issue of whether gravity measured in the abstract or the concrete is driving these results, but they do tell us that there is something of a hierarchy of crimes that both scholars and practitioners should be aware of.

While these findings speak to the impact of qualitative factors on sentencing, we see that the quantity of the crimes committed also plays a crucial role. The coefficient for the variable measuring the number of counts on which individuals are convicted is both statistically significant and powerful. For each count on which the trial chamber finds the accused guilty, the individual can expect to receive an additional eight months in prison. The scope and scale of the criminal offenses play a powerful role in judicial decision making. The number of aggravating factors for which the accused is cited by the trial chamber is also a powerful explanatory factor. For every additional aggravating factor that is discussed by the judges as relevant in their determinations, the convicted party can expect to receive an additional twenty-four months in prison. The judges have found numerous such circumstances as critical in their judgments.

The level of power held by the accused is one of the most critical sentencing determinants – the coefficient for this variable is positive and statistically significant. For every one-unit increase in this variable (corresponding to a step up in the three-value categorization of level of responsibility), the convicted party can expect to receive fifty-four additional months in prison. In the *Martic* case the trial chamber asserted that:

> in principle, a person's guilt must be described as increasing in tandem with his position in the hierarchy: The higher in rank or further detached the mastermind is from the person who commits a crime with his own hands, the greater is the responsibility.[53]

As can be seen in Table 5.4, there are forty-three individuals at the low end of the scale (25 percent); fifty-nine convicted persons who occupied mid-rung levels of responsibility (35 percent); and sixty-eight individuals who held the highest levels of power and were found guilty by the tribunals (40 percent). The tribunals have

[53] The Prosecutor v. Milan Martic, Separate Opinion of Judge Schomburg, Case No. IT-95-11, October 8, 2008, x 9.

consistently argued that in order for deterrence to work, those who organize and order human rights atrocities must perceive that justice will eventually catch up with them. Yet, while domestic law enforcement often emphasizes the instrumental reasons that explain obedience – the fear of detection and punishment that restrains individuals from violating the law for personal gain (from stealing, speeding, or cheating on taxes) – there is substantial research that suggests deterrence plays only a limited role in influencing individual behavior (MacCoun 1993; Tyler 1990; Tyler and Darley 2000). Rather, individuals are more apt to obey the law because they accord legitimacy to those entrusted with authority and because they perceive such behavior as morally correct.

Thus, even though the tribunals have gained the apprehension of nearly all those individuals they have indicted and convicted the vast majority of them, the extent to which their effectiveness in this regard has penetrated the decision making process of would-be war criminals elsewhere in the world is uncertain. Nonetheless, as we emphasized earlier, one must also think in terms of the potential impact of a counter-factual situation in which none of the tribunals were established. Would potential war criminals have been emboldened to act in the belief that there would always be impunity? As ICTY President Judge Meron has written, "Without the establishment of the tribunal . . . the perception that even the most egregious violations of international humanitarian law can be committed with impunity would have been confirmed." One cannot know this, but such a future would seem to be a dangerous and insecure one indeed.[54] Thus, we find that the tribunals punish those most responsible most severely to both condemn the behavior and dissuade others from embarking on such enterprises.

Surrenders also play a key role in reducing sentences. Regardless of whether judges cite defendants for such behavior or not, those who surrender tend to receive approximately forty-three months in sentence reduction (Table 5.3). Such behaviors lessen the amount of political wrangling the tribunals must engage in to induce major powers, such as the United States and the European Union to exert pressure on recalcitrant states. Their financial inducements, such as the prospect of membership in the EU was instrumental in gaining compliance from Serbia and Croatia. The Serbian government also passed legislation that offered financial rewards for those who surrendered and for their families:

> The law gives indictees a full salary, plus unspecified "compensation" for family and legal expenses. In the Republic of Srpska, the Serb-controlled part of Bosnia, benefits are even more generous: a full salary to the indictee himself, a double salary paid to his family, plus 80 euro a month to each of his school-age children. (A typical Bosnian Serbian salary is only 200 euro a month.) Family members also

54 Meron, Theodor (1997). "Answering for War Crimes – Lessons from the Balkans." *Foreign Affairs* 76(1): 1–8, at 7.

get four expense-paid trips a year to The Hague to visit indicted loved ones. And last year Srpska added a cash bonus of 25,000 euro for anyone who surrenders.[55]

In total, 51 out of 166 individuals have surrendered to the tribunals, with the vast majority coming to the ICTY (results not shown). We include in this calculation only those individuals who were ultimately found guilty. There were no surrenders to the SCSL and just six surrenders to the ICTR. In contrast, forty-five individuals surrendered to the ICTY, which represents nearly half of the total number of individuals who were convicted on at least one charge (48 percent). When we examine the total of all individuals who surrendered to the tribunals, regardless of the final outcome of their case, we find that out of a grand total of 215 individuals who were indicted and in the custody of the tribunals, sixty-five (30 percent) surrendered to the tribunals. We note that this population includes both those whose cases were later referred to a national court and those who were acquitted. In fact, of the twenty-four defendants who were acquitted of all charges, eight or 33 percent were individuals who had surrendered.

The coefficient for the variable measuring the total number of mitigating factors cited by the judges as influential in their sentencing is also statistically significant. The negative relationship indicates that each mitigating factor cited by the judges as influential tends to decrease the sentence by approximately twenty-three months. In fact, this coefficient is very close in size, albeit in the opposite direction as the coefficient for the number of aggravating factors cited by the judges. In the former case, the tendency is to diminish sentences by approximately two years for every factor cited, while in the latter the trend is to increase sentences by about two years for every factor cited as determinative.

Those who plead guilty, cooperate with the tribunal and show remorse for the crimes perpetrated tend to receive lighter sentences, although the coefficient for this variable is statistically insignificant. However, there is a significant degree of overlap or collinearity between this variable and our measure of the number of mitigating factors. Because this variable consists of the presence of three such factors, we reran the model without the variable measuring the total number of mitigating factors and found that indeed, those who plead guilty, cooperate and show remorse receive lighter sentences. The new results are found in Table 5.5. The coefficient for this variable is negative and now statistically significant. It indicates that such individuals can expect to receive, on average, a sentence reduction of approximately fifty-eight months. It has been argued that such pleas can provide many benefits for international justice, as noted by the Trial Chamber in the *Bagaragaza* case:

[55] Nordland, Ron, and Zoran Cirjakovic. "Pensions For War Criminals." *Newsweek International* July 25, 2005, US edition.

TABLE 5.5. *Revised Regression Estimates of Trial Chamber Sentences at the Ad Hoc Tribunals*

Variable	Coefficient	Standard Error	T Statistic	P Value
Genocide	252.170	40.615	6.210	0.000
Crimes Against Humanity	127.140	28.646	4.440	0.000
Number Guilty Counts	9.832	1.989	4.940	0.000
Aggravating Factors	25.933	6.905	3.760	0.000
Power	53.390	13.476	3.960	0.000
Plea/Cooperate/Remorse	− 58.084	32.461	− 1.790	0.075
Surrender	− 72.102	24.138	− 2.990	0.003
ICTR	− 51.482	41.578	− 1.240	0.217
constant	− 67.309	41.450	− 1.620	0.106

$N = 170$
$R^2 = 58$

The jurisprudence has established that a guilty plea may have mitigating effects because it shows remorse and repentance and contributes to reconciliation, the establishment of the truth, the encouragement of other perpetrators to do so, the sparing of a lengthy investigation and trial and thus resources and time, and relieves witnesses from giving evidence in court.[56]

Ewald (2010) argues that regardless of their benefits to the tribunal in the form of reduced costs and increased efficiency, guilty pleas serve an even more critical function in helping advance peace. In the Srebrenica case involving Momir Nikolic the judges provide strong evidence of the impact of guilty pleas when combined with cooperation and expressions of remorse, when they write, "The Trial Chamber finds that Momir Nikolić's guilty plea is significant and can contribute to fulfilling the Tribunal's mandate of restoring peace and promoting reconciliation."[57] The judges then go on to provide even more tangible evidence of the impact when they quote at length from a victim of the atrocities committed by the Bosnian Serb forces:

> Mr Suljagić writes that, while the confession of Mr. Nikolić (and that of Mr. Obrenović) will likely not transform Bosnian Serb views, for him personally: the confessions have brought me a sense of relief I have not known since the fall of Srebrenica in 1995. 'They have given me the acknowledgement I have been looking for these past eight years. While far from an apology, these admissions are a start. We Bosnian Muslims no longer have to prove we were victims. Our friends and cousins, fathers and brothers were killed − we no longer have to prove they were innocent'.[58]

[56] The Prosecutor v. Michel Bagaragaza, Case No. ICTR-05–86-S, November 17, 2009, para 38.
[57] The Prosecutor Momir Nikolic, Case No. IT-02–60/1-S, December 2, 2003, para 145.
[58] The Prosecutor Momir Nikolic, Case No. IT-02–60/1-S, December 2, 2003, para 146.

While the tribunals' abilities to advance reconciliation and peace in these nations that have experienced horrific violence are limited, there is no doubt great power to be found in such statements as these that demonstrate the value of the guilty plea.

Finally, we see that the coefficient for the ICTR variable is statistically insignificant. When controlling for all other relevant sentencing determinants, the ICTR is no more likely to sentence individuals to longer or lighter terms of incarceration. As we noted earlier, the ICTR has handed down significantly more life sentences. This is most likely a result of the greater numbers of genocide convictions. It has been (mis)perceptions such as this that have caused many observers to argue that there is a lack of consistency in sentencing within and across the tribunals. Consistency in sentencing is critical in many respects, not the least of which is that inapposite practices risk undermining public confidence in these institutions (Clark 2007). The judges too have been quite cognizant of these charges and have written in their opinions numerous times that each case is treated on its own unique circumstances. This debate has now carried over to the ICC. In a very revealing discussion in its very first sentencing judgment in the case of the Congolese war criminal, Thomas Dyilo, judges take note of the Prosecutor's desire to avoid charges of inconsistency and develop a sentencing regime. It is worth quoting at length from their opinion:

> The prosecution argues that in order "to avoid inexplicable sentencing discrepancies," the sentencing policy of the Court should presume a "consistent baseline" for sentences, which should not be adjusted on the basis that some crimes are less serious than others. It is submitted that the appropriate "baseline" or starting point for all sentences should be set at approximately 80% of the statutory maximum, and this should then be adjusted in accordance with Rule 145 to take into account any aggravating and mitigating circumstances and other factors relevant to the convicted person and the circumstances of the crimes. No established principle of law or relevant jurisprudence under Article 21 of the Statute has been relied on in support of this suggested approach, which would bind the judges to a minimum starting point of 24 years in all cases. In the judgment of the Chamber, the sentence passed by a Trial Chamber should always be proportionate to the crime (see Article 81(2)(a)), and an automatic starting point – as proposed by the prosecution – that is the same for all offences would tend to undermine that fundamental principle.[59]

Once again, we see judges defending the principle that each case must be judged based on its own characteristics and that any kind of sentencing guidelines would tend to undermine such an important principle, especially one that has been written into the founding documents of all the tribunals. Perhaps once practitioners and scholars examine the evidence as presented in research like this and other work

---

[59] *The Prosecutor v. Thomas Lubanga Dyilo*, Case No. ICC-01/04–01/06, July 10, 2012, paras 92 and 93.

(Hola, Bijleveld and Smeulers 2011a, 2011b; King and Meernik 2011; Meernik 2011) there will be greater awareness of the significant consistency that does exist.

This is not to argue that the sentences at the Trial Chamber are without fault. Many have been revised at the level of the appeals chamber, especially in a downward direction, which may suggest that the trial chambers tend to sentence some individuals to excessively lengthy sentences. In general, however, the Appeals Chamber will only revise sentences, ". . . unless the Trial Chamber has committed a 'discernible error' in exercising its discretion or has failed to follow the applicable law."[60] In particular:

> To show that the Trial Chamber committed a discernible error in exercising its discretion, appellants must demonstrate that the Trial Chamber gave weight to extraneous or irrelevant considerations, failed to give weight or sufficient weight to relevant considerations, made a clear error as to the facts upon which it exercised its discretion, or that the Trial Chamber's decision was so unreasonable or plainly unjust that the Appeals Chamber is able to infer that the Trial Chamber must have failed to exercise its discretion properly.[61]

When we examine what happens at the Appeals Chamber level, we find that fifty-two or 56 percent of Appeals Chamber decisions resulted in no change to the sentence; forty or 37 percent of the sentences are reduced; and only eleven or 10 percent of the sentences are increased on appeal (results not shown). While most sentences are left unchanged, when the judges are compelled to revise them, they tend to diminish the penalty provided at the trial chamber level. In one sense, the Appeals Chamber might appear to be easing back on what turn out to be excessively severe punishments.

The appeals chambers, in reducing sentences in a number of cases, may be responding to several different concerns. First, given their remove from the vivid and emotionally compelling testimony of eye witnesses to the crimes committed specifically and the facts of the case more generally, it is possible appellate judges may not be as influenced by the horrific nature of these human rights atrocities. Second, and relatedly, the appellate focus on the more procedural aspects of the trial may lead judges to strike down some grounds for conviction that did not meet their more stringent legal expectations. Third, the defendants generally lodge every sort of appeal possible against their convictions and sentences, which may increase the likelihood that they will find at least some element of their judgment that was lacking. Regardless, it is important to emphasize that the appellate process that is now a basic feature of international tribunals does serve a key purpose in reviewing trial judgments and providing a key procedural safeguard to protect the rights of

---

[60] The Prosecutor v. Stanislav Galic, Case No. IT-98–29-T 5, December 5, 2003, para 393.
[61] The Prosecutor v. Enver Hadzihasanovic and Amir Kubura, Case No. IT-01–47-A, April 22, 2008, para 2068.

defendants, and even, on occasion, the interests of victims and the larger national and international communities.

CONCLUSION

Punishments represent the culmination and in many ways are the most essential aspect of the work of the international tribunals. As Harmon and Gaynor (2007, 707) write, "Sentencing, therefore, arguably means more to victims, the accused and the public at large than almost any other issue that arises during trial." Sentences are an expression of the legal, political and moral values not just of the tribunals, but of the international community, and as such, are intended to speak to the victims, the villains and the world. As we have noted, however, many have criticized the tribunals' sentences for being inconsistent, for lacking in rationale, and to the extent there is an underlying basis for the punishments, too rooted in retributivist norms of justice that are not so relevant to the people of the affected states. We have shown that there is a great deal of consistency in sentencing, and certainly an emphasis on retribution as reflected in the severity of the punishments that have been handed down by the judges.

Despite the evidence of consistency and severity in sentencing, we must recognize that such punishments may not always resonate with the victims. Many sadly conclude that the punishments available can never match the gravity of war crimes, crimes against humanity and genocide for such offenses do violence to all of society whose full measure of retribution could never be encapsulated in the punishment meted out to an individual or even those few responsible at the highest level. As one witness recounted:

> The International Tribunal in the Hague is following the laws and facts, and any punishment to be determined is too lenient for their crime; only we, the people who witnessed the terror, lost our closest and dearest ones, watched and listened to descriptions of the crimes inconceivable to the human spirit, know that there is no adequate punishment for such crimes. (Ivkovic 2001, 321)

Indeed, even while the judgments of these international tribunals can provide a necessary level of condemnation that the international community desires when its' most cherished norms are violated, the more immediate victims and the citizens of the affected societies cannot repair the damage wrought with lofty words. As we saw in the previous chapter, however, judges have sought to use these occasions to utilize the expressive capacity of the law. They have condemned the atrocities and made stirring proclamations that such behaviors should never be tolerated again.

Can we expect the ICC to continue this tradition and resist developing a more rigorously defined theory and practice of punishment? ICC judges are given less discretion in the sentencing process than their colleagues at the ad hoc tribunals (e.g., significant restrictions on sentences beyond thirty years; requirement that a punishment be provided for each count on which an individual is convicted found in the Rome Statute and a detailed listing of mitigating and especially aggravating factors in the Rules of Procedure and Evidence[62]). On the one hand, these limitations may at some point become too restrictive on the judges, who may then seek greater flexibility from the Assembly of States Parties. On the other hand, since these individual circumstances have long been cited by the ad hoc tribunals, it seems likely that the ICC judges would find them useful as well. Therefore, it would appear doubtful that they would find it necessary to develop a theory of punishment either. As long as the guidance provided in the founding documents comports with the practice of the tribunals and as long as the judges still retain significant capacity to individualize sentences according to their own needs, they have the necessary discretion to proceed without their own theory of punishment. Judges seek to go beyond the written word when that word no longer reflects the realities with which they must contend.

We have argued that judges are not typically behaving in an expressly entrepreneurial fashion when sentencing individuals, although we must emphasize that we draw a distinction between the practice of sentencing analyzed here and the jurisprudence of sentencing evaluated in Chapter Three. That is, judges are not generally motivated to move beyond the guidance found in their statutes and rules of procedure and evidence when sentencing because their authority is already quite substantial in this area. The founding documents are flexible enough to permit the judges to ground punishment in various rationales (e.g., retribution, deterrence, peace and reconciliation) and utilize whatever sentencing determinants are most appropriate. Thus, judges are not expressly entrepreneurial in the more specific sense that they seek to protect human rights and advance the legacy of international justice by pushing the boundaries of their rights, responsibilities and powers. Rather, they are we might say, more generally entrepreneurial in advancing their right and judicial power to continue to sentence individuals according to the open-ended criteria they find most useful. By referencing those elements of sentencing objectives and criteria that are most useful in ensuring judicial discretion, judges seek to strengthen the role of their institutions in advancing human rights and ensuring their judicial legacies.

We would argue that the goal that unites judicial behavior in the progressive development of the law, the use of expressive language in judgments and sentencing behavior is the cementing of judicial authority. By asserting their authority to develop the law, speak through the law and punish through the law, judges rely on the authority granted them when possible and move beyond it in an entrepreneurial fashion when the need and opportunity arise. Thus in sentencing, as in the progressive development of the law and the use of expressive language, judges have evinced a marked determination to assert judicial authority to achieve the broad

---

[62] ICC Treaty, Article 77 and Rules of Procedure and Evidence, Rule 145, Part 2.

aims of the tribunals to provide justice, retribution, deterrence and protection of human rights. In matters of sentencing where judges possess nearly all the requisite authority necessary to advance human rights and ensure their judicial legacy, we see judges clearly asserting their authority to decide on such matters as they see fit. Ultimately, whether judges act as bold entrepreneurs in matters of law or confident arbiters of punishment, they are custodians of international justice seeking to establish its rightful place in international relations.

6

Conclusions

Judges are the fulcrum upon which international law turns. Their judgments at the international criminal tribunals are the ultimate expression of the mandate to provide justice, but they are much more than the final words that conclude a trial or an appeal. Judges use them as a tool to realize goals that can empower the legacy and effectiveness of international criminal law beyond the goals stated in the founding documents. This is particularly important given that international criminal justice had remained mostly dormant for more than fifty years after Nuremberg and Tokyo. On the one hand, our arguments are not especially remarkable, for those who practice and study international law understand the critical role played by judges and their rulings. On the other hand, we conceive of judges as conscious players in this process of the development of international justice. Where much scholarship has analyzed the content of their decisions the focus has been on the law itself rather than the human agency that drives change. We have argued throughout that judges are judicial entrepreneurs who seek to achieve professional and ideological goals in the business of the development of international jurisprudence. Identifying the import and role of these goals for the judges represents a shift in our analysis of the law from one where law is the object to one in which judges are the subject.

We find ourselves at a critical turning point in the history of the development of the system of international justice that makes our scholarly task and our theoretical focus all the more important. At the time of writing two of the four international tribunals we analyze have shuttered their doors – the SCSL and the ICTR. The end of the ICTY is now in sight as its last cases conclude. With their business ended, our analysis of new developments in international law and judicial decision making must turn its focus almost entirely to the International Criminal Court.[1]

---

[1] With all due respect to the Lebanese tribunal, the Extraordinary Chambers in the Courts of Cambodia and the Special Panels for Serious Crimes in East Timor, these institutions have experienced significant problems with conducting trials such that their impact upon international law development is likely to be limited.

What theoretical paradigm(s) or model(s) will now guide our understanding of international jurisprudence as we focus our attention increasingly upon this institution that has, not without coincidence, established, at the time of writing, its permanent headquarters in The Hague? We suggest a diversity of approaches to understand the increasingly critical role that is played by international justice in international relations. Not surprisingly, we believe it is important that we chart the development of international law and jurisprudence as guided by judges with legal and ideological preferences regarding its direction. Judges, acting as decision makers, are both reactive and proactive; they are both agents of the international community and agents of judicial change; and most especially judges are judicial entrepreneurs. The law matters, but so do the individuals who write the law.

In the preceding pages we have sought to draw a portrait of judges as individuals guided by these professional and ideological goals in advancing human rights and the legacy of their institutions. Their judgments are informed by the progressive development of the law, the desire to speak beyond the legal community to the victims and the wider international community, and the need to provide a punishment that is grounded in a commitment to human rights and the preservation of judicial prerogative. Professional goals animate their rulings as they seek to convince the legal community of the necessity of progressive jurisprudential development and as they work to achieve a lasting historical legacy. We see evidence of their ideological interest in human rights and the concern for the victims of human rights atrocities in many of their legal arguments and most especially in their expressive use of language and the sentences handed down. Judges also advance the more political goals the tribunals were bequeathed by the international community that sought not only justice, but deterrence, reconciliation and ultimately peace through their efforts. Indeed, some maintain that such goals are truly the most important and consequential of all the tribunals' aims (Futumura and Gow 2014). They have acted as judicial entrepreneurs to realize these goals on judgment day. Understanding the importance of what these judges do through their judgments is critical for several reasons.

Judgments are the ultimate expression of condemnation of violations of international humanitarian law. They represent not just a legal verdict, important though this may be, but also the verdict of the international community. The judges speak on behalf of this community when they communicate through their decisions and express moral judgments and understanding of human rights. Judgments represent a "historical archive" of the atrocities committed. They are the ledger books upon which we assess the damage wrought by genocide, war, and violence, and the allocation of blame among the actors involved. They create a history of conflict through which the history of the affected peoples is informed. We would hope that most of those in whose name the tribunals dispense justice would seek to genuinely understand and act upon the true meaning of these judgments. But we must recognize that many will interpret these judgments to suit their own political use of history or deny the truths articulated by the tribunals. And despite the absence of a fully-formed system of 'stare decisis' in international law, judgments are the jurisprudence upon which future international tribunals will base their decisions. Judgments are the repository of the major developments of international criminal law. They are the reference book to which future judges and scholars will turn to understand our world and to inform their contemporary laws. What, exactly then, have we learned about how judges act as judicial entrepreneurs?

PROGRESSIVE DEVELOPMENT OF THE LAW

In the numerous judgments handed down by the appeals chambers of the post-Nuremberg international criminal tribunals, judges have very often gone beyond their mandate of dispensing justice, establishing a historic and judicial record of the perpetrated crimes, and punishing the perpetrators. Many of the judgments develop international criminal law, define new typologies of violations of international humanitarian law, and improve upon the definition of crimes to eliminate the disconnect between the law and facts adjudicated. In our theoretical framework we have analyzed the legal and political reasons why judges go beyond their mandate and have demonstrated how judges push the boundaries of legal and political constraints to advance international law. We have spoken of entrepreneurial judges, who out of concern for the protection of human rights and the establishment of the tribunals' legacy and legitimacy, have used the gaps and ambiguities of international law to develop and enhance international law.

We suggested that the appeals chamber judgments are the documents in which judges repeatedly reaffirm important, particularly new and emerging principles of international criminal law that are subsequently cited by other appellate decisions. The appeals chamber decisions represent the final conclusion of a case and the last judicial word on the definition of crimes and procedures. We also suggested that the higher number of citations of paragraphs contained in the appeals chamber decisions as well as some of the trial chamber judgments, the greater the likelihood that that paragraph or that case contains an important development of international criminal law. Our findings indicate that some of the most groundbreaking cases, such as *Celebici* and *Tadic*, which deal with some of the most critical issues international judges face, are indeed the most cited cases. We also found that aspects of crimes that were not clearly defined by existing international criminal law, such as elements of joint criminal enterprise, issues related to the definition of "aiding and abetting," "common design" or "purpose," are the issues on which judges have progressively enhanced international criminal law. Judges also cited many key rulings on sentencing that demonstrate the vital import of punishment in jurisprudence but also in the realization of the tribunals' political goals. The development of international law on both modes of liability and in sentencing demonstrate that judges have widened the scope of the law to either ensure individuals may be held accountable or that those who are, are punished appropriately. In both cases, the end result is greater protection for individual human rights, which in turn, is one of the key legacies of international tribunals.

The frequent reference to these case paragraphs, we believe, demonstrates the critical role of the judicial reasoning in these opinions, and also suggests a progressive development of the law. The cases to which the judges refer are setting important, new precedents on subjects that heretofore were often absent, ambiguous, or lacking in definition. Judges have acted as entrepreneurs to develop jurisprudence in these areas to better protect human rights through ensuring liability of leaders and effective punishment of the guilty, and to secure their legacy.

However, we were surprised to find that for one of the crimes that has attracted considerable attention from scholars and practitioners alike – the crime of rape or sexual assault – there has been significantly less evidence of judicial ferment and citation of key cases regarding its definition (Schabas 2012, 158). The crime of rape has been defined as a violation of international humanitarian law for the very first time by the tribunals and the elements of the crime have been expanded to comprehend a variety of criminal behavior. Yet, in the extensive jurisprudence produced by the appeals chamber of the ad hoc tribunals, issues pertaining to the crime of rape are noticeably sparse. The absence of the appeals chamber's jurisprudence is even more puzzling in the case of the ICTR, which has adjudicated some of the most heinous sexual violations in the history of humanity. The SCSL has also reached important decisions on issues such as sexual slavery, but its rulings are not cited nearly so often yet. What does this tell us about judicial behavior at the ad hoc tribunals and what does it means for our theoretical argument?

To be sure, the jurisprudence on rape developed by the ad hoc tribunals has been groundbreaking and of pivotal importance for the future of international criminal justice. The trial chambers' decisions that have dealt with the crime of rape have revolutionized the way rape in times of war is adjudicated by, for example, making clearer the role of coercion in sexual slavery cases. We suggest that the relative lack of an extensive network of citations on the subject, however, may be due in part to judges seeking to balance the *need* to dispense certain and expeditious justice with a perceived need to avoid lengthy and difficult debates on the definition of crimes, which could hinder the effective adjudication of cases. Judges seem to have readily accepted the definitions set forth in *Akayesu*, *Furundzija* and *Kunarac*. Many of the cases involving sexual assault have also involved the actual perpetrators, a class of defendants whose presence has gradually diminished as the tribunals sought more high level officials in cases that have involved command responsibility. Thus, another critical reason for the comparative lack of progressive development of the law has been the scarcity of additional cases involving sexual assault.

The comparative lack of extensive citation of issues involving sexual assault may suggest that when the actual criminal behavior involves principally the conduct of the direct perpetrator, there will be less prosecutorial involvement in bringing such cases and hence, less judicial development of the law. Rather, we may need to await cases where superiors are involved directly or indirectly in the commission of crimes for such charges to be brought and for the law to be further developed. The progressive development of law on sexual assault and other specific criminal offenses may depend on whether the ICC is able to bring cases involving superiors who exercised authority over perpetrators of such crimes.

Lastly, one of our unanticipated findings is that appeals chamber judges spend a considerable amount of time detailing appeals procedures, creating rules about the relationship between appeals chambers and trial chambers, and overseeing the formal requirements of the appellants' briefs. All appellate judgments, before dealing with the more substantive issues of a case, feature a list of formal procedures. We believe that there is a very basic reason for this type of judicial behavior, which is that these tribunals are the first to have appellate chambers (Drumbl and Gallant 2001; Fleming 2002). Thus, lacking precedents on which to rely and scant statutory directions on appeals rules and regulations, the procedural aspects of the appellate jurisdiction have necessitated some level of judicial entrepreneurialism and the development of international criminal courts' procedures. Judges have contributed to the creation of a significant body of regulations, which tackles the most compelling concerns of appellate courts, from the admissibility and criteria of justiciable issues at the appellate level, to the novel relationship in international criminal justice between the appeals chambers and the trial chambers.

We believe that the progressive development of law accomplished by judges on these appellate procedures, while perhaps not as far-reaching as their development of the more substantive areas of the law, do play a critical role in the broader effort to realize the legitimacy and legacy of international justice. The development of proper appellate procedures and formal requirements enhance the institutionalization of this system of international justice by creating greater clarity and certainty in its administration. They provide a solid foundation upon which the more substantive matters can be adjudicated thereby lessening the risk that such developments in the law are perceived as resting on less than a firm and fair legal footing. In frequently citing paragraphs pertaining to technical requirements, judges have paid particular attention to procedural aspects that could invalidate or considerably slow down the proceedings and have also made sure to establish appellate procedures to guarantee the rights of the accused. Thus, the frequent reference to appellate procedures helps ensure the legacy and legitimacy of the progressive development of the law.

Overall, our findings demonstrate that there are a set of issues, as we had predicted, that would result in a substantial number of citations because of the embryonic state of international law in several key areas. These key issues were those, we contended, that were particularly ripe for jurisprudential development because of their central importance to the administration of justice, such as sentencing, but also to the types of crimes and modes of liability that characterize warfare and atrocities in the present day. We contend that it is on these issues where we should expect to find progressive development of the law. Increasing numbers of citations we argued represent not just the relevance of these prior cases, but the development of the law as subsequent cases not only cement the importance of prior judgments, but also clarify and expand upon jurisprudence. The judges have acted as entrepreneurs largely, although certainly not always, in the ways we had hypothesized. As we conclude our analysis of the cases and issues of the past that have led to the progressive development of the law, we naturally turn our attention next to the future, progressive development of the law.

While still at the beginning of its operations and lacking jurisprudence on which to rely, we can only make some suggestions as to how we predict judicial entrepreneurship will play out at the ICC. Contrary to the ad hoc tribunals, the ICC statutory and procedural documents are far more detailed. Worrying about judicial independence and a prosecutor who could independently charge crimes under the jurisdiction of the court, the state parties proceeded with extreme caution in determining the jurisdiction of the court, the elements of the crimes and the laws upon which cases can be adjudicated. The ICC has a limited jurisdiction "over the most serious crimes of international concern";[2] the elements of these crimes are further detailed according to Article 9 of the Rome Statute by a separate document called "Elements of Crimes," which specifically lists all subjective and objective elements of the crimes;[3] and the sources of law upon which judges can adjudicate cases mandates the application of the elements of crimes, before any other source.[4] In addition ICC judges have at their disposal a considerable amount of authoritative jurisprudence that simply was not available to the judges of the ICTY and ICTR. That said, we still would argue that when possible and necessary judges will interpret and expand international law. However, we suggest that the chances for them to find unchartered territory fertile for progressive development may be more limited.

Lastly, we turn to reflecting on the substantive legacy of the international jurisprudence we studied. What exactly has come from this judicial entrepreneurialism? What will be the most important judicial legacy left by these tribunals? In the years to come these tribunals will be remembered for many reasons, such as the progressive development of the law, the convictions and punishments of the ringleaders of international crimes and in particular by their legitimacy in the eyes of the citizens of the affected nations and the world. Most especially, these tribunals have lifted the curtains on the perpetration of atrocities by human beings *against* human beings. Judges have given names and voice to victims and perpetrators. They have warned us again that "the wrongs [perpetrated] have been so calculated, so malignant, and so

[2] Rome Statute of the International Criminal Court, Art. 1.
[3] Elements of Crimes can be found at https://www.icc-cpi.int/NR/rdonlyres/336923D8-A6AD-40EC-AD7B-45BF9DE73D56/0/ElementsOfCrimesEng.pdf.
[4] Rome Statute of the International Criminal Court, Art. 21.

devastating, that civilization cannot tolerate their being ignored, because it cannot survive their being repeated."[5] We believe that a proper and useful way to conclude this section would be to speculate on which judgments will exhibit ongoing ferment and thus become ripe for continued progressive development of the law. Given the jurisprudential record of the tribunals and most especially considering the prevalence in today's world of conflicts involving ethnicity, religion and other deeply-felt types of identities as well as violence that is often sponsored and masterminded by powerful actors at some remove from the scene of the violence that will be adjudicated in international courts, we offer two predictions to conclude. We suggest two types of decisions will be talked about the most in the years to come. The jurisprudence on genocide, while still in evolution to an extent, will be critical even though we did not find nearly the amount of jurisprudence citing such crimes as we expected. Second, we predict that the issue of "specific direction," although also still a work in progress, will pose critical legal and political issues for many years to come.

First, of the many judgments handed down by the tribunals we believe that the ones which will remain long impressed in international jurisprudence and in the memories of practitioners, scholars and the many affected people are very likely those associated with the crime of genocide. The ICTY and the ICTR have been the first tribunals to charge the crime of genocide, thus they will be constantly referred to as the original jurisprudential source on the subject matter. As well, the cases in which genocide was charged are those that have seen the most prominent political figures standing trials; the leaders and the masterminds of a political campaign of extermination; the elected governments and the highest levels of the military hierarchy. In a way these cases, such as *Krstic, Popovic et al., Karadzic, Milosevic,* and *Akayesu,* have been the most emblematic in wiping out the myth of impunity and political immunity. We suggest that these cases will resonate in history not only for jurisprudential issues, but also because of the judicial acknowledgement of the human suffering of the thousands of people. Ultimately evocative of Justice Jackson's words, the *Krstic* Appeals Chamber stated that the cases in which genocide has been adjudicated remind us that:

> Those who devise and implement genocide seek to deprive humanity of the manifold richness its nationalities, races, ethnicities and religions provide. This is a crime against all humankind, its harm being felt not only by the group targeted for destruction, but by all of humanity.[6]

We believe that important legal issues surrounding genocide are still in need of further clarification, especially regarding the definition of protected groups, which

[5] Robert H. Jackson Opening Statement before the International Military Tribunal, November 21, 1945.
[6] Prosecutor v. Radislav Krstic, Case No. IT-98–33-A, April 19, 2004, para 36.

makes likely the need for further legal development. While the tribunals did reach several landmark decisions in this area, there has not yet been a clear resolution to how such groups are to be defined. There is also the issue of political groups, which are not currently protected under the Genocide Convention, but which are often the target of violence and massacres. We can foresee a time when judges in the future will be poring over the *Akayesu* and *Krstic* decisions, among others, seeking to determine how judges of the ad hoc tribunals grappled with these issues. The potential remains for the definitional elements of genocide to become one of the most important legacies of the ad hoc tribunals.

The second jurisprudential legacy we believe will continue to resonate in future international criminal prosecutions concerns the status of the notion of specific direction in aiding and abetting. The reader will recall our discussion of the evolution of the use of this terminology across a series of cases at all three of the ad hoc tribunals that continues to generate debate in the present. To be sure, there are other methods via which superiors may be convicted for their roles in the formulation and execution of plans that violate human rights. Nonetheless, if there is an expectation by appellate chambers that the prosecution establish that political and military leaders operating from afar and managing the actions of their agents on the battlefield (whether public or private forces) be shown to have given specific orders rather than more general forms of support in the commission of international crimes, the evidentiary bar will be lifted considerably. A specific direction requirement would increase the likelihood of acquittal in cases where evidence of command authority or failure to prevent and punish may also be lacking. We see this as an especially critical issue in light of the many conflicts around the world in which various pro-governmental and anti-governmental forces receive support from state sponsors, and who are at risk of committing human rights atrocities. Interestingly at this point in jurisprudential development future judges might find sufficient precedent on either side of the issue to buttress the use of this requirement or its rejection. Nonetheless, given the difficulties we have seen already with prosecutorial efforts at the ICC, a specific direction requirement may further complicate its role in the protection of human rights.

EXPRESSIVE USE OF LANGUAGE

One of our most fascinating findings is that judges, primarily at the ICTY and SCSL, will sometimes use expressive language to communicate messages that reach beyond the community of lawyers and fellow judges to speak to the victims, those affected by violence and to the people of the international community writ large. So many of our analyses of courts, whether domestic or international, are oriented toward identifying the predictable forms of behavior and decisions that we can quantify or understand within an intellectual paradigm that we forget that judges, defendants, and victims have human interests in communicating other kinds of ideas whose meaning is not found within the law or rules of adjudication. Judges, it would seem, do seek to reach beyond the immediate requirements of a tribunal and pronounce statements of a moral or philosophical nature. As judicial entrepreneurs we found that judges used expressive language to condemn atrocities when the crimes were especially heinous or enormous. They will use the words of witnesses and victims whose language comes from heart-felt, personal experience when the lexicon of the law may seem hollow in comparison. Indeed, even when such testimony comes from the accused, such as when defendants confess their crimes and show genuine remorse, judges spotlight their words to demonstrate to the victims that their suffering has been acknowledged and to prove to those who would deny such crimes took place, that they are wrong.

And judges speak to history with these expressive uses of language. They link the suffering of the victims in their court to the suffering and crimes of past wars almost, one might say, as a caution to the world that the ultimate tragedy is that these tragedies keep repeating. We must be cautious, however, as we are inferring motives based on the usage of words that we perceive as resonating beyond the findings and the verdicts. We do not know what is truly motivating these judges inside their own thought processes, only that certain of the words and writings go beyond what is necessary and achieve an emotional connection with the reader that suggests judges have larger purposes in mind. Nonetheless, given all of the usual caveats, we do believe that judges, acting as judicial entrepreneurs, employ expressive language intentionally to help achieve the tribunals' aims of advancing justice, peace and reconciliation. To be sure, many people who read these judgments may remember little beyond the verdicts and sentences. So, perhaps even mindful of the stirring words delivered by US Chief Prosecutor Robert Jackson at the Nuremberg Tribunal, they aim to deliver a message that will change behavior and advance the cause of peace by aiming at the heart and not just the mind.

We are, however, puzzled by the near total absence of such language in the judgments of the ICTR, given our search strategy. It is still too early to determine if the ICC judges will behave more like their counterparts at the ICTY and SCSL, or if they will show the same sort of reticence to utilize expressive language as the ICTR judges. Perhaps institutional differences, such as the need to parse through the testimony of multiple witnesses to arrive at a verdict, or the near-universal agreement that genocide did occur in Rwanda does not lend itself to such moral condemnations. Perhaps there is a different role orientation or culture at the tribunals that encourages or discourages such displays of emotion.

We believe that a much deeper analysis of this expressive language is warranted. We suggest that the use of more sophisticated programs of text analysis might assist in analyzing the language of judgments to determine not just when particular words or phrases are used, but to ascertain whether the writing makes use of a constellation of words or terms that denote an expressive purpose. Researchers should also explore whether there are relationships between certain cases or particular judges and the use of expressive language to not only understand when such language is employed, but to better understand its purposes and its context. Are there some judges, for example, who are more comfortable using such language because of a background in human rights work? Are there some cases marked by particularly heinous actions that lend themselves more easily to the use of expressive language? Finally, it will be interesting to see what kind of life the words of these judges have twenty to thirty years in the future. Will they be remembered? Will they resonate like the words of Justice Jackson? Or will their full impact gradually dissipate over time? Will these judgments live on more for their jurisprudential contributions or will they be more remembered for their stirring language?

PUNISHMENT

One of the most important moments in judicial decision making is the punishment handed down by judges for those found responsible for international crimes. Punishment is the final act, which, together with the final judgment, speaks to the peoples of the affected nations, the international judicial community, those who created the tribunals, and the international community writ large – those who will ultimately evaluate the legacy of the tribunals. We have examined two fundamental elements of punishment. The first issue regards how the punishment handed down by international judges addresses the overarching goals of the tribunals – namely retribution, deterrence, and the establishment of peace and reconciliation. The second concerns the identification of specific sentencing determinants.

We suggest that judges have considerable discretion on sentencing matters and that they have sought to preserve this power through reliance on their mandate to let individual circumstances guide punishment, rather than articulating a theory of punishment or a set of sentencing determinants that would tie their hands. Our analyses also show that, despite judicial statements to the contrary and criticism from the International legal community, judges do accord some factors special emphasis and have reached fairly consistent sentences across a broad range of cases. Especially monumental crimes like genocide, aggravating circumstances, and higher levels of responsibility are strong and statistically significant predictors of lengthier sentences, while mitigating circumstances, guilty pleas, and surrender are predictors of lower sentences. We believe that the consistency of the punishment handed down by judges is particularly important for the legitimacy of international tribunals. Those found guilty have often lamented the length of their prison term when comparing it to other cases. Many scholars and practitioners have criticized the international tribunals for failing to devise a consistent system of punishment, while others have charged that reliance upon a human rights rationale for sentencing has interfered with a more legally grounded methodology. Danner and Martinez (2005, 101) pointedly argue that:

Importing the interpretive techniques and analytical modes drawn from a human rights paradigm, which is based on ensuring that all serious harms to human life and well-being find protection within its ambit, to a system designed to punish individuals for transgressions of previously-articulated crimes, poses clear dangers for the integrity of a criminal law system.

The judges have answered that it is not their place to devise a theory of punishment from which a sentencing schedule may be derived to ensure equitable treatment for those found guilty. Again and again judges stress that sentencing is premised on the particular circumstances of a case and that to depart from such guidance in their founding documents would truly undermine the instructions of those international authorities that created these courts and potentially injure the rights of the accused. Critics have suggested that the lack of a penological theory of sentencing is harmful to both the law and the accused and there is room for debate on this question. We interpret the evidence found here to suggest that the judges have explicitly succeeded in adhering to a conception of their primacy in sentencing formulation while maintaining a fairly consistent record of sentencing that has often escaped notice by both the scholarly and legal communities. The preservation of judicial discretion in sentencing represents a validation of the judges' interest in preserving the primacy of judicial decision making in general.

In addition to adhering to judicial authority in determining individual sentences, punishments have also been shaped by their relationship to the overarching goals set out for the tribunals in their founding documents. The expressed aims of providing redress, eroding the norm of impunity and contributing to a reduction in human rights atrocities have combined to elevate sentence severity as the appropriate manifestation of the retribution and deterrence goals. To right the scales of justice and communicate international condemnation for the violations of its laws tends to lead toward increasing sentences. At the same time, the need to consider larger notions of peace as human security and reconciliation can also lead to a reduction in sentence length as a means to acknowledge the acceptance of responsibility, cooperation with the prosecution and contrition by those found guilty. To be sure, however, the retributivist rationale emerges as the most powerful determinant of sentencing.

The goals of peace and reconciliation are probably the most nebulous and difficult to advance of all the goals of the tribunals. They may also be the most important legacy the tribunals bequeath to the affected peoples. Based on the spare reference to such goals in the tribunals' founding documents, it is not immediately apparent how punishment can help to reconcile ethnic divisions. We argued that one method by which judges might advance peace and reconciliation is through the encouragement of guilty pleas and the expressions of remorse that often accompany such case resolutions. Yet, victims are likely to see the punishment that acknowledges the contributions of the remorseful as too light and not commensurate with their suffering. Conversely, those groups who identify with the accused may perceive judgments that are a product of plea bargaining as a political bargain that justifies their perception of bias and victimization. Ultimately, when considering the legal criticisms described above, complaints from victims that some sentences do not fully right the scales of justice (as we have seen most recently in criticism of the Karadzic sentence as too lenient in comparison to his role in the commission of so many crimes) and the charges of bias by those groups punished most severely (e.g., Serbs, Hutus) there are few communities that seem to naturally support tribunal practices regarding punishment.

If punishment fails to be perceived as such; if the conviction of higher ranking officials fosters anger and desire for vindication; if victims and their families are left with no sense of justice, and if the communities at large fear retaliation, then punishment would have failed to achieve the goals of international justice. This may be an inescapable fact in a world where international justice must continually collide with local politics, inter-ethnic group enmities and powerful historical narratives that continue to shape present understandings of who did what to whom in the course of war and human rights atrocities. Perhaps more powerful and clear messages about the goals of peace and reconciliation will resonate more with at least some of these communities and address some of this criticism. Such efforts, we believe, may be better conveyed by the judges through the expressive use of language.

Nonetheless, our findings here demonstrate again the importance of the judges in advancing their goals of protecting human rights and ensuring the legacy of the tribunals. While judges acted more explicitly in an entrepreneurial fashion in the progressive development of the law and in the use of expressive language, in the case of punishment there was little or no need to act as boldly. Rather, the scant guidance given judges on the theory and practice of sentencing has essentially given them all the discretionary power they would need to sentence the guilty according to those goals and circumstances they found most relevant. Thus, judges have been able to advance the protection of human rights and the legacy of the tribunals through punishment as well. We argue that what unites the progressive development of the law, the expressive use of language, and the punishment of the guilty is the preservation and enhancement of judicial influence to use judgments as the vehicle for the realization of the goals of human rights protection and judicial legacy. Ultimately, our theory of judicial entrepreneurialism is distinguished by the pivotal role of judges in advancing the work of the tribunals.

FINAL JUDGMENTS

Our principal goal was to advance our theory of judicial entrepreneurship and in that effort we believe we have shown that judges do take on this role orientation and engage in several activities that move them beyond the guidance of their founding documents. Indeed, because these documents not only charged the tribunals with advancing far-reaching political goals, such as deterrence, reconciliation and peace, but were also quite silent on how these aims were to be achieved, the judges of the international tribunals have been afforded significant discretion. Their founding documents are often ambiguous or even bereft of guidance on such important matters as sentencing that it hardly seems possible the judges could accomplish their immediate and more far-reaching goals without becoming judicial entrepreneurs. Developing international tribunals and international jurisprudence under such circumstances is not a job for the sticklers to detail or the faint of heart. As in the beginning of any novel political experiment strong leadership, a willingness to experiment and take risks and commitment to change are almost prerequisites for success. Perhaps, when decades down the road international justice is woven more deeply into the fabric of international relations, we will find judges more strictly conforming to their institutional roles. But the rebirth of international justice has seemed to require something more. It will fall to the next generation of judges to cement the gains made by their judicial ancestors.

After years of operation, the ad hoc tribunals have established themselves as legitimate institutions advancing justice and human rights. The undeniable achievements of the tribunals over the years have lifted the "burden of proof" of legitimacy and efficiency off the shoulder of international judges, giving them more confidence in tackling challenging legal questions more independently, while still navigating the labyrinth of the multiple sources of international humanitarian and criminal law. We suggest that once tribunal judges and their institutions found their sea legs in the early years of the tribunals, they sought to realize the goals outlined in their founding documents and develop a historical legacy that went beyond the mere execution of the law. Freed from the uncertainty that pervaded the initial establishment of their institutions, international judges have seized opportunities to shape international humanitarian and criminal law. Since the early 1990s a significant number of landmark decisions have been handed down by trial and appeals chambers of the ad hoc tribunals, defining crimes and criminal procedures as well as expanding the reach of international law to advance human rights. Today, international jurisprudence is the result of years of judicial interpretation and expansion performed by entrepreneurial judges who understand their role and the significance of their judgments more extensively than originally envisioned within their mandate.

Through our analyses of the judgments of the tribunals we have shed new light on the role of judges and the importance of these decisions. These international judges are neither referees that manage trials nor bureaucrats who simply apply a black and white law. Judges were bequeathed a disparate and embryonic international jurisprudence to apply to complex and horrific conflicts in order to achieve ambitious international goals. Their success and the success of the larger international judicial enterprise depended on the judges delivering just verdicts that would advance these goals, which in turn necessitated an entrepreneurial spirit to their decision making. Without a willingness to act as entrepreneurs it is quite likely these tribunals would have been judged as falling short of the ambitions so many have had for them.

Whether judges at the ICC and other ad hoc tribunals that may be established in the future continue this tradition remains to be seen. It may be that conditions will not be as propitious for the degree of judicial entrepreneurialism we have seen thus far in the jurisprudence of the ad hoc tribunals. There may be less room for expansion of the substance and process of international law as more gaps and ambiguities are filled in and clarified and international justice becomes more fully institutionalized. We argued throughout that key to understanding the judicial entrepreneurial spirit was a concern for human rights and ensuring that the law could both protect those whose rights were violated and could be used to prosecute those who violate the law, as well as a concern for their legacy. Their regard for human rights has been the guiding spirit of judicial entrepreneurialism while their judgments are the vehicles.

Judges have acted in an entrepreneurial fashion in the progressive development of the law, the use of expressive language in judgments and to a lesser extent in their sentencing. Such entrepreneurial behavior is most clearly in evidence in the first two types of judicial actions. As we have argued, judges have had little reason to act in an entrepreneurial fashion when sentencing the guilty as their founding documents provide them with such ample discretion over sentencing that there has been little need to expand their authority in this area. The common denominator that ties these three behaviors together, however, is the expansion and preservation of judicial authority. Judges step beyond the bounds of what is expressly permitted when they find a compelling legal justification, such as ambiguous statutory guidance or when crimes are particularly shocking. They exercise their discretionary power to do what they believe is legally appropriate and morally compelling when legal and factual circumstances would seem to demand a response. In matters of sentencing, judgments are noteworthy more for their insistence on adherence to guidance that provides for substantial judicial independence in meting out punishment. In all three cases these actions preserve judicial power and prerogative. Judges are, in a sense, entrepreneurial institution builders. Their decisions are ultimately grounded in jurisprudence and their founding documents and their respect for human rights, but all come together in enhancing the authority of the institutions within which they reside and labor.

The legacy of the judicial entrepreneurialism we have described will ultimately depend on the legacy of the International Criminal Court. If the ICC is able to establish an acknowledged record of effectiveness, can further erode the norm of impunity and can continue to advance the protection of human rights, the jurisprudence of the ad hoc tribunals will likely be seen as the foundation on which these advances rest. If, by contrast, the ICC's record is perceived as inconsistent or ineffective, the work of the ad hoc tribunals may be viewed as an interesting, but *sui generis* period of jurisprudential evolution bookended by its irrelevance during the Cold War and an increasing erosion brought about by an overly ambitious agenda for international justice whose reach exceeded its grasp. We will wait to see if the spirit of judicial entrepreneurialism continues on.

Judges are guardians of international law specifically and the guardians of the legacy of international justice more generally, and as such would seem to be conscious of both the need to solidify and expand its protections of human rights and embed international jurisprudence into international relations. They are judicial entrepreneurs in the service of human rights and their judicial legacy, just as they are custodians of the international justice enterprise their superiors have established.

APPENDIX

Expressive quotes

PROSECUTOR V. RADISLAV KRSTIC, CASE NO.: IT-98-33-T, 02 AUGUST 2001, PARA. 2

2. The events of the nine days from July 10–19 1995 in Srebrenica defy description in their horror and their implications for humankind's capacity to revert to acts of brutality under the stresses of conflict. In little over one week, thousands of lives were extinguished, irreparably rent or simply wiped from the pages of history. The Trial Chamber leaves it to historians and social psychologist to plumb the depths of this episode of the Balkan conflict and to probe for deep-seated causes. The task at hand is a more modest one: to find, from the evidence presented during the trial, what happened during that period of about nine days and, ultimately, whether the defendant in this case, General Krstic, was criminally responsible, under the tenets of international law, for his participation in them. The Trial Chamber cannot permit itself the indulgence of expressing how it feels about what happened in Srebrenica, or even how individuals as well as national and international groups not the subject of this case contributed to the tragedy. This defendant, like all others, deserves individualised consideration and can be convicted only if the evidence presented in court shows, beyond a reasonable doubt, that he is guilty of acts that constitute crimes covered by the Statute of the Tribunal ("Statute"). Thus, the Trial Chamber concentrates on setting forth, in detail, the facts surrounding this compacted nine days of hell and avoids expressing rhetorical indignation that these events should ever have occurred at all. In the end, no words of comment can lay bare the saga of Srebrenica more graphically than a plain narrative of the events themselves, or expose more poignantly the waste of war and ethnic hatreds and the long road that must still be travelled to ease their bitter legacy.

PROSECUTOR V. RADISLAV KRSTIC, CASE NO.: IT-98–33-T,
02 AUGUST 2001, PARA. 93

93. The Trial Chamber heard that the survivors of Srebrenica have unique impediments to their recovery and staff members at Vive Zene speak of the "Srebrenica Syndrome" as a new pathology category. One of the primary factors giving rise to the syndrome is that, with few exceptions, the fate of the survivor's loved ones is not officially known: the majority of men of Srebrenica are still listed as missing. For Bosnian Muslim women it is essential to have a clear marital status, whether widowed, divorced or married: a woman whose husband is missing does not fit within any of these categories. Moreover, on a psychological level, these women are unable to move forward with the process of recovery without the closure that comes from knowing with certainty what has happened to their family members and properly grieving for them. The Trial Chamber also heard of the collective guilt experienced by women because they survived the events in Potocari and their husbands, brothers and fathers did not. The level of trauma experienced by the women and children who were transported out of Srebrenica was assessed by Vive Zene as being "exceptionally high" and this, in large part, was attributed to the fact that the women and men had been separated following the take-over of Srebrenica. This heartbreak and anguish is no better reflected than in the words of Witness DD whose young son was torn away from her in Potocari:

　　... I keep dreaming about him. I dream of him bringing flowers and saying, "Mother, I've come" I hug him and say, "Where have you been, my son?" and he says, "I've been in Vlasenica all this time."

PROSECUTOR V. RADISLAV KRSTIC, CASE NO.: IT-98–33-T,
02 AUGUST 2001, PARA. 724

724. The Trial Chamber's overall assessment is that General Krstic is a professional soldier who willingly participated in the forcible transfer of all women, children and elderly from Srebrenica, but would not likely, on his own, have embarked on a genocidal venture; however, he allowed himself, as he assumed command responsibility for the Drina Corps, to be drawn into the heinous scheme and to sanction the use of Corps assets to assist with the genocide. After he had assumed command of the Drina Corps, on 13 July 1995, he could have tried to halt the use of Drina Corps resources in the implementation of the genocide. His own commander, General Mladic, was calling the shots and personally supervising the killings. General Krstic's participation in the genocide consisted primarily of allowing Drina Corps assets to be used in connection with the executions from 14 July onwards and assisting with the provision of men to be deployed to participate in executions that occurred on 16 July 1995. General Krstic remained largely passive in the face of his knowledge of what was going on; he is guilty, but his guilt is palpably less than others who devised

and supervised the executions all through that week and who remain at large. When pressured, he assisted the effort in deploying some men for the task, but on his own he would not likely have initiated such a plan. Afterwards, as word of the executions filtered in, he kept silent and even expressed sentiments lionising the Bosnian Serb campaign in Srebrenica. After the signing of the Dayton Accords, he co-operated with the implementers of the accord and continued with his professional career although he insisted that his fruitless effort to unseat one of his officers, whom he believed to have directly participated in the killings, meant he would not be trusted or treated as a devoted loyalist by the Bosnian Serb authorities thereafter. His story is one of a respected professional soldier who could not balk his superiors' insane desire to forever rid the Srebrenica area of Muslim civilians, and who, finally, participated in the unlawful realisation of this hideous design.

PROSECUTOR V. RADISLAV KRSTIC, CASE NO.: IT-98–33-A, JUDGMENT, 19 APRIL 2004, PARA. 37

37. The gravity of genocide is reflected in the stringent requirements which must be satisfied before this conviction is imposed. These requirements – the demanding proof of specific intent and the showing that the group was targeted for destruction in its entirety or in substantial part – guard against a danger that convictions for this crime will be imposed lightly. Where these requirements are satisfied, however, the law must not shy away from referring to the crime committed by its proper name. By seeking to eliminate a part of the Bosnian Muslims, the Bosnian Serb forces committed genocide. They targeted for extinction the forty thousand Bosnian Muslims living in Srebrenica, a group which was emblematic of the Bosnian Muslims in general. They stripped all the male Muslim prisoners, military and civilian, elderly and young, of their personal belongings and identification, and deliberately and methodically killed them solely on the basis of their identity. The Bosnian Serb forces were aware, when they embarked on this genocidal venture, that the harm they caused would continue to plague the Bosnian Muslims. The Appeals Chamber unequivocally that the law condemns, in appropriate terms, the deep and lasting injury inflicted, and calls the massacre at Srebrenica by its proper name: genocide. Those responsible will bear this stigma, and it will serve as a warning to those who may in future contemplate the commission of such a heinous act.

PROSECUTOR V. ZLATKO ALEKSOVSKI, CASE NO.: IT-95–14/1-A, 24 MARCH 2000, PARA. 37

37. The Appeals Chamber, having considered the various acts for which the Appellant was convicted, can find no reason whatsoever to doubt the seriousness of these crimes. Under any circumstances, the outrages upon personal dignity that the victims in this instance suffered would be serious. The victims were not merely

inconvenienced or made uncomfortable – what they had to endure, under the prevailing circumstances, were physical and psychological abuse and outrages that any human being would have experienced as such.

PROSECUTOR V. MILAN BABIC, CASE NO.: IT-03–72-S, 29 JUNE 2004, PARA. 82

82. The Trial Chamber notes that during one of the interviews given to investigators of the Office of the Prosecutor on 23 February 2002, Babic stated:

> Today with this awareness, consciousness I have and the knowledge I have, I certainly wouldn't act in that way, I wouldn't conduct myself in that way, but at that time my role could have been much better, or not at all, to have no role at all. And in some way I feel shame and … I feel shame for what happened and I also regret it, regret for having participated in a certain way in these events, which were ugly.

PROSECUTOR V. MILAN BABIC, CASE NO.: IT-03–72-S, 29 JUNE 2004, PARA. 83

83. After his guilty plea was entered before the Trial Chamber, Babic again expressed his remorse:

> I come before this Tribunal with a deep sense of shame and remorse. I have allowed myself to take part in the worst kind of persecution of people simply because they were Croats and not Serbs. Innocent people were persecuted; innocent people were evicted forcibly from their houses; and innocent people were killed. Even when I learned what had happened, I kept silent. Even worse, I continued in my office, and I became personally responsible for the inhumane treatment of innocent people.

He continued:

> These crimes and my participation therein can never be justified. I'm speechless when I have to express the depth of my remorse for what I have done and for the effect that my sins have had on the others. I can only hope that by expressing the truth, by admitting to my guilt, and expressing the remorse can serve as an example to those who still mistakenly believe that such inhuman acts can ever be justified. Only truth can give the opportunity for the Serbian people to relieve itself of its collective burden of guilt. Only an admission of guilt on my part makes it possible for me to take responsibility for all the wrongs that I have done.

PROSECUTOR V. ZEJNIL DELALIC ET AL., CASE NO.: IT-96–21-T, 16 NOVEMBER 1998, PARA. 495

495. The Trial Chamber considers the rape of any person to be a despicable act which strikes at the very core of human dignity and physical integrity. The condemnation

and punishment of rape becomes all the more urgent where it is committed by, or at the instigation of, a public official, or with the consent or acquiescence of such an official. Rape causes severe pain and suffering, both physical and psychological. The psychological suffering of persons upon whom rape is inflicted may be exacerbated by social and cultural conditions and can be particularly acute and long lasting. Furthermore, it is difficult to envisage circumstances in which rape, by, or at the instigation of a public official, or with the consent or acquiescence of an official, could be considered as occurring for a purpose that does not, in some way, involve punishment, coercion, discrimination or intimidation. In the view of this Trial Chamber this is inherent in situations of armed conflict.

PROSECUTOR V. ZEJNIL DELALIC ET AL., CASE NO.: IT-96–21-T, 16 NOVEMBER 1998, PARA. 1262

1262. Hazim Delic is guilty of torture by way of the deplorable rapes of two women detainees in the Celebici prison-camp. He subjected Grozdana Cecez not only to the inherent suffering involved in rape, but exacerbated her humiliation and degradation by raping her in the presence of his colleagues. The effects of this crime are readily apparent from the testimony of the victim when she said " . . . he trampled on my pride and I will never be able to be the woman that I was."

PROSECUTOR V. DRAZEN ERDEMOVIC, CASE NO.: IT-96–22-T, 29 NOVEMBER 1996, PARA. 19

19. With regard to a crime against humanity, the Trial Chamber considers that the life of the accused and that of the victim are not fully equivalent. As opposed to ordinary law, the violation here is no longer directed at the physical welfare of the victim alone but at humanity as a whole.

PROSECUTOR V. STANISLAV GALIC, CASE NO.: IT-98–29-T, 5 DECEMBER 2003, PARA. 764

764. The gravity of the offences committed by General Galic is established by their scale, pattern and virtually continuous repetition, almost daily, over many months. Inhabitants of Sarajevo – men, women, children and elderly persons – were terrorized and hundreds of civilians were killed and thousands wounded during daily activities such as attending funerals, tending vegetable plots, fetching water, shopping, going to hospital, commuting within the city, or while at home. The Majority of the Trial Chamber also takes into consideration the physical and psychological suffering inflicted on the victims. Sarajevo was not a city where occasional random acts of violence against civilians occurred or where living conditions were simply hard. This was an anguishing environment in which, at a minimum hundreds of men, women,

children, and elderly people were killed, and thousands were wounded and more generally terrorized.

PROSECUTOR V. STANISLAV GALIC, CASE NO.: IT-98–29-A, 30 NOVEMBER 2006, PARA. 455

455. Although the Trial Chamber did not err in its factual findings and correctly noted the principles governing sentencing, it committed an error in finding that the sentence imposed adequately reflects the level of gravity of the crimes committed by Galić and his degree of participation. The sentence rendered was taken from the wrong shelf. Galić's crimes were characterized by exceptional brutality and cruelty, his participation was systematic, prolonged and premeditated and he abused his senior position of VRS Corps commander. In the Appeals Chamber's view, the sentence imposed on Galić by the Trial Chamber falls outside the range of sentences available to it in the circumstances of this case. The Appeals Chamber considers that the sentence of only 20 years was so unreasonable and plainly unjust, in that it underestimated the gravity of Galić's criminal conduct,that it is able to infer that the Trial Chamber failed to exercise its discretion properly.

THE PROSECUTOR V. ANTE GOTOVINA, IVAN CERMAK & MLADEN MARKAC, CASE NO: IT-06–90, 15 APRIL 2011, PARA. 2600

2600. First and foremost, the Trial Chamber considers that Ante Gotovina and Mladen Markač were found responsible for their participation in a joint criminal enterprise. Its objective was the permanent removal of the Serb civilian population from the Krajina by force or threat of force, which amounted to and involved persecution (deportation, unlawful attacks against civilians and civilian objects and discriminatory and restrictive measures), deportation and forcible transfer. Gotovina and Markač were thereby found responsible for a large number of crimes that occurred in a wide geographical area and during a period of approximately two months. This is set out in detail in chapters 4, 5, 6.3, and 6.5. The crimes include persecution, deportation, plunder, wanton destruction, inhumane acts, cruel treatment, and murder. Without being able to retell each of the countless individual stories of suffering and loss inflicted by these crimes, the Trial Chamber leaves it at the exemplary mentioning of the following. It recalls the great number of dead for which criminal responsibility under this Indictment could be established. It notes that through the acts of wanton destruction some settlements were almost entirely destroyed as was the case with, for instance, Kistanje, thereby destroying what was home for so many and making it practically impossible for them to return. Thousands were forced from what was their home, condemning most of them to live the uncertain lives of refugees who have to rebuild their lives abroad, and depriving them of their property through comprehensive wanton destruction and looting.

PROSECUTOR V. MOMCILO KRAJISNIK, CASE NO.: IT-00–39-T, 27 SEPTEMBER 2006, PARA. 1146

1146. There is no need to retell here the countless stories of brutality, violence, and depravation that were brought to the Chamber's attention. But hidden amidst the cold statistics on the number of people killed and forced away from their homes, lies a multitude of individual stories of suffering and ordeal – psychological violence, mutilation, outrages upon personal dignity, rape, suffering for loved ones, despair, death. A sentence, however harsh, will never be able to rectify the wrongs, and will be able to soothe only to a limited extent the suffering of the victims, their feelings of deprivation, anguish, and hopelessness.

PROSECUTOR V. KUNARAC ET AL., CASE NO.: IT-96–23-A & IT-96–23/1-A, 12 JUNE 2002, PARA. 858

858. The Appeals Chamber in the *Tadic* case held that a Trial Chamber also has to consider adequately the need for sentences to reflect the relative significance of the role of the accused in the broader context of the conflict in the former Yugoslavia.1489 The Appeals Chamber in the *Delalic* case interpreted that consideration as follows: That judgement did not purport to require that, in every case before it, an accused's level in the overall hierarchy in the conflict in the former Yugoslavia should be compared with those at the highest level, such that if the accused's place was by comparison low, a low sentence should automatically be imposed. Establishing a gradation does not entail a low sentence for all those in a low level of the overall command structure. On the contrary, a sentence must always reflect the inherent level of gravity of a crime [. . .].

It cannot be said that any of the accused played relatively significant roles in the broader context of the conflict in the former Yugoslavia. None of them were commanders, their crimes were geographically relatively limited and there is no evidence that their specific offences affected other perpetrators of violations of international humanitarian law or other victims of such crimes within that broader context. That said, the three accused committed, by any measure, particularly serious offences against the most vulnerable of persons in any conflict, namely, women and girls, in the Foča region of Bosnia and Herzegovina. The Trial Chamber considered this fact in the context of the consideration of the gravity of the offences.

PROSECUTOR V. ZORAN KUPRESKIC ET AL., CASE NO.: IT-95–16-T, 14 JANUARY 2000, PARA. 754

754. The massacre carried out in the village of Ahmici on 16 April 1993 comprises an individual yet appalling episode of that widespread pattern of persecutory violence. The tragedy which unfolded that day carried all the hallmarks of an ancient tragedy.

For one thing, it possessed unity of time, space and action. The killing, wounding and burning took place in the same area, within a few hours and was carried out by a relatively small groups of members of the Bosnian Croatian military forces: the HVO and the special units of the Croatian Military Police, the so-called Jokers. Over the course of the several months taken up by these trial proceedings, we have seen before us, through the narration of the victims and the survivors, the unfolding of a great tragedy. And just as in the ancient tragedies where the misdeeds are never shown but are only recounted by the actors, numerous witnesses have told the Trial Chamber of the human tragedies which befell so many of the ordinary inhabitants of that small village.

PROSECUTOR V. ZORAN KUPRESKIC ET AL., CASE NO.: IT-95–16-T, 14 JANUARY 2000, PARA. 755

755. Indisputably, what happened on 16 April 1993 in Ahmici has gone down in history as comprising one of the most vicious illustrations of man's inhumanity to man. Today, the name of that small village must be added to the long list of previously unknown hamlets and towns that recall abhorrent misdeeds and make us all shudder with horror and shame: Dachau, Oradour sur Glâne, Katijn, Marzabotto, Soweto, My Lai, Sabra and Shatila, and so many others.

PROSECUTOR V. MILAN LUKIC AND SREDOJE LUKIC, CASE NO.: IT-98–32/1, 20 JULY 2009, PARA. 740

740. In the all too long, sad and wretched history of man's inhumanity to man, the Pionirska street and Bikavac fires must rank high. At the close of the 20th century, a century marked by war and bloodshed on a colossal scale, these horrific events remain imprinted on the memory for the viciousness of the incendiary attack, for the obvious premeditation and calculation that defined it, for the sheer callousness, monstrosity and brutality of herding, trapping and locking the victims in the two houses, thereby rendering them helpless in the ensuing inferno and for the degree of pain and suffering inflicted on the victims as they were burnt alive.

PROSECUTOR V. MILAN LUKIC AND SREDOJE LUKIC, CASE NO.: IT-98–32/1, 20 JULY 2009, PARA. 1061

1061. The serious gravity of these multiple murders and savage beatings must be recognized individually, even as the Trial Chamber considers the particular gravity of the monstrous mass killings that Milan Lukić committed in the Pionirska street fire and the Bikavac fire. The Trial Chamber reiterates that the Pionirska street fire and the Bikavac fires exemplify the worst acts of inhumanity that one person may inflict upon others. The Trial Chamber recalls its observations that these horrific events remain imprinted on the memory for the viciousness of the incendiary attack, for the sheer callousness and cruelty of herding, trapping, and locking the victims in the two houses, thereby rendering them helpless in the ensuing inferno, and for the degree of pain and suffering inflicted on the victims as they were burned alive.

PROSECUTOR V. MILAN LUKIC AND SREDOJE LUKIC, CASE NO.: IT-98–32/1, 20 JULY 2009, PARA. 1066

1066. The survivors of these crimes now live with permanent physical injuries and with the mental anguish that accompanies those who have witnessed and survived the brutality and violence which Milan Lukic inflicted upon them. The Trial Chamber particularly recalls Zehra Turjačanin, who presented a sad, tragic but heroic figure as the sole survivor of the Bikavac fire. The survivors of both fires were forced to leave behind family members or neighbours in their escape. Several survivors bear the scars and physical pain of having been burned, shot by bullets and hit by shrapnel. The Uzamnica detainees bear scars, ill-health and serious physical disabilities as a result of the beatings they received in detention. Family members watched their loved ones being taken away, and after the Drina river incident and Varda factory incident, had to live with the fear and uncertainty that resulted from Milan Lukić's random selection of Muslim victims.

PROSECUTOR V. MIODRAG JOKIĆ, CASE NO.: IT-01–42/1-S, 18 MARCH 2004, PARA. 77

77. The Trial Chamber recognizes that Miodrag Jokić's guilty plea prior to the commencement of the trial contributes to establishing the truth about the events in and around the Old Town of Dubrovnik on 6 December 1991. Mutual understanding and conciliation presuppose, to some extent, a true and acknowledged record of the events which made up the conflict in the former Yugoslavia. The Trial Chamber believes that such mutual appreciation of the events can be only advanced by Miodrag Jokić's guilty plea. His plea has the potential to strengthen the foundations for reconciliation between the peoples of the former Yugoslavia and for the restoration of a lasting peace in the region. The Trial Chamber finally notes that Miodrag Jokić's plea saves considerable time and resources for the Tribunal.

PROSECUTOR V. DARKO MRDA, CASE NO.: IT-02–59-S 31, MARCH 2004, PARA. 55

55. The Trial Chamber is convinced beyond a reasonable doubt that some of the victims, if not all, were subjected to a level of suffering that went beyond what is usually suffered by victims of murder or inhumane acts. Once separated from the other persons in the convoy, the men must have feared for their lives, and must

have felt desperate when they were ordered to kneel down by the edge of the cliff
or when they witnessed the execution of others. Those who survived only did so
by desperately seeking to escape what must have seemed to be a certain death and
subsequently faced suffering of an extreme nature.

PROSECUTOR V. POPOVIC ET AL., CASE NO.: IT-05–88-T, 10 JUNE 2010, PARA. 844

844. The Trial Chamber finds that the killing operation inflicted serious bodily
and mental harm on the Muslims of Eastern Bosnia. The males in Potočari first
had to endure a painful separation process and the anxiety that followed from not
knowing what would happen to their families. Once detained, the men had their
personal property – including identification cards and passports – removed and
uncertainty as to their ultimate fate turned to fear and terror. They were detained in
intolerable conditions of overcrowded facilities with no food, little if any water and
abhorrent sanitary conditions. In many instances they were subjected to taunting and
physical abuse. Similar rudimentary and cruel conditions awaited the men who were
captured from the column. For all of them, any hope of survival was extinguished
in the terrifying moments when they were brought to execution sites, in many
instances already filled with bodies, and realized their fate. The Trial Chamber
finds that through the operation to detain and kill, serious bodily and mental harm
was inflicted on the males who were the subject of this murderous enterprise.

PROSECUTOR V. POPOVIC ET AL., CASE NO.: IT-05–88-T, 10 JUNE 2010, PARA. 845

845. The Trial Chamber also finds that serious bodily and mental harm was caused to
those who survived the killing operation. Those few who lived were often physically
injured and all endured the extreme anguish and terror of a close encounter with
violent death. Several were forced by circumstance to pretend to be dead and to hide
under the cover of and surrounded by the bodies of those killed around them. They
then endured harrowing circumstances in order to escape. The Trial Chamber has
no doubt as to the intense physical suffering and mental anguish endured by these
survivors as a direct result of the implementation of the plan to murder.

PROSECUTOR V. POPOVIC ET AL., CASE NO.: IT-05–88-T, 10 JUNE 2010, PARA. 846

846. The Trial Chamber further finds that the killing operation and executions
inflicted serious mental harm on the surviving family members and loved ones of
those killed. These survivors also had to endure the separation process at Potočari
with the heightened anxiety it created among the Bosnian Muslim population. The

women, children and the elderly – who had been torn from their homes and all which was familiar to them – then had their brothers, fathers, husbands and sons taken from them. They were left with uncertainty about their future and fear about the fate of those they loved.

PROSECUTOR V. POPOVIC ET AL., CASE NO.: IT-05–88-T, 10 JUNE 2010, PARA. 2150

2150. The campaign of persecution on the basis of the ethnicity of the victims was massive in scale and was the underlying motif of both joint criminal enterprises. The manifold persecutory acts that were committed with discriminatory intent were not random or isolated incidents; these were crimes committed in a pattern on a large scale accompanied by brutality. These factors increase the gravity of the crimes.

PROSECUTOR V. POPOVIC ET AL., CASE NO.: IT-05–88-T, 10 JUNE 2010, PARA. 2151

2151. The gravity of these crimes is further demonstrated by their terrible impact on the victims and their relatives. For the thousands who lost their lives at the many execution sites, the consequences were absolute. Those few who survived the executions underwent extreme suffering and severe mental and physical trauma, some only to be later recaptured and killed. Like the few survivors of the executions, the Bosnian Muslim women, children and elderly people forcibly removed from Srebrenica suffered not only their own physical and mental trauma as a result of the conditions of life in Potočari and their separation from their men, but also the sudden loss and disappearance of their male family members or the uncertainty about the fates of the men yet unaccounted for. This has been termed the "Srebrenica Syndrome." Those who were forcibly removed from Srebrenica also experienced a sharp decline in their standard of life due to the loss of their homes and possessions as a result of the expulsions.

PROSECUTOR V. POPOVIC ET AL., CASE NO.: IT-05–88-T, 10 JUNE 2010, PARA. 2152

2152. The sheer scale and cruelty of these crimes and the continuing impact they have had and still have on so many victims and their relatives is overwhelming.

PROSECUTOR V. BILJANA PLAVSIC, CASE NO.: IT-00–39&40/1, 27 FEBRUARY 2003, PARA. 80

80. The Trial Chamber accepts that acknowledgement and full disclosure of serious crimes are very important when establishing the truth in relation to such

crimes. This, together with acceptance of responsibility for the committed wrongs, will promote reconciliation. In this respect, the Trial Chamber concludes that the guilty plea of Mrs. Plavšić and her acknowledgement of responsibility, particularly in the light of her former position as President of Republika Srpska, should promote reconciliation in Bosnia and Herzegovina and the region as a whole.

PROSECUTOR V. DUSKO TADIC, CASE NO.: IT-94–1-T, 14 JULY 1997, PARA. 71

71. In his final statement, Dusko Tadic offered a list of persons whom he suggested were more responsible than he for the horrific events that transpired. At trial, he testified that "I do not think that anybody is guilty." TP 6137 (Tuesday, 29 October 1996). Likewise, in closing submissions at trial, his counsel at that time quoted from a letter from the then President of the United States, Abraham Lincoln, in the period of the Civil War in the United States in the mid-nineteenth century, in which he stated: "Each man feels an impulse to kill his neighbour, lest he be first killed by him." *Abraham Lincoln: Speeches and Writings 1859–1865* (1989), p 523. However, what was not pointed out by that counsel was that the Executive Order which President Lincoln issued in response to that conflict, the Instructions for the Government of Armies of the United States in the Field, better known as the Lieber Code, has been recognised as one of the foundations of the Law of The Hague, setting limits on the conduct of armed conflicts. *See* Frits Kalshoven, *Constraints on the Waging of War* (2 ed., 1991), pp 11, 12, 13. Thus, this quote from President Lincoln should not be construed as excusing criminal conduct even when committed during a time of armed conflict. The International Tribunal was established to adjudge individual guilt or innocence, and it discharges that responsibility without recognising as justifications the exigencies some say are inherent in the nature of armed conflict.

PROSECUTOR V. DUSKO TADIC, CASE NO.: IT-94–1-T, 14 JULY 1997, PARA. 72

72. Thus, the Trial Chamber does not accept that Dusko Tadic's actions were anything but criminal, constituting offences against individuals, and indeed, against all mankind. To condone Dusko Tadic's actions is to give effect to a base view of morality and invite anarchy. However, the virulent propaganda that stoked the passions of the citizenry in opstina Prijedor was endemic and contributed to the crimes committed in the conflict and, as such, has been taken into account in the sentences imposed on Dusko Tadic. As two writers have noted

When victims are dehumanised . . . the moral restraints against killing or harming them become less effective. Groups of people who are systematically demonized, assigned to inferior or dangerous categories, and identified by derogatory labels are readily excluded from the bonds of human empathy and the protection of moral and legal precepts.

HC Kelman and VL Hamilton, *Crimes of Obedience: Toward a Social Psychology of Authority and Responsibility* (1989), p 163.

Dusko Tadic himself in part responded to this campaign. In this respect, the Trial Chamber has recognised Dusko Tadic's personal circumstances and considered them in determining the appropriate sentence.

PROSECUTOR V. ZDRAVKO TOLIMIR, CASE NO.: IT-05–88/2-T, 12 DECEMBER 2012, PARA. 428

428. Bursts of gunfire erupted as soon as the trucks which had brought the prisoners departed, hitting the prisoners in the back. When the shooting stopped, one of the Bosnian Serb soldiers walked amongst the bodies lying on the ground, shooting them in the head. The Bosnian Serb soldiers cursed the wounded and would sometimes let them suffer in agony for a while before killing them. They also shot at survivors trying to escape. Although no evidence before the Chamber conclusively establishes which unit of soldiers carried out the shootings, one member of the 4th Battalion of the Zvornik Brigade, Gojko Simic, appeared to be in charge.

PROSECUTOR V. ZDRAVKO TOLIMIR, CASE NO.: IT-05–88/2-T, 12 DECEMBER 2012, PARA. 429

429. Trucks arrived approximately every four or five minutes. At one point, a boy of approximately five or six years old stood up from the pile of bodies and began to move towards the soldiers, calling out "Baba, where are you?" He was in shock and covered with dark blood stains and bits of others' bowel and tissue. The soldiers lowered their rifles and froze.

PROSECUTOR V. ZDRAVKO TOLIMIR, CASE NO.: IT-05–88/2-T, 12 DECEMBER 2012, PARA. 430

430. The tall, moustachioed "lieutenant colonel or colonel" turned to the soldiers and asked what they were waiting for, telling them to "finish him off." The soldiers replied that the "lieutenant colonel or colonel" had a weapon and that he should do it himself because they could not. The "lieutenant colonel or colonel" then ordered the soldiers to take the boy on the truck and to bring him back with the next "batch"

to be finished off. The boy, however, was taken to a hospital in Zvornik, where he received treatment for his injuries.

PROSECUTOR V. BRIMA, KAMARA AND KANU, CASE NO.: SCSL-2004–16-T, 19 JULY 2007, PARA. 16

16. International criminal tribunals have held further that the element of deterrence is important in demonstrating "that the international community is not ready to tolerate serious violations of international humanitarian law and human rights." It follows that the penalties imposed by the Trial Chamber must be sufficient to deter others from committing similar crimes. In the context of international criminal justice, it is recognised that one of the main purposes of a sentence is to "influence the legal awareness of the accused, the surviving victims, their relatives, the witnesses and the general public in order to reassure them that the legal system is implemented and enforced. Additionally, sentencing is intended to convey the message that globally accepted laws and rules have to be obeyed by everybody."

PROSECUTOR V. BRIMA, KAMARA AND KANU, CASE NO.: SCSL-2004–16-T, 19 JULY 2007, PARA. 34

34. Brima, Kamara and Kanu have been found responsible for some of the most heinous, brutal and atrocious crimes ever recorded in human history. Innocent civilians – babies, children, men and women of all ages – were murdered by being shot, hacked to death, burned alive, beaten to death. Women and young girls were gang raped to death. Some had their genitals mutilated by the insertion of foreign objects. Sons were forced to rape mothers, brothers were forced to rape sisters. Pregnant women were killed by having their stomachs slit open and the foetus removed merely to settle a bet amongst the troops as to the gender of the foetus. Men were disembowelled and their intestines stretched across a road to form a barrier. Human heads were placed on sticks on either side of the road to mark such barriers. Hacking off the limbs of innocent civilians was commonplace. The victims were babies, young children and men and women of all ages. Some had one arm amputated, others lost both arms. For those victims who survived an amputation, life was instantly and forever changed into one of dependence. Most were turned into beggars unable to earn any other living and even today cannot perform even the simplest of tasks without the help of others. Children were forcibly taken away from their families, often drugged and used as child soldiers who were trained to kill and commit other brutal crimes against the civilian population. Those child soldiers who survived the war were robbed of a childhood and most of them lost the chance of an education.

PROSECUTOR V. BRIMA, KAMARA AND KANU, CASE NO.: SCSL-2004–16-T, 19 JULY 2007, PARA. 35

35. The Trial Chamber cannot recall any other conflict in the history of warfare in which innocent civilians were subjected to such savage and inhumane treatment.

PROSECUTOR V. MOININA FOFANA AND ALLIEU KONDEWA, CASE NO.: SCSL-04–14-A, 28 MAY 2008, PARA. 561

561. In exercising its sentencing discretion, the Appeals Chamber re-emphasizes that it is an international court with responsibility to protect and promote the norms and values of the international community, expressed not only as part of customary international law but also, in several international instruments.

PROSECUTOR V. MOININA FOFANA AND ALLIEU KONDEWA, CASE NO.: SCSL-04–14-A, 28 MAY 2008, PARA. 563

563. The Appeals Chamber here emphasizes that the crimes of which the accused have been convicted are international crimes and not political crimes, in which consideration of national interest may be a relevant issue. What has to be paramount are international interests in protecting humanity. Such offences as Fofana and Kondewa have been convicted of are of the nature of such "offences that do not affect the interests of one State alone, but shock the conscience of mankind."

PROSECUTOR V. MOININA FOFANA AND ALLIEU KONDEWA, CASE NO.: SCSL-04–14-A, 28 MAY 2008, PARA. 564

564. What should be one of the paramount considerations in the sentencing of an accused person convicted of crimes against humanity and war crimes is the revulsion of mankind, represented by the international community, to the crime and not the tolerance by a local community of the crime; or lack of public revulsion in relation to the crimes of such community; or local sentiments about the persons who have been found guilty of the crimes. In describing what it described as the *"Justice Phase"* of the armed conflict that took place in Sierra Leone, the Appeals Chamber stated this in *"Decision on Immunity from Jurisdiction"*: The *Justice Phase* is that phase in which participants in the armed conflict have to answer for crimes committed in the course of the armed conflict. The *Justice Phase* itself involves separating what is in the exclusive domain of the municipal authority to be resolved under municipal law from what is in the concurrent jurisdiction of that authority and of the international community' to be resolved by application purely of international law." The Appeals Chamber had earlier stated in that Decision that: "The parties, whether from the

Government side or the insurgents, were … subjected to the obligations imposed by international law in a situation of internal armed conflicts."

PROSECUTOR V. MOININA FOFANA AND ALLIEU KONDEWA, CASE NO.: SCSL-04-14-J, 9 OCTOBER 2007, PARA. 49

49. The Chamber considers these crimes to have had a significant physical and psychological impact on the victims of such crimes, on the relatives of the victims, and on those in the broader community. The testimony of witnesses heard by the Chamber during the trial, and appended to the Prosecution Brief in Annex D, indicates the impact which events such as amputations and the loss of family members have had on the lives of victims and witnesses. As appropriately described and summarized by our sister Trial Chamber II, victims who had their limbs hacked off not only endured extreme pain and suffering, if they survived, but lost their mobility and capacity to earn a living or even to undertake simple daily tasks. They have been rendered dependent on others for the rest of their lives. In particular, the Chamber notes the lasting effect of these crimes on victims such as TF2–015, who was the only survivor of an attack on 65 civilians who were hacked to death by machetes or shot, and who was himself hacked with a machete and rolled into a swamp on top of the dead bodies in the: belief that he was dead.

PROSECUTOR V. MOININA FOFANA AND ALLIEU KONDEWA, CASE NO.: SCSL-04-14-J, 9 OCTOBER 2007, PARA. 96

96. We again observe, however, that the crimes for which the Accused were tried and convicted remain very serious crimes, and both Fofana and Kondeva will bear the stigma of a conviction after we have pronounced their sentences. The Chamber hopes that this Judgement will send a message to future pro-democracy armed forces or militia groups that notwithstanding the justness or propriety of their cause, they must observe the laws of war in pursuing and defending legitimate causes, and that they must not recruit or use children as agents or instruments of war. It will, in addition, remind them of their obligation to protect civilians who are unarmed and not participating in hostilities, and whose aspirations is only to protection, regardless of their perceived affiliation.

PROSECUTOR V. ISSA HASSAN SESAY, MORRIS KALLON AND AUGUSTINE GBAO, CASE NO.: SCSL-04-15-T, 8 APRIL 2009, PARA. 109

109. Killings were done arbitrarily, brutally and cruelly. A man was shot in the chest and had his head severed and his legs broken. A Limba man was killed because he

refused to surrender palm wine, Rebels would routinely sing, celebrate murders and taunt survivors. Men were disembowelled with their intestines subsequently used as makeshift checkpoints. The severed heads of victims were placed on sticks and displayed publicly. A boy had all four limbs hacked off before being thrown into a latrine pit and left to die. Civilians were made to choose between their own lives or those of their family members and, and one instance, a civilian was made to watch as rebels cast lots on whether he would live or die.

PROSECUTOR V. ISSA HASSAN SESAY, MORRIS KALLON AND AUGUSTINE GBAO, CASE NO.: SCSL-04–15, SENTENCING JUDGMENT, 8 APRIL 2009, PARA. 115

115. The Chamber observes that the killing of civilians in such circumstances brings along with it a lot of suffering on families and the community. In several of these incidents the Chamber made findings as to the grief of the civilian populations and their ordeal in burying the corpses, estimated in the hundreds. Some were exposed to the decomposing bodies, left in the streets for days, or to the severed heads of victims, also left on the street. Many were subjected to the ordeal of observing one of several family members killed in their presence.

PROSECUTOR V. ISSA HASSAN SESAY, MORRIS KALLON AND AUGUSTINE GBAO, CASE NO.: SCSL-04–15-T, 8 APRIL 2009, PARA. 133–135

133. The Chamber further considers that the crimes of sexual violence were committed in a society where cultural values greatly dictate the sacred manner in which any form of sexual acts take place. Such violations in a society where the sexual lives of women and girls are strictly scrutinised would have an adverse impact on the family as a whole and the society at large.

134. We therefore recall our finding that the brutal manner in which women and girls were debased and molested, in the naked view of their protectors, the fathers, husbands and brothers deliberately destroyed the existing family nucleus, and flagrantly undermined the cultural values and relationships which held the societies together. The Chamber observes that the shame and fear experienced by victims of sexual violence, alienated and tore apart communities, creating vacuums where bonds and relations were initially established.

135. In the Chamber's view the AFR /RUF inflicted physical and psychological pain and harm which transcended the individual "victim and relatives to an entire society. These acts of sexual violence left several women and girls extremely traumatised and scarred for life, consequently destroying the bearers of future generations. The Chamber infers that crimes of sexual violence further erode the moral fibre of society.

PROSECUTOR V. ISSA HASSAN SESAY, MORRIS KALLON AND AUGUSTINE GBAO, CASE NO.: SCSL-04–15-T, 8 APRIL 2009, PARA. 155

155. The Chamber considers that these crimes had a significant adverse physical and psychological effect on the victims. Many victims of these crimes of physical violence have found themselves permanently disfigured and incapacitated. For instance, during his oral testimony, TF1-015 mentioned that he still feels the pain in his mouth, and that he is still unable to chew any food. The Chamber particularly notes the cruel suffering imposed upon those civilians who had hands, feet, or limbs amputated. The immediate degree of suffering involved in amputations is immense. Amputees are also left to bear the consequences of a permanent and serious physical disability, which in many cases has led to a degree of dependency upon family, and in some cases total and permanent reliance upon others for their every need. The Chamber notes the lasting effects of these crimes on victims, on their dependants and relatives.

PROSECUTOR V. ISSA HASSAN SESAY, MORRIS KALLON AND AUGUSTINE GBAO, CASE NO.: SCSL-04–15-T, 8 APRIL 2009, PARA. 218

218. The Chamber considers it utter y reprehensible that such a senior military commander, who was in a position of authority and had effective control of subordinate commanders and troops, would allow, or would allow to go unchecked, attacks directed against a UN Peacekeeping Force that had been deployed as a result of the Lome Peace Accord, to which the RUF was one of the signatories. UN Peacekeepers act at the behest of the international community in order to preserve the peace for the benefit of ordinary civilians. Sesav's conduct as overall military commander can only be condemned in the strongest terms possible, and the Chamber considers the gravity of Sesay's criminal conduct in this regard to reach the highest level.

PROSECUTOR V. CHARLES TAYLOR, CASE NO.: SCSL-03–01-T, 30 MAY 2012, PARA. 71

71. In determining an appropriate sentence for the Accused, the Trial Chamber has taken into account the tremendous suffering caused by the commission of the crimes for which the Accused is convicted of planning and aiding and abetting, and the impact of these crimes on the victims, physically, emotionally and psychologically. The Trial Chamber recalls the tremendous loss of life – innocent civilians burned to death in their homes, or brutally killed by maiming and torture. The amputation of limbs was a hallmark of terror and cruelty visited upon innocent civilians. For those who survived these crimes, the long-term impact on their lives is devastating – amputees without arms who now have to live on charity because they can no longer work; young girls who have been publicly stigmatized and will never recover from

the trauma of rape and sexual slavery to which they were subjected, in some cases resulting in pregnancy and additional stigma from the children born thereof; child soldiers, boys and girls who are suffering from public stigma, highlighted by the identifying marks carved on their bodies, and enduring the after-effects of years of brutality, often irreparable alienation from their family and community, all as a consequence of the crimes for which Mr. Taylor stands convicted of aiding and abetting and planning. The Defense aptly described "the pain of lost limbs, he agony not only of rape in its commonly understood sense, but also the rape of childhood, the rape of innocence, possibly the rape of hope." The Trial Chamber witnessed many survivors weeping as they testified, a decade after the end of the conflict. Their suffering will be life-long.

PROSECUTOR V. CHARLES TAYLOR, CASE NO.: SCSL-03–01-T, 30 MAY 2012, PARA. 74

74. The Trial Chamber notes that the effects of these crimes on the families of the victims, as well as the society as a whole, are devastating. A large number of physically handicapped Sierra Leoneans have been left unable to do the simplest tasks we take for granted as a direct result of amputation. Many of the victims were productive members of society, breadwinners for their families, and are now reduced to beggars, unable to work as a result of the injuries inflicted to them. They are no longer productive members of society.

PROSECUTOR V. CHARLES TAYLOR, CASE NO.: SCSL-03–01-T, 30 MAY 2012, PARA. 102

102. Leadership must be carried out by example, by the prosecution of crimes not the commission of crimes. As we enter a new era of accountability, there are no true comparators to which the Trial Chamber can look for precedent in determining an appropriate sentence in this case. However, the Trial Chamber wishes to underscore the gravity it attaches to Mr. Taylor's betrayal of public trust. In the Trial Chamber's view this betrayal outweighs the distinctions that might otherwise pertain to the modes of liability discussed above.

PROSECUTOR V. THOMAS LUBANGA DYILO, CASE NO.: ICC-01/04–01/06, 10 JULY 2012, PARA. 60

60. The Chamber strongly deprecates the attitude of the former Prosecutor in relation to the issue of sexual violence. He advanced extensive submissions as regards sexual violence in his opening and closing submissions at trial, and in his arguments on sentence he contended that sexual violence is an aggravating factor that should be reflected by the Chamber. However, not only did the former Prosecutor fail to apply

to include sexual violence or sexual slavery at any stage during these roceedings, including in the original charges, but he actively opposed taking this step during the trial when he submitted that it would cause unfairness to the accused if he was convicted on this basis. Notwithstanding this stance on his part throughout these proceedings, he suggested that sexual violence ought to be considered for the purposes of sentencing.

References

Akhavan, Payam. 2001. "Beyond Impunity: Can International Criminal Justice Prevent Future Atrocities." *American Journal of International Law* 95(1): 7–31.

Akhavan, Payam. 2005. "The Crime of Genocide in the ICTR Jurisprudence." *Journal of International Criminal Justice* 3(4): 989–1006.

Akhavan, Payam. 2008. "Reconciling Crimes Against Humanity with the Laws of War Human Rights, Armed Conflict, and the Limits of Progressive Jurisprudence." *Journal of International Criminal Justice* 6: 21–37, p. 26.

Regulation 15/2000, 13 Criminal Law Forum (2002) 190, at 24.

Amann, Diane Marie. 2013. "Children and the First Verdict of the International Criminal Court." *Washington University Global Studies Law Review* 12: 411–432.

Amann, Günter. 2002. "Group Mentality, Expressivism, and Genocide." *International Criminal Law Review* 2(2): 93–143.

Arendt, Hannah. 1992 [1963]. *Eichmann in Jerusalem: A Report on the Banality of Evil*. New York: Penguin.

Ashworth, Andrew. 2010. *Sentencing and Criminal Justice*. Cambridge: Cambridge University Press.

Askin, Kelly Dawn. 1997. *War Crimes against Women: Prosecution in International War Crimes Tribunals*. Vol. 1. Martinus Nijhoff Publishers.

Askin, Kelly Dawn. 2002. "Reflections on Some of the Most Significant Achievements of the ICTY." *New England Law Review* 37(4): 903–914.

Askin, Kelly Dawn. 2003. "Prosecuting Wartime Rape and Other Gender-Related Crimes under International Law: Extraordinary Advances, Enduring Obstacles." *Berkley Journal of International Law* 21(2): 288–349.

Askin, Kelly Dawn. 2004. "A Decade of the Development of Gender Crimes at the International Courts and Tribunals: 1993–2003." *Human Rights Brief* 11(3): 16–19.

Bagaric, Mirko and John Morss. 2006. "International Sentencing Law: In Search of a Justification and Coherent Framework." *International Criminal Law Review* 6(2): 191–255.

Banjeglav, Tamara. 2013. "Dealing with the Past in Post-War Croatia: Perceptions, Problems, and Perspectives." *Transitional Justice and Civil Society in the Balkans*: 33–50.

Bantekas, Ilias. 1999. "The Contemporary Law of Superior Responsibility." *American Journal of International Law* 93(Jul.):573–595.

Bassiouni, Cherif. 2008. *International Criminal Law* Vol. 3. Martinus Nijhoff.

Bettwy, David Shea. 2011. "Genocide Convention and Unprotected Groups: Is the Scope of Protection Expanding under Customary International Law?" *Notre Dame J. Int'l & Comp. L.* 2: 167–196.

Blavoukos, Spyrous and Dimitris Bourantonis. 2011. "Chairs as Policy Entrepreneurs in Multilateral Negotiations." *Review of International Studies* 37: 653–672.

Boas, Gideon, James Bischoff and Natalie Reid. 2011. *Forms of Responsibility in International Criminal Law*. Cambridge: Cambridge University Press.

Boas, G., J. Jackson, B. Rocke and B. Done Taylor III. 2013. "Appeals, Reviews, and Reconsiderations," in *International Criminal Procedure, Principle and Rules*, Eds. Goran Sluiter, Hakan Friman, Suzannah Linton, Salvatore Zappala, Sergey Vasiliev, pp. 939–1014.

Book, Jan Philipp. 2011. *Appeal and Sentence in International Criminal Law*. Berlin: BWV Berliner Wissenschafts-Verlag.

Boelaert-Suominen, Sonja. 2001. "Prosecuting Superiors for Crimes Committed by Subordinates: A Discussion of the First Significant Case Law Since the Second World War." *Virginia Journal of International Law* 41: 747–785.

Calvo-Goller, Notburga K. 2006. *The Trial Proceedings of the International Criminal Court: ICTY and ICTR Precedents*. BRILL.

Carter, Ralph, James Scott and Charles Rowling. 2004. "Setting a Course: Congressional Foreign Policy Entrepreneurs in Post–World War II US Foreign Policy." *International Studies Perspectives* 5: 278–299.

Carter, Ralph and James Scott. 2010. "Understanding Congressional Foreign Policy Innovators: Mapping Entrepreneurs and Their Strategies." *The Social Science Journal* 47: 418–438.

Cassese, Antonio. 2000. "The Martens Clause: Half a Loaf or Simply Pie in the Sky?" *European Journal of International Law* 11(1): 187–216.

Cassese, Antonio. 2001. *International Criminal Law: A Commentary on the Rome Statute for an International Criminal Court*. Oxford: Oxford University Press.

Cassese, Antonio. 2003. "A Big Step Forward for International Justice." Crimes of War Project. http://bigo.zgeist.org/students/readings/cassese2003.pdf.

Cassese, Antonio. 2004. "The ICTY: A Living and Vital Reality." *Journal of International Criminal Justice* 2: 585–597.

Cassese, Antonio. 2007–2008. "Freedman Award Address." *Colombia Journal of Transnational Law* 46: 1–13.

Cepeda-Espinosa, Manuel Jose. 2004. "Judicial Activism in a Violent Country: The Origin, Role and Impact of the Colombian Constitutional Court." *Washington University Global Studies Law Review* 3:529–700.

Checkel, Jeff. 1993. "Ideas, Institutions, and the Gorbachev Foreign Policy Revolution." *World Politics* 452 (1993): 271–300.

Clark, Janine Natalya. 2014. *International Trials and Reconciliation: Assessing the Impact of the International Criminal Tribunal for the Former Yugoslavia*. Routledge.

Clark, Janine. 2009. "The Limits of Retributive Justice." *Journal of International Criminal Justice* 7: 463–487.

Clark, Jennifer J. 2008. "Zero to Life: Sentencing Appeals at the International Criminal Tribunals for the Former Yugoslavia and Rwanda." *The Georgetown Law Journal* 96 (5): 1685–1723.

Clark, Phil. 2013. "The Challenges of International Criminal Law in Addressing Mass Atrocity" in *The Routledge Handbook of International Crime and Justice Studies*, Eds. Bruce Arrigo and Heather Bersot, pp. 147–168. Routledge.

Coco, Antonio and Tom Gal. 2014. "Losing Direction: The ICTY Appeals Chamber's Controversial Approach to Aiding and Abetting in *Perisic*." *Journal of International Criminal Justice* 12(2): 345–366.

Combs, Nancy. 2013. *Fact Finding Without Facts: The Uncertain Evidentiary Foundations of International Criminal Convictions*. Cambridge: Cambridge University Press.

Copelon, Rhonda. 2000. "Gender Crimes as War Crimes: Integrating Crimes against Women into International Criminal Law (Hate, Genocide and Human Rights Fifty Years Later: What Have We Learned? What Must We Do?)." *McGill Law Journal* 46(1): 217–241.

Costain, Anne and Steven Majstorovic. 1994. "Congress, Social Movements and Public Opinion: Multiple Origins of Women's Rights Legislation." *Political Research Quarterly* 47 (1): 111–135.

Cross, Frank B., James F. Spriggs Jr, Timothy R. Johnson and Paul J. Wahlbeck. 2010. "Citations in the U.S. Supreme Court: An Empirical Study of Their Use and Significance." *University of Illinois Law Review* (2): 489–576.

Crow, Deserai. 2010. "Policy Entrepreneurs, Issue Experts and Water Rights Policy Change in Colorado." *Review of Policy Research* 27: 299–315.

Cryer, Robert, Hakan Friman, Darryl Robinson and Elizabeth Wilmhurst. 2007. *An Introduction to International Criminal Law and Procedure*. Cambridge: Cambridge University Press.

D'Ascoli, Silvia. 2011. *Sentencing in International Criminal Law the UN ad hoc Tribunals and Future Perspectives for the ICC*. Oxford: Hart Publishing.

Damaska, Mirjan R. 2008. "What is the Point of International Criminal Justice?" *Chicago-Kent Law Review* 83(1): 329–365.

Dana, Shahram. 2004. "Revisiting the Blaškić Sentence: Some Reflections on the Sentencing Jurisprudence of the ICTY." *International Criminal Law Review* 4(3): 321–348.

Danner, Allison M. 2001. "Constructing a Hierarchy of Crimes in International Criminal Law Sentencing." *Virginia Law Review* 87(3): 415–501.

Danner, Allison Marston. 2006. "When Courts make Law: How the International Criminal Tribunals Recast the Laws of War." *Vanderbilt Law Review* 59(1): 1–65.

Danner, Allison M. and Jenny S. Martinez. 2005. "Guilty Associations: Joint Criminal Enterprise, Command Responsibility, and the Development of International Criminal Law." *California Law Review* 93(1): 75–169.

Darcy, Shane and Joseph Powderly. 2010. *Judicial Creativity at the International Criminal Tribunals*. Oxford: Oxford University Press.

DeGuzman, Margaret. 2012. "How Serious are International Crimes? The Gravity Problem in International Criminal Law." *Columbia Journal of Transnational Law* 51: 18–68.

DeGuzman, Margaret. 2012. "Choosing to Prosecute: Expressive Selection at the International Criminal Court." *Michigan Journal of International Law* 33(2): 265–320.

Drumbl, Mark A. 2007a. *Atrocity, Punishment and International Law*. Cambridge: Cambridge University Press.

Drumbl, Mark A. 2007b. "The Expressive Value of Prosecuting and Punishing Terrorists: Hamdam, the Geneva Conventions and International Criminal Law." *The George Washington Law Review* 75: 1165–1199.

Eskridge, William. 1994. *Dynamic Statutory Interpretation*. Cambridge, MA: Harvard University Press.

Evangelista, Michael. 1995. "The Paradox of State Strength: Transnational Relations, Domestic Structures, and Security Policy in Russia and the Soviet Union." *International Organization* 49: 1–38.

Ewald, Uwe. 2010. "'Predictably Irrational' – International Sentencing and its Discourse against the Backdrop of Preliminary Empirical Findings on ICTY Sentencing Practices." *International Criminal Law Review* 10: 365–402.

Farhang, Cliff. 2010. "Point of No Return: Joint Criminal Enterprise in *Brdanin*." *Leiden Journal of International Law* 23(1): 137–164.

Fedorova, Mascha. 2012. *The Principle of Equality of Arms in International Criminal Proceedings*. Cambridge, UK: Intersentia.

Feinberg, Joel. 1970. *Doing & Deserving; Essays in the Theory of Responsibility*. Princeton, NJ: Princeton University Press.

Findlay, Mark and Ralph J. Henham. 2005. *Transforming International Criminal Justice: Retributive and Restorative Justice in the Trial Process*. Cullompton, UK: Willan.

Findlay, Mark, and Ralph J. Henham. 2010. *Beyond Punishment: Achieving International Criminal Justice*. Basingstoke, UK: Palgrave Macmillan.

Fiori, Matteo. 2007. "A Further Step in the Development of the Joint Criminal Enterprise Doctrine." *Hague Justice Journal* 2(2): 60–68.

Fleming, Mark. 2002. "Appellate Review in the International Criminal Tribunals." *Texas International Law Journal* 37: 111–156.

Fletcher, Laurel E. 2004. "From Indifference to Engagement: Bystanders and International Criminal Justice." *Michigan Journal of International Law* 26(4): 1013–1095.

Fournet, Caroline and Clotilde Pegorier. 2010. "'Only One Step Away from Genocide': The Crime of Persecution in International Criminal Law." *International Criminal Law Review* 10: 713–738.

Fowler, James H., Timothy R. Johnson, James F. Spriggs, Sangick Jeon and Paul J. Wahlbeck. 2007. "Network Analysis and the Law: Measuring the Legal Importance of Precedents at the U.S. Supreme Court." *Political Analysis* 15(3): 324–346.

Franke, Katherine M. 2006. "Gendered Subjects of Transitional Justice." *Columbia Journal of Gender and Law* 15(3): 813–828.

Freeman, Mark. 2006. *Truth Commissions and Procedural Fairness*. Cambridge: Cambridge University Press.

Gamble, John King and Charlotte Ku. 2000. "International Law – New Actors and New Technologies: Centre Stage for NGOs?" *Law and Policy in International Business* 31(2): 221–262.

Gekker, Elena. 2014. "Rape, Sexual Slavery, and Forced Marriage at the International Criminal Court: How Katanga Utilizes a Ten-Year-Old Rule but Overlooks New Jurisprudence." *Hastings Women's Law Journal* 25: 105–133.

George, Tracey and Jeffrey Berger. 2005. "Judicial Entrepreneurs on the U.S. Courts of Appeals: A Citation Analysis of Judicial Influence." Vanderbilt Law and Economics Research Paper.

Gibson, James L. 2004. "Does Truth Lead to Reconciliation? Testing the Causal Assumptions of the South African Truth and Reconciliation Process." *American Journal of Political Science* 48(2): 201–217.

Ginsburg, Tom. 2005. "Bounded Discretion in International Judicial Lawmaking." *Virginia Journal of International Law* 45: 631–673.

Goldstone, Richard J. 2002. "Prosecuting Rape as a War Crime." *Case Western Reserve Journal International Law* 34: 277–285.

Goodman, Ryan and Derek Jinks. 2004. "How to Influence States: Socialization and International Human Rights Law." *Duke Law Journal* 54(3): 621–703.

Greenwalt, Alexander K.A. 2014. "International Criminal Law for Retributivists." *University of Pennsylvania Journal of International Law* 35(4): 969–1044.

Guillaume, Gilbert. 2011. "The Use of Precedent by International Judges and Arbitrators." *Journal of International Dispute Settlement* 2: 5–23.

Gustafson, Carrie. 1998. "International Criminal Courts: Some Dissident Views on the Continuation of War by Penal Means." *Houston Journal of International Law* 21(1): 51–84.

Gustafson, Katrina. 2007. "The Requirement of an 'Express Agreement' for Joint Criminal Enterprise Liability: a Critique of Brđanin." *Journal of International Criminal Justice* 5(1): 134–158.

Haan, Verena. 2005. "The Development of the Concept of Joint Criminal Enterprise at the International Criminal Tribunal for the Former Yugoslavia." *International Criminal Law Review* 5: 167–201.

Haas, Peter M. 1992. *Knowledge, Power, and International Policy Coordination*. Columbia, SC: University of South Carolina Press.

Haffajee, Rebecca L. 2006. "Prosecuting Crimes of Rape and Sexual Violence at the ICTR: The Application of the Joint Criminal Enterprise Theory." *Harvard Journal of Law and Gender* 29: 201–221.

Haider-Markel, Donald P., Mark R. Joslyn and Chad J. Kniss. 2000. "Minority Group Interests and Political Representation: Gay Elected Officials in the Policy Process." *The Journal of Politics* 62(2): 568–577.

Harmon, Mark and Fergal Gaynor. 2007. "Ordinary Sentences for Extraordinary Crimes." *Journal of International Criminal Justice* 5: 683–712.

Hazan, Pierre. 2004. *Justice in a time of war: The true story behind the International Criminal Tribunal for the Former Yugoslavia*. Texas A&M University Press.

Hayashi, Nubuo. 2010. "Requirements of Military Necessity in International Humanitarian Law and International Criminal Law." *Boston University International Law Journal* 28(1): 39–140.

Hayes, Niam. 2015. "La Lutte Continue: Investigating and Prosecuting Sexual Violence at the ICC" in *The Law and Practice of the International Criminal Court*, Ed. Carsten Stahn, pp. 801–839. Cambridge: Cambridge University Press.

Helfer, Laurence R. and Anne-Marie Slaughter. 2005. "Why States Create International Tribunals: A Response to Professors Posner and Yoo." *California Law Review* 93(3): 899–956.

Henham, Ralph. 2003. "The Philosophical Foundations of International Sentencing." *Journal of International Criminal Justice* 1: 64–85.

Henham, Ralph. 2007. "Developing Contextualized Rationales for Sentencing in International Criminal Trials." *Journal of International Criminal Justice* 5: 757–778.

Hola, Barbara, Alette Smeulers and Catrien Bijleveld. 2009. "Is ICTY Sentencing Predictable? An Empirical Analysis of ICTY Sentencing Practice." *Leiden Journal of International Law* 22(1): 79–97.

Hola, Barbara, Alette Smeulers and Catrien Bijleveld. 2011a. "International Sentencing Facts and Figures." *International Journal of Criminal Justice* 9: 411–439.

Hola, Barbara, Alette Smeulers and Catrien Bijleveld. 2011b. "Punishment for Genocide: Exploratory Analysis of ICTR Sentencing." *International Criminal Law Review* 114: 745–773.

Hola, Barbara, Alette Smeulers and Catrien Bijleveld. 2012. "Consistency of International Sentencing: ICTY and ICTR Case Study." *European Journal of Criminology* 9(5): 539–552.

Hola, Barbara, Alette Smeulers and Catrien Bijleveld. 2011. "International Sentencing Facts and Figures." *International Journal of Criminal Justice* 9: 411–439.

Ivkovic, Sanja. 2001. "Justice by the International Criminal Tribunal for the Former Yugoslavia." *Stanford Journal of International Law* 37(Summer): 255–346.

Jain, Neha. 2014. *Perpetrators and Accessories in International Criminal Law: Individual Modes of Responsibility for Collective Crimes*. Oxford: Hart Publishing.

Jayawardane, Sash and Charlotte Divin. September 2014. "The Gotovina, Perisic, and Sain-ovic Appeal Judgments: Implications for International Criminal Justice Mechanisms." *Policy Brief 13*, The Hague Institute for Global Justice. http://thehagueinstituteforglobaljustice. org/cp/uploads/publications/Policypaper_13-The_Gotovina-Perisic-Sainovic-Appeal-Judgments_1409068649.pdf.

Jodoin, Sebastien. 2010. "Understanding the Behavior of International Courts – An Exam-ination of Decision Making at the *ad hoc* International Criminal Tribunals." *Journal of International Law and International Relations* 6(1): 1–34.

Karnavas, Michael G. 2011. "The ICTY Legacy: A Defense Counsel's Perspective." *Goettingen Journal of International Law* 3(3): 1052–1092.

Keck, Margaret and Kathryn Sikkink. 1998. *Activists Beyond Borders*. Ithaca, NY: Cornell University Press.

Kelsall, Tim. 2009. *Culture Under Cross-Examination: International Justice and the Special Court for Sierra Leone*. Cambridge: Cambridge University Press.

Kelsen, Hans. 1943. "Collective and Individual Responsibility in International Law with Particular Regard to the Punishment of War Criminals." *California Law Review* 31(5): 530–571.

King, Kimi and Megan Greening. 2007. "Gender Justice or Just Gender? The Role of Gen-der in Sexual Assault Decisions at the International Criminal Tribunal for the Former Yugoslavia." *Social Science Quarterly* 88(5): 1049–1071.

King, Kimi and James Meernik. 2011. "A Distant Court: Assessing the Impact of the Inter-national Criminal Tribunal for the Former Yugoslavia" (with Prof. Kimi King, University of North Texas) in *The Legacy of the International Criminal Tribunal for the Former Yugoslavia*, Eds. Göran Sluiter, Bert Swart, and Alexander Zahar, pp. 7–54. Oxford: Oxford University Press.

King, Kimi and James Meernik. Forthcoming. "Deborah's Voice: The Role of Women in Sexual Assault Cases at the International Criminal Tribunals for the Former Yugoslavia." To appear in *Social Science Quarterly*.

Kingdon, John W. 1995. *Agendas, Alternatives, and Public Policies*. New York: Longman.

Kmiec, Keenan. 2004. The Origin and Current Meaning of Judicial Activism. *California Law Review* 92: 1441–1478.

Koskenniemi, Martti and Päivi Leino. 2002. "Fragmentation of International Law? Postmod-ern Anxieties." *Leiden Journal of International Law* 15(3): 553–579.

Kuo, Peggy. 2002. "Prosecuting Crimes of Sexual Violence in an International Tribunal." *Case Western Reserve Journal of International Law* 34: 305–321.

Ku, Charlotte. 1996. "Catholicism, the Peace of Westphalia, and the Origins of Modern International Law." *The European Legacy* 1(2): 734–739.

Ku, Julian and Jide Nzelibe. 2006. "Do International Criminal Tribunals Deter or Exacerbate Humanitarian Atrocities?" *Washington University Law Review* 84: 777–833.

Kwon, O-Gon. 2007. "The Challenge of an International Criminal Trial as Seen from the Bench." *Journal of International Criminal Justice* 5: 360–376.

Lederach, Jean Paul. 1999. *The Journey toward Reconciliation*. Scottdale, PA: Herald Press.

Lindquist, Stephanie and Cross, Frank. 2009. *Measuring Judicial Activism*. Oxford: Oxford University Press.

Luban, David. 2010. "Fairness to Rightness: Jurisdiction, Legality, and the Legitimacy of International Criminal" in *Philosophy of International Law*, Eds. Samantha Besson and John Tasioulas, pp. 569–588. Oxford: Oxford University Press.

MacCoun, Robert J. 1993. "Drugs and the Law: A Psychological Analysis of Drug Prohibition." *Psychological Bulletin* 113: 497–512.

Manacorda, Stefano and Chantal Meloni. 2011. "Indirect Perpetration *versus* Joint Criminal Enterprise Concurring Approaches in the Practice of International Criminal Law?." *Journal of International Criminal Justice* 9: 159–178.

McDonald, Gabrielle. 2000. "The International Criminal Tribunals: Crime & Punishment in the International Arena." *Nova Law Review* 25: 463–484.

McDonald, Gabrielle Kirk. 2005. "Problems, Obstacles and Achievements of the ICTY." *Journal of International Criminal Justice* 2: 558–571.

McGuire, Kevin T. and Barbara Palmer. 1996. "Issues, Agendas, and Decision Making on the Supreme Court." *The American Political Science Review* 90(4): 853–865.

McIntosh, Wayne V. and Cynthia L. Cates. 1997. *Judicial Entrepreneurship: The Role of the Judge in the Marketplace of Ideas*. Westport, CT: Greenwood Press.

Meernik, James and Kimi King. 2003. "The Determinants of ICTY Sentencing: An Empirical and Doctrinal Analysis." *Leiden Journal of International Law* 16(4): 717–750.

Meernik, James, Kimi King and Geoff Dancy. 2005. "Judicial Decision Making and International Tribunals: Assessing the Impact of Individual, National and International Factors." *Social Science Quarterly* 86: 683–703.

Meernik, James. 2003. "Victor's Justice or the Law: Judging and Punishing at the International Criminal Tribunal for the Former Yugoslavia." *Journal of Conflict Resolution* 47: 140–162.

Meernik, James. 2005. "Justice or Peace: How the International Criminal Tribunal Affects Societal Peace in Bosnia." *Journal of Peace Research* 42: 271–290.

Meernik, James. 2011. "Sentencing Rationales and Judicial Decision-Making at the International Criminal Tribunals." *Social Science Quarterly* 92(3): 588–608.

Mendeloff, David. 2004. "Truth-Seeking, Truth-Telling, and Postconflict Peacebuilding: Curb the Enthusiasm?" *International Studies Review* 6(3): 355–380.

Meron, Theodor. 1993. "Rape as a Crime under International Humanitarian Law." *The American Journal of International Law* 87(3): 424–428.

Meron, Theodor. 1996. "The Normative Impact on International Law of the International Tribunal for Former Yugoslavia." *War Crimes in International Law*, Eds. Yoram Dinstein and Mala Tabory, pp. 211–231. The Hague: Martinus Nijhoff.

Meron, Theodor. 2000. "The Humanization of Humanitarian Law." *The American Journal of International Law* 94(2): 239–278.

Meron, Theodor. 2000. "The Martens Clause, Principles of Humanity, and Dictates of Public Conscience." *The American Journal of International Law* 94(1): 78–89.

Meron, Theodor. 2004. "Procedural Evolution in the ICTY." *Journal of International Criminal Justice* 2: 520–525.

Meron, Theodor. 2005. "Revival of Customary Humanitarian Law." *American Journal of International Law* 99(4): 817–834.

Meron, Theodor. 2006. "Reflections on the Prosecution of War Crimes by International Tribunals." *American Journal of International Law* 100: 551–575.

Mettraux, Guenael. 2005. *International Crimes and the Ad Hoc Tribunals*. Oxford: Oxford University Press.

Mintrom, Michael. 1997. "Policy Entrepreneurs and the Diffusion of Innovation." *American Journal of Political Science* 41(3): 738–770.

Mintrom, Michael. 2000. *Policy Entrepreneurs and School Choice*. Washington, DC: Georgetown University Press.

Mintrom, Michael and Philippa Norman. 2009. "Policy Entrepreneurship and Policy Change." *Policy Studies Journal* 37: 649–667.

Mitchell, Andrew D. 2000. "Failure to Halt, Prevent or Punish: The Doctrine of Command Responsibility for War Crimes." *Sydney Law Review* 22: 381–410.

Moffett, Luke. 2014. *Realising Justice for Victims before the International Criminal Court*. The Hague: International Crimes Database.

Moffett, Luke. 2015. "Elaborating Justice for Victims at the International Criminal Court – Beyond Rhetoric and The Hague." *Journal of International Criminal Justice* 13: 281–311.

Mose, Erik. 2005. "Main Achievements of the ICTR." *Journal of International Criminal Justice* 3(4): 920–943.

Mundis, Daryl A. 2001. "The Legal Character and Status of the Rules of Procedure and Evidence of the ad hoc International Criminal Tribunals." *International Criminal Law Review* 1.3: 191–239.

Nerlich, Volker. 2013. "Daring Diversity – Why There Is Nothing Wrong with 'Fragmentation' in International Criminal Procedures." *Leiden Journal of International Law* 26: 777–781.

Nilsson, Cecilia. 2011. "Contextualizing the Agreement on the Privileges and Immunities of the International Criminal Court." *Leiden Journal of International Law* 17: 559–578.

Nollkaemper, André. 2001. "The Legitimacy of International Law in the Case Law of the International Criminal Tribunal for the Former Yugoslavia." *Ambiguity in the Rule of Law: the Interface between National and International Legal Systems*: 11–23.

Oberleitner, Gerd. 2015. *Human Rights in Armed Conflict: Law, Practice, Policy*. Cambridge: Cambridge University Press.

Olusanya, Olaoluwa. 2005. *Sentencing War Crimes and Crimes against Humanity Under the International Criminal Tribunal for the Former Yugoslavia*. Groningen: Europa Law Pub.

O'Rourke, Allen. 2006. "Joint Criminal Enterprise and Brdanin: Misguided Overcorrection." *Harvard International Law Journal* 47(1): 307–325.

Orie, Alphons. 2012. "Stare Decisis in the ICTY Appeal System?" *Journal of International Criminal Justice* 10: 635–644.

Pelc, Krzysztof J. 2014. "The Politics of Precedent in International Law: A Social Network Application." *American Political Science Review* 108(3): 547–564.

Phelps, Andrea R. 2006. "Gender Based War Crimes: Incidence and Effectiveness of International Criminal Prosecution." *William and Mary Journal of the Women and the Law* 12(2): 499–520.

Pollack, Mark A. 1997. "Delegation, Agency, and Agenda Setting in the European Community." *International Organization* 51: 99–134.

Rasler, Karen A. 2000. *Shocks, Expectancy Revision, and the Deescalation of Protracted Conflicts: The Israeli-Palestinian Case*. Jerusalem: Leonard Davis Institute for International Relations, the Hebrew University of Jerusalem.

Ratner, Steven R., Jason S. Abrams and James L. Bischoff. 2009. *Accountability for Human Rights Atrocities in International Law: Beyond the Nuremberg Legacy*. Oxford: Oxford University Press.

Robinson, Patrick. 2009. "The Interaction of Legal Systems in the Work of the International Criminal Tribunal for the Former Yugoslavia." *International Law Students Association Journal of International and Comparative Law* 16: 5–18.

Rohan, Colleen M. 2010. "Rules Governing the Presentation of Testimonial Evidence" in *Principles of Evidence in International Criminal Justice*, Eds. Karim A. A. Khan, Caroline Buisman, and Christopher Gosnell, pp. 499–550. Oxford: Oxford University Press.

Rosenberg, Gerald. 1991. *Hollow Hope: Can Courts Bring About Social Change*. Chicago: University of Chicago Press.

Roosevelt, Kermit III. 2006. *The Myth of Judicial Activism*. New Haven, CT: Yale University Press.

Rothe, Dawn and Christopher Mullins. 2010. "Beyond the Juristic Orientation of International Criminal Justice: The Relevance of Criminological Insight to International Criminal Law and its Control A Commentary." *International Criminal Law Review* 10: 97–110.

Schabas, William A. 1997. "Sentencing by International Tribunals: A Human Rights Approach." *Duke Journal of Comparative and International Law* 7: 461–517.

Schabas, William A. 2006a. *The UN International Criminal Tribunals.* Cambridge: Cambridge University Press.

Schabas, William A. 2006b. "The Crime of Torture and the International Criminal Tribunals." *Case Western Reserve Journal of International Law* 37(2): 349–364.

Schabas, William A. 2007. *An Introduction to the International Criminal Court.* Cambridge: Cambridge University Press.

Schabas, William A. 2008. "Prosecutorial Discretion v. Judicial Activism at the International Criminal Court." *Journal of International Criminal Justice* 6(4): 731–761.

Schmitt, Michael N. 2010. "Military Necessity and Humanity in International Humanitarian Law: Preserving the Delicate Balance." *Virginia Journal of International Law* 50(4): 795–839.

Schneider, Mark, Paul Teske and Michael Mintrom. 1995. *Public Entrepreneurs Agents for Change in American Government.* Princeton, NJ: Princeton University Press.

Schomburg, Wolfgang and Ines Peterson. 2007. "Genuine Consent to Sexual Violence Under International Criminal Law." *The American Journal of International Law* 101: 121–141.

Scobbie, Iain. 1997. "The Theorist as Judge: Hersch Lauterpacht's Concept of the International Judicial Function." *European Journal of International Law* 8: 264–298

Segal, Jeffrey A. and Harold J. Spaeth. 1993. *The Supreme Court and the Attitudinal Model.* Cambridge: Cambridge University Press.

Shapiro, Ian. 1986. *The Evolution of Rights in Liberal Theory.* Cambridge: Cambridge University Press.

Shapiro, Martin. 1994. "Judges as Liars." *Harvard Journal of Law and Public Policy* 17: 155–156.

Sharp, Gene. 1994. *From Dictatorship to Democracy.* Cambridge, MA: Committee for the Restoration of Democracy in Burma.

Sikkink, Kathryn. 1993. "Human Rights, Principled Issue-Networks, and Sovereignty in Latin America." *International Organization* 1993: 411–441.

Sikkink, Kathryn. 2011. *The Justice Cascade.* New York: W.W. Norton.

Sloane, Robert. 2006. "The Expressive Capacity of International Punishment." *Columbia Public Law & Legal Theory Working Papers* Paper 06100.

Sloane, Robert D. 2007a. "The Expressive Capacity of International Punishment: The Limits of National Law Analogy and the Potential of International Criminal Law." *Stanford Journal of International Law* 43(Winter): 39–94.

Sloane, Robert D. 2007b. "Sentencing for the Crime of Crimes: The Evolving Common Law of Sentencing of the International Criminal Tribunal for Rwanda." *Journal of International Criminal Justice* 5: 713–734.

Smithey, Shannon and John Ishiyama. 2002. "Judicial Activism in Post-Communist Politics." *Law and Society Review* 36: 719–742.

Snyder, Jack and Wright L. Vinjamuri. 2003. "Trials and Errors: Principle and Pragmatism in Strategies of International Justice." *International Security* 283: 5–44.

Staub, Ervin. 2006. "Reconciliation after Genocide, Mass Killing, or Intractable Conflict: Understanding the Roots of Violence, Psychological Recovery, and Steps toward a General Theory." *Political Psychology* 27: 867–894.

Sunstein, Cass R. 1996. "On the Expressive Function of Law." *University of Pennsylvania Law Review* 144(5): 2021–2053.

Swart, Mia. 2010. "Judicial Lawmaking at the Ad Hoc Tribunals: The Creative use of the Sources of International Law and 'Adventurous Interpretation'." *Zeitschrift für ausländisches öffentliches Recht und Völkerrecht* 70.3: 459–486.

Szoke-Burke, Sam. 2012. "Avoiding Belittlement of Human Suffering: A Retributivist Critique of Ictr Sentencing Practices." *Journal of International Criminal Justice* 10(3): 561–580.

Szpak, Agnieszka. 2012. "National, Ethnic, Racial, and Religious Groups Protected against Genocide in the Jurisprudence of the Ad Hoc International Criminal Tribunals." *European Journal of International Law* 23(1): 155–173.

Tallgren, Immi. 2002. "The Sensibility and Sense of International Criminal Law." *European Journal of International Law* 13(3): 561–595.

Tezcur, Gunes Murat. 2009. "Judicial Activism in Perilous Times: The Turkish Case." *Law and Society Review* 54: 305–336.

Tonry, Michael. 2001. "Punishment Policies and Patterns in Western Countries" in *Sentencing and Sanctions in Western Countries*, Eds. Michael Tonry and Richard S. Frase, pp. 3–28. Oxford: Oxford University Press.

Tyler, Tom and John Darley. 2000. "Building a Law-Abiding Society: Taking Public Views about Morality and the Legitimacy of Legal Authority into Account when Formulating Substantive Law." *Hofstra Law Review* 28: 707–739.

Tyler, Tom. 1990. *Why People Obey the Law.* New Haven, CT: Yale University Press.

Van Schaack, Beth. 2008. "Crimen Sine Lege: Judicial Lawmaking at the Intersection of Law and Morals." *Georgetown Law Journal* 97(1): 119–192.

Ventura, Manuel. 2013. "Farewell 'Specific Direction': Aiding and Abetting War Crimes and Crimes Against Humanity in *Perišić, Taylor, Šainović et al.*, and US Alien Tort Statute Jurisprudence" in "The War Report." Geneva Academy of International Humanitarian Law and Human Rights.

Wald, Patricia. 2001. "The International Criminal Tribunal for the Former Yugoslavia Comes of Age: Some Observations on Day-To-Day Dilemmas of an International Court." *Journal of Law and Policy* 5: 87–118.

Wald, Patricia. 2010. "Notes from the Bench" in *Judicial Creativity at the International Tribunals*, Eds. Shane Darcy and Joseph Powderly, pp. xxxv–xl. Oxford: Oxford University Press.

Weinberg de Roca, Inés Mónica and Christopher M. Rassi. 2008. "Sentencing and Incarceration in the Ad Hoc Tribunals." *Stanford Journal of International Law* 441: 1–62.

Wessel, Jared. 2006. "Judicial Policy-Making at the International Criminal Court: An Institutional Guide to Analyzing International Adjudication." *Columbia Journal of Transnational Law.* 442: 377–452.

Williamson, Jamie Alan. 2008. "Some Considerations on Command Responsibility and Criminal Liability." *International Review of the Red Cross* 90: 303–317.

Wippman, David. 1999. "Atrocities, Deterrence, and the Limits of International Justice." *Fordham International Law Journal* 23(2): 473–488.

Woods, Andrew K. 2012. "Moral Judgments & International Crimes: Disutility of Desert." *Virginia Journal of International Law* 52(3): 633–681.

Wringe, Bill. 2006. "Why Punish War Crimes? Victor's Justice and Expressive Justifications of Punishment." *Law and Philosophy: An International Journal for Jurisprudence and Legal Philosophy* 25(2): 159–191.

Zacklin, Ralph. 2004. "The Failings of Ad Hoc International Tribunals." *Journal of International Criminal Justice* 2(2): 541–545.

Zarbiyev, Fuad. 2012. "Judicial Activism in International Law – A Conceptual Framework for Analysis." *Journal of International Dispute Settlement* 3: 247–278.

Index